THE
POETICAL WORKS
OF
ABRAHAM COWLEY

VOLUME IV

Elibron Classics
www.elibron.com

BELL'S EDITION
The POETS of GREAT BRITAIN
COMPLETE FROM
CHAUCER to CHURCHILL.

COWLEY VOLUME IV.
Affift me Phæbus! wit of Heav'n, whofe care
So bounteoufly both Plants & Poets fhare.
Book 1 Invocation to his Book of Plants

Mortimer del.

Grignion fc.

Printed for John Bell near Exchange Strand London Jan.ʸ 14ᵗʰ 1778.

THE
POETICAL WORKS
OF
ABRAHAM COWLEY.

IN FOUR VOLUMES.

FROM THE TEXT OF DR. SPRAT, &c.

WITH THE LIFE OF THE AUTHOR.

Begin the song, and strike the living lyre!
Lo! how the Years to come, a num'rous and well-fitted quire!
All hand in hand do decently advance,
And to my song with smooth and equal measures dance.
Whilst the dance lasts, how long soe'er it be,
My Music's voice shall bear it company,
Till all gentle notes be drown'd
In the last trumpet's dreadful sound.   THE RESURRECTION.

COWLEY does to Jove belong,
Jove and COWLEY claim my song.-----
The Muses did young COWLEY raise,
They stole thee from thy nurse's arms,
Fed thee with sacred love of praise,
And taught thee all their charms:
As if Apollo's self had been thy sire,
They daily rock'd thee on his lyre.   VERSES TO COWLEY.

VOL. IV.

EDINBURG:
AT THE Apollo Press, BY THE MARTINS.
Anno 1777.

THE
POETICAL WORKS
OF
ABRAHAM COWLEY.

VOL. IV.

CONTAINING HIS

SIXTH BOOK OF PLANTS,	DAVIDEIS. BOOK THIRD,
DAVIDEIS. BOOK FIRST,	DITTO. BOOK FOURTH,
DITTO. BOOK SECOND,	IMITATIONS, FRAGMENTS,

&c. &c. &c.

Alone exempted from the common fate,
The forward COWLEY held a lafting date:
For Envy's blaft, and pow'rful Time, too ftrong,
He bloffom'd early, and he flourifh'd long:
In whom the double miracle was feen,
Ripe in his fpring, and in his autumn green.
With us he left his gen'rous fruit behind,
The feaft of wit, and banquet of the mind:
While the fair tree, tranfplanted to the fkies,
In verdure with th' Elyfian garden vies,
The pride of Earth before, and now of Paradife.----
VER. TO MEM. OF COWLEY.

EDINBURGH:
AT THE Apollo Prefs, BY THE MARTINS.
Anno 1777.

OF PLANTS.

BOOK VI. OF TREES.

Tranſlated by Mrs. A. Behn.

SYLVA.

Cease, O my Muſe! the ſoft delights to ſing
Of flow'ry gardens in their fragrant ſpring,
And trace the rougher paths of obſcure woods,
All gloom aloft, beneath o'ergrown with ſhrubs,
Where Phœbus, once thy guide, can dart nó ray   5
T' inſpire thy flight, and make the ſcene look gay.
   Courage, my Huntreſs! let us range the glades,
And ſearch the inmoſt grottos of the ſhades;
Ev'n to the lone receſſes let us paſs,
Where the green goddeſs reſts on beds of moſs: 10
Let looſe my Fancy, ſwift of foot to trace,
With a ſagacious ſcent, the noble chaſe,
And with a joyful cry purſue the prey;
'Tis hidden Nature we muſt rouze to-day:
Set all your gins, let ev'ry toil be plac'd,   15
Thro' all her tracks let flying Truth be chas'd,
And ſeize her panting with her eager haſte.
Nor yet diſdain, my Muſe! in groves to range,
Or humbler woods for nobler orchards change;

A iij

Here deities, of old, have made abode,   20
And once fecur'd great Charles, our earthly god.
The royal youth, born to outbrave his fate,
Within a neighb'ring Oak maintain'd his ftate:
The faithful boughs, in kind allegiance, fpread
Their fhelt'ring branches round his awful head,25
Twin'd their rough arms, and thicken'd all the
        fhade.

    To thee, belov'd of Heav'n! to thee we fing
Of facred groves, blooming perpetual fpring:
May'ft thou be to my rural verfe and me
A prefent and affifting deity: 30
Difdain not in this leafy court to dwell,
Who its lov'd Monarch did fecure fo well.
Th' eternal Oak, now confecrate to thee,
No more thy refuge, but thy throne, fhall be.
We'll place thee conqu'ror now, and crown thy brows
With garlands made of its young gayeft boughs, 36
While from our oaten pipes the world fhall know
How much they to this facred fhelter owe.

    And you, the foft Inhabitants of the groves!
You Wood-nymphs! Hamadryades, and Loves,   40
Satyrs and Fauns! who in thefe arbours play,
Permit my fong, and give my Mufe her way:
She tells of ancient woods the wondrous things,
Of groves, long veil'd in facred darknefs, fings,
And a new light into your gloom fhe brings.   45
Let it be lawful for me to unfold
Divine decrees that never yet were told;

The harangues of the wood-gods to rehearse,
And sing of flow'ry senates in my verse:
Voices unknown to man he now shall hear,   50
Who, always ignorant of what they were,
Have pass'd 'em by with a regardless ear;
Thought 'em the murm'rings of the ruffled Trees,
That mov'd and wanton'd with the sporting breeze.
But Daphne knew the mysteries of the wood,   55
And made discov'ries to her am'rous god;
Apollo me inform'd, and did inspire
My soul with his divine prophetic fire;
And I, the priest of Plants, their sense expound;
Hear, O ye Worlds! and listen all around.   60
   'Twas now when royal Charles, that prince of peace,
(That pious offspring of the Olive-race)
Sway'd England's sceptre with a godlike hand,
Scattering soft ease and plenty o'er the land;
Happy 'bove all the neighb'ring kings, while yet   65
Unruffled by the rudest storms of Fate;
More fortunate the people, till their pride
Disdain'd obedience to the sovereign guide,
And to a base plebeian Senate gave
The arbitrary priv'lege to enslave;   70
Who thro' a sea of noblest blood did wade,
To tear the diadem from the sacred head.
Now above envy, far above the clouds,
The Martyr sits, triumphing with the gods.
While Peace before did o'er the ocean fly,   75
On our bless'd shore to find security,

In Britiſh groves ſhe built her downy neſt,
No other climate could afford her reſt;
For warring winds o'er wretched Europe range,
Threat'ning deſtruction, univerſal change: 80
The raging tempeſt tore the aged woods,
Shook the vaſt earth, and troubled all the floods.
Nor did the fruitful goddeſs brood in vain,
But here in ſafety hatch'd her golden train:
Juſtice and Faith one cornucopia fill,   85
Of uſeful med'cines known to many an ill.
    Such was the Golden Age in Saturn's ſway;
Eaſy and innocent it paſs'd away;
But too much lux'ry and good fortune cloys,
And virtues ſhe ſhould cheriſh ſhe deſtroys.   90
What we moſt wiſh, what we moſt toil to gain,
Enjoyment palls, and turns the bliſs to pain.
Poſſeſſion makes us ſhift our happineſs
From peaceful wives to noiſy miſtreſſes.
The repetition makes the pleaſure dull;   95
'Tis only Change that's gay and beautiful.
O notion falſe! O appetite deprav'd!
That has the nobler part of man enſlav'd:
Man! born to reaſon, does that ſafety quit,
To ſplit upon the dang'rous rock of wit.   100
Phyſicians ſay there is no ſuch danger near
As when, tho' no ſigns manifeſt appear,
Self-tir'd, and dull, man knows not what he ails,
And, without toil, his ſtrength and vigour fails.

Such was the ſtate of England, ſick with eaſe, 105
Too happy, if ſhe knew her happineſs.
Their crime no ign'rance for excuſe can plead,
That wretched refuge for ingratitude.
'Twas then that from the pitying gods there came⎫
A kind admoniſhing anger to reclaim,   110⎬
In dreadful prodigies*; but, alas! in vain.   ⎭
So rapid thunderbolts, before the flame
Fly, the conſuming vengeance to proclaim.
I, then a boy, arriv'd to my tenth year,
And ſtill thoſe horrid images I bear;   115
The mournful ſigns are preſent to my eyes:
I ſaw o'er all the region of the ſkies
The hiſtory of our approaching wars,
Writ in the heav'ns in wondrous characters:
The vaulted firmament with lightning burns,   120
And all the clouds were kindled into ſtorms,
And form'd an image of th' infernal hell;
(I ſhake with the portentous things I tell)
Like ſulph'rous waves the horrid flames did roll,
Whoſe raging tides were hurl'd from pole to pole; 125
Then ſuddenly the burſting clouds divide,
A fire like burning mounts on either ſide,
Diſcovering (to th' aſtoniſh'd world) within
At once a dreadful and a beauteous ſcene:
Two mighty armies clad in battle-array,   130
Ready, by combat, to diſpute the day;

---

* This relation of prodigies M. Cowley aſſures to be true.
Veram eſſe in me recipio, in the margin of the original.

Their waving plumes and glitt'ring armour fhone,
Mov'd by the winds, and gilded by the fun :
So well in order feem'd each fearlefs rank,
As they'd been marfhall'd by our hero Monk ;   135
Monk! born for mighty things and great command,
The glorious pillar of our falling land :
Perhaps his Genius on the royal fide
One of thofe heav'nly figures did defcribe,
Here pointed out to us his noble force,   140
And form'd him conqu'ror on a flaming horfe.
We heard, or fancy'd that we heard, around,
The fignal giv'n by drum and trumpet found ;
We faw the fire-wing'd horfes fiercely meet,
And with their fatal fpears each other greet :   145
Here fhining brandifh'd pikes like lightning fhook,
While from ethereal guns true thunder broke :
With gloomy mifts they' involv'd the plains of heav'n,
And to the cloud-begotten men was given
A memorable fate——   150
By the dire fplendour which their arms difplay'd,
And dreadful lightning that from cannons play'd,
We faw extended o'er the aerial plain
The wounded bodies of the numerous flain,
(Their faces fierce with anger underftood)   155
Turning the fky red with their gufhing blood :
At laft that army we the juft efteem'd,
And which adorn'd by nobleft figures feem'd

Of arms and men, alas! was put to flight;
The reft was veil'd in the deep fhades of night, 160
And fates to come fecur'd from human fight.

   But ftupid England, touch'd with no remorfe,
Beholds thefe prodigies as things of courfe:
(With many more, which to the juft appear'd
As ominous prefages) then who fear'd   165
The monfters of the Caledonian woods,
Or the hid ferments of fchifmatic crowds?
Nor had the impious Cromwell then a name,
For England's ruin, and for England's fhame:
Nor were the gods pleas'd only to exhort   170
By figns the reftive City and the Court:
Th' impending fates o'er all the thickets reign'd,
And ruin to the Englifh wood proclaim'd.
We faw the fturdy Oaks, of monftrous growth,
Whofe fpreading roots, fix'd in their native earth,
Where for a thoufand years in peace they grew, 176
Torn from the foil, tho' none but Zeph'rus blew.
But who fuch violent outrages could find
To be th' effects of the foft Weftern wind?
The Dryads faw the right hand of the gods   180
O'erturn the nobleft fhelters of the woods;
Others their arms with baneful leaves were clad,
That new unufual forms and colours had,
Whence now no aromatic moifture flows,
Or noble Miffeltoe enrich the boughs;   185
But, bow'd with galls, within thofe boding hulls
Lurk'd flies, diviners of enfuing ills,

Whofe fetal buzz did future flaughters threat,
And confus'd murmurs, full of dread, repeat.
When no rude winds difturb'd the ambient air,   190
The Trees, as weary of repofe, made war;
With horrid noife grappling their knotty arms,
Like meeting tides they ruffle into ftorms;
But when the winds to rattling tempefts rife,
Inftead of warring Trees, we heard the cries   195
Of warring men, whofe dying groans around
The woods and mournful echoes did refound.

    The difmal fhade with birds obfcene were fill'd,
Which, fpight of Phœbus, he himfelf beheld.
On the wild Afhes' tops the bats and owls,   200
With all night ominous and baneful fowls,
Sate brooding, while the fcreeches of thefe droves
Profan'd and violated all the groves.
If ought that poets do relate be true,
The ftrange Spinturnix * led the feather'd crew : 205
Of all the monfters of the earth and air,
Spinturnix bears the cruelleft character.
The barbarous bird, to mortal eyes unknown,
Is feen but by the goddeffes alone,
And then they tremble; for fhe always bodes   210
Some fatal difcord ev'n among the gods.
But that which gave more wonder than the reft,
Within an Afh a ferpent built her neft †,

    * What this bird truly was is not known, but it was much
dreaded by the Arufpices. *Plin. Servius,* &c.
    † For the truth hereof take Pliny's word, l. 16, 17.

And laid her eggs, when once to come beneath
The very shadow of an Ash was death;　　　215
Rather, if chance should force, she thro' the fire
From its fall'n leaves, so baneful, would retire.
But none of all the sylvan prodigies
Did more surprise the rural deities;
Than when the lightning did the Laurel blast;　220
The lightning their lov'd Laurels all defac'd:
The Laurel! which, by Jove's divine decree,
Since ancient time from injuring tempests free,
No angry threats from the celestial powers
Could make her fear the ruin of her bowers;　225
But always she enjoy'd a certain fate,
Which she could ne'er secure the victor yet.
In vain these signs and monsters were not sent
From angry Heav'n; the wise knew what they meant:
Their coming by conjectures understood,　230
As did the Dryads of the British wood.

　There is an ancient forest * known to Fame,
On this side sep'rate from the Cambrian plain
By wand'ring Wye, whose winding current glides,
And murm'ring leaves behind its flow'ry sides;　235
On that 'tis wash'd by nobler Severn's streams,
Whose beauties scarce will yield to famous Thames:
Of yore 'twas Arden call'd, but that great name,
As like herself, diminish'd into Dean:

　　　* The forest of Dean.

The cùrfed weapons of deftructive war   240
In all their cruelties have made her fhare;
'The iron has its nobleft fhades deftroy'd,
'Then to melt iron is its wood employ'd;
And fo unhappy 'tis, as it prefents
Of its own death the fatal inftruments;   245
With induftry its ruin to improve,
Bears minerals below and Trees above.
Oh, Poverty! thou happinefs extreme,
(When no afflicting want can intervene)
And. oh! thou fubtle treafure of the earth,   250
From whence all rapes and mifchiefs take their birth.
And you, triumphing Woods! fecur'd from fpoil,
By the fafe blefling of your barren foil,
Here, unconfum'd, how fmall a part remains
Of that rich ftore that once adorn'd the plains!   255
Yet that fmall part that has efcap'd the ire
Of lawlefs fteel, and avaricious fire,
By many nymphs and deities poffefs'd,
Of all the Britifh fhades continues ftill the beft.
Herè the long reverend Dryas (who had. been   260
Of all thofe fhady verdant regions queen,
To which by conqueft fhe had forc'd the fea
His conflant tributary waves to pay)
Proclaim'd a gen'ral council thro' her court,
To which the fylvan nymphs fhould all refort.   265
    All the wood-goddeffes do ftraight appear,
At leaft who could the Britifh climate bear,

And on a foft afcent of rifing ground
Their queen, their charming Dryas! they furround,
Who, all adorn'd, was in the middle plac'd,   270
And by a thoufand awful beauties grac'd.

Thefe goddeffes alike were drefs'd in green,
The ornaments and liv'ries of their queen.
Had travellers at any diftance view'd
The beauteous order of this ftately crowd,   275
They would not guefs they 'ad been divinities,
But groves all facred to the deities.
Such was the image of this leafy fcene,
On one fide water'd by a cooling ftream,
Upon whofe brink the Poplar took her place,   280
The Poplar! whom Alcides once did grace,
Whofe double colour'd fhadow'd leaves exprefs
The labours of our hero Hercules,
Whofe upper fides are black, the under white,
To reprefent his toil and his delight.   285

The Phaetonian Alder next took place,
Still fenfible of the burnt youth's difgrace;
She loves the purling ftreams, and often laves
Beneath the floods, and wantons with the waves.

Clofe by her fide the penfive Willows join'd,   290
Chafte fifters all, to lovers moft unkind,
Oleficarpians * call'd, in youth fevere,
Before the winter-age had fnow'd their hair;

* That is, a tribe which early drops its feed; or which
an enemy to venery.

In rivers take delight, whofe chilling ftreams
Mix'd with the native coldnefs of their veins,   295
Like falamanders, can all heat remove,
And quite extinguifh the quick fire of love:
Firm lafting bonds they yield to all befide,
But take delight the lovers to divide.

 The Elders next, who, tho' they waters love,   300
The fame from human bodies yet remove,
And quite difperfe the humid moifture thence,
And parley with the dropfy in this fenfe :
 " Why do you linger here, O lazy Flood !
 " This foil belongs to rivulets of blood.   305
 " Why do you men torment, when many a fhade,
 " And honeft Trees and Plants, do want your aid ?
 " Be gone, from human bodies quick be gone.
 " And back into your native channels run
 " By every pore, by all the ways you can".   310
The moifture, frighten'd, flies at the command,
And awful terror of her pow'rful wand.

 The hofpitable Birch does next appear,
Joyful and gay in hot or frigid air;
Flowing her hair, her garments foft and white,   315
And yet in cruelty fhe takes delight;
No wild inhabitant o' the woods can be
So quick in wrath, and in revenge, as fhe;
In houfes great authority affumes,
And is the fole punifher of petty crimes;   320
But moft of all her malice fhe employs
In fchools, to terrify and awe young boys:

If ſhe chaſtiſe 'tis for the patient's good,
Tho' oft' ſhe bluſhes with her tender blood.

Not ſo the gen'rous Maples; they preſent 325
Whate'er the city lux'ry can invent,
Who with induſtrious management and pains
Divide the labyrinth of their curious grains,
And many neceſſary things produce,
That ſerve at once for ornament and uſe. 330

But thou, O Pteleas *! to the ſwain allows
Shades to his cattle, timber for his ploughs;
Ennobled thou above the leafy race,
In that an amorous god † does thee embrace.

Next thee the Oxias ‡, of herſelf a grove, 335
Whoſe wide-ſpread ſhade the flocks and ſhepherds
Whether thy murmurs do to ſleep invite, [love;
Or thy ſoft noiſe inſpire the rural pipe,
Alike thou 'rt grateful, and canſt always charm,
In ſummer cooling, and in winter warm: 340
Tityrus, of yore, the nymph with garlands hung,
And all his love-lays in her ſhadow ſung.
When firſt the Infant-world her reign began,
Ere pride and lux'ry had corrupted man,
Before for gold the earth they did invade, 345
The uſeful houſehold-ſtuff of Beech was made;
No other plate the humble ſideboard dreſs'd,
No other bowls adorn'd the wholeſome feaſt,

---

* The Elm. † Bacchus; or, the Vine.
‡ The Beech.

Which no voluptuous cookery could boaſt,
The home-bred kid or lamb was all the coſt;   350
The mirth, the innocence, and little care,
Surpaſs'd the loaded boards of high-priz'd fare:
There came no gueſt for int'reſt or deſign,
For guilty love, fine eating, or rich wine:
The Beechen bowl without debauch went round, 355
And was with harmleſs mirth and roſes crown'd:
In theſe—the Ancients in their happy ſtate
Their feaſts and banquets us'd to celebrate:
Fill'd to the brim with uncorrupted wine,
They made libations to the powers divine,   360
To keep 'em ſtill benign; no ſacrifice
They need perform the angry gods t' appeaſe;
They knew no crimes the deities t' offend,
But all their care was ſtill to keep 'em kind:
No poiſon ever did thoſe bowls infeſt,   365
Securely here the ſhepherd quench'd his thirſt;
'Twas not that any virtue in the wood
Againſt the baneful liquor was thought good,
But poverty and innocence were here
The antidotes againſt all ills and fear.   370
    Such was the Aſh, the nymph was Melias nam'd,
For peaceful uſe and lib'ral virtues fam'd;
But when Achilles' ſpear was of her wood
Fatally form'd, and drank of Hector's blood,
O wretched glory! O unhappy power!   375
She loves the rain and neighb'ring floods no more;

No more the falling fhowers delight her now,
She only thirfts to drink of bloody dew.

Philyra *, not inferior to her race,
For her bel-taille, good mien, and handfome grace, 380
For pious ufe and nobleft ftudies fit,
Minerva here might exercife her wit,
And on the lafting vellum which fhe brings,
May in fmall volumes write feraphic things;
'Mongft all the nymphs and hamadryades, 385
None are fo fair and fo adorn'd as this:
All foft her body, innocent and white,
In her green flowing hair fhe takes delight;
Proud of her perfum'd bloffoms, far fhe fpreads
Her lovely, charming, odoriferous, fhades: 390
Her native beauties even excelling art,
Her virtues many med'cines ftill impart;
The dowry of each Plant in her does reft,
And fhe deferv'dly triumphs o'er the beft.

Next her Orcimelis and Achras † ftood, 395
Whofe offspring is a fharp and rigid brood;
A fruit no feafon e'er could work upon,
Not to be mellow'd by th' all-ripening fun.

Hither the fair amphibious nymphs refort,
Who both in woods and gardens keep their court; 400
The Ouas ‡, but of no ignoble fame,
Altho' fhe bears a bafe and fervile name;

---

* The Lime Tree. † Wood Pear and Crab Apple.
‡ Service Tree.

Sharp Oxyacantha* next the Mulberry ſtood,
The Mulberry, dy'd in haplefs lovers' † blood.

Craneia ‡, a nymph too lean to be admir'd,   405
But hard-gain'd Carya ‖ is by all defir'd;
The pretty Corylus **, ſo neat and trim,
And Caſtanis, with rough ungrateful ſkin.
Theſe nymphs, of all their race, live rich and high, ⎫
They taſte the city golden luxury,   410 ⎬
And woods their country villas do ſupply.   ⎭
Nor was the Hawthorn abſent from this place,
All ſoils are native to her harden'd race;
Tho' her the fields and gardens do reject,
She with a thorny hedge does both protect :   415
Helvetia ††, rough with cold and ſtones, firſt bred
The nymph, who thence to other climates fled;
Of her a warlike ſturdy race was born,
Whoſe dreſs nor court nor city can adorn,
But with a faithful hand they both defend,   420
While they upon no garriſon depend;
No ſhow, or noiſy grandeur, they affect,
But to their truſt they're conſtant and exact :
Should you behold 'em rang'd in battle-array,   ⎫
All muſter'd in due order, you would ſay   425 ⎬
That no Militia were ſo fine and gay.   ⎭
Let the Ancients raſhly then reproach,
Who cut from hence the hymeneal torch,

---

* Barberry.   † Pyramus and Thiſbe.
‡ Cornelian-Berry.   ‖ Wallnuts.
** Small nuts.   †† Switzerland.

Since they fuch fafeguard were'gainft thieves and beafts,
Which with an equal force their charge molefts ; 430
And 'twas commanded they fhould always bear
Their watchful twigs before the married pair.

   With the Helvetian nymph a pretty train,
All her companions, to the circle came ;
The fruitful Bullace firft, whofe offspring are,   435
Tho' harfh and fharp, yet moderately fair.

   The prickly Bramble, neat and lovely Rofe,
So nice and coy, they never will difpofe
Their valu'd favours, but fome wounds they give
To thofe who will their guarded joys receive.   440

   No lefs a troop of thofe gay nymphs were feen,
Who nobly flourifh in eternal green ;
Unfubject to the laws o' th' changing year,
They want no aids of kindly beams or air ;
But happy in their own peculiar fpring,   445
While the pole weeps in fhowers, they laugh and fing.
The generous Pyxias *, who a conqueft gains
O'er armed Winter, with her hofts of rains,
All ages fhe fubdues ; devouring Time
In vain endeavours to deftroy her prime ;   450
Still in her youth and beauty fhe furvives ;
When all the fpring is dead fhe fmiles and lives ;
Yet tho' fhe's obftinate to time and ftorms,
She's kindly pliable to all curious forms :
To artful mafters fhe obedience lends,   455
And to th' ingenious hand, with eafe, fhe bends ;

        * The Box Tree.

Into a thousand true-love's knots she twines,
And with a verdant wall the flowers confines,
Still looking up with gay and youthful love
To the triumphing flow'rs that reign above :   460
Or, if you please, she will advance on high,
And with the lofty Trees her stature vie;
And cheerfully will any figure take,
Whether man, lion, or a bird you make;
Or on her trunk like a green parrot show,   465
Or sometimes like a Hercules she'll grow :
And hence Praxiteles fair statues forms,
When with green gods the gardens he adorns;
Nor yet, being dead, does of less use appear
To the industrious artificer :   470
From her the noblest figures do arise,
And almost are immortal deities;
Of her the Berecynthian pipe is made,
That charms its native mountain and its shade,
That in such tuneful harmonies express   475
The praises of their goddess Cybeles.
With this the lovely females dress their hair,
That not least pow'rful beauty of the fair,
Their noblest ornament, and th' lover's snare.
This into form the beauteous nets still lay,   480
That the poor heedless gazer does betray.
Agrias * is content with easier spoils,
Only for silly birds she pitches toils :

* The Holly. Hereof bird-lime is made.

The wanton bird fhe ftops upon the wing,
And can forbid the infolence of men :   485
With a defence the garden fhe fupplies,
And does perpetually delight the eyes;
Her fhining leaves a lovely green produce,
And ferve at once for ornament and ufe.
Deform'd December, by her pofy-boughs   490
All deck'd and drefs'd, like joyful April fhows :
Cold winter-days fhe both adorns and cheers,
While fhe her conftant fpringing livery wears.
 Camaris *, who in winter give their birth,
Not humbly creeping on the fervile earth,   495
But rear aloft their nobler fruitful heads,
Whofe fylvan food unhappy Janus feeds;
His hungry appetite he here deftroys,
And both his rav'nous mouths at once deftroys.
 Phillyrea † here, and Pyracantha, rife,   500
Whofe beauty only gratifies the eyes
Of gods and men; no banquets they afford
But to the welcome, tho' unbidden, bird;
Here, gratefully, in winter they repay
For all the fummer-fongs that made their groves fogay.
 Next came the melancholy Yew, who mourns   506
With filent languor at the warrior's urns.
See, where fhe comes! all in black fhadow veil'd ;
Ah! too unhappy nymph, on every fide affail'd!

---

 * Strawberry Tree.   † Ever-green Privet, and Prickly
Coral Tree.
 2

Whom the Greek poets and hiftorians blame,   510
(Deceiv'd by eafy Faith and common Fame)
Thee as a guilty poifoner they prefent;
Oh! falfe afperfers of the innocent!
If poets may find credit when they fpeak,
(At leaft all thofe who are not of the Greek)   515
No baneful poifon, no malignant dew,
Lurks in, or hangs about, the harmlefs Yew;
No fecret mifchief dares the nymph invade,
And thofe are fafe that fleep beneath her fhade.

 Nor thou, Arceuthis *! art an enemy   520
To the foft notes of charming harmony:
Falfely the chief of poets would perfuade
That evil's lodg'd in thy eternal fhade;
Thy aromatic fhade, whofe verdant arms
Ev'n thy own ufeful fruits fecures from harms: 525
Many falfe crimes to thee they attribute;
Would no falfe virtues, too, they would to thee impute.

 But thou, Sabina †! my impartial Mufe
Cannot with any honefty excufe;
By thee the firft new fparks of life, not yet   530
Struck up to fhining flame, to mature heat,
Sprinkled by thy moift poifon fade and die;
Fatal Sabina! nymph of infamy.
For this the Cyprefs thee companion calls,
Who pioufly attends at funerals;   535
But thou, more barbarous, doft thy pow'r employ,
And even the unborn innocent deftroy.

   * Juniper Tree. † Savin.

Like Fate deftructive thou, without remorfe,
While fhe the death of even the ag'd deplores.
   Such Cypariffus was, that bafhful boy,   540
Who was belov'd by the bright god of Day;
Of fuch a tender mind, fo foft a breaft,
With fo compaffionate a grief opprefs'd,
For wounding his lov'd dear, that down he lay
And wept, and pin'd his fighing foul away;   545
Apollo pitying it renew'd his fate,
And to the Cyprefs did the boy tranflate,
And gave his haplefs life a longer date;
Then thus decreed the god—"And thou, oh, Tree!
" Chief mourner at all funerals fhalt be;   550
" And fince fo fmall a caufe fuch grief could give,
" Be it ftill thy talent (pitying Youth!) to grieve:
" Sacred be thou in Pluto's dark abodes,
" For ever facred to th' infernal gods!"
This faid, well'd fkill'd in truth, he did bequeath
Eternal life to the dire Tree of death,   556
A fubftance that no worm can ere fubdue,
Whofe never-dying leaves each day renew,
Whofe figures, like afpiring flames, ftill rife,
And with a noble pride falute the fkies.   560
   Next the fair nymph that Phœbus does adore,
But yet as nice and cold as heretofore;
She hates all fires, and with averfion ftill
She chides and crackles, if the flame fhe feel:

Yet tho' fhe is chafte the burning god no lefs 565
Adores, and makes his love his prophetefs;
And ev'n the murmurs of her fcorn do now
For joyful founds and happy omens go :
Nor does the humble tho' the facred Tree
Fear wounds from any earthly enemy ; 570
For fhe beholds, when loudeft ftorms abound,
The flying thunder of the gods around :
Let all the flaming heav'ns threat as they will,
Unmov'd th' undaunted nymph outbraves it ftill.
 Oh, thou!——   575
Of all the woody nations happieft made,
Thou greateft princefs of the fragrant fhade;
But fhould the goddefs Dryas not allow
That royal title to thy virtue due,
At leaft her juftice muft this truth confefs, 580
If not a princefs, thou 'rt a prophetefs;
And all the glories of immortal fame,
Which conqu'ring monarchs fo much ftrive to gain,
Is but at beft from thy triumphing boughs,
To reach a garland to adorn their brows; 585
And after monarchs poets claim a fhare,
As the next worthy, thy priz'd wreaths to wear:
Among that number do not me difdain,
Me, the moft humble of that glorious train :
I by a double right thy bounties claim *, 590
Both from my fex, and in Apollo's name:

  * The Tranflatrefs in her own perfon fpeaks.

Let me with Sappho and Orinda be,
Oh! ever facred Nymph! adorn'd by thee,
And give my verfes immortality.

 The tall Elate next, and Peuce ftood, 595
The ftatelieft fifter-nymphs of all the wood ;
The flying winds fport with their flowing hair,
While to the dewy clouds their lofty heads they rear.
As mighty hills above the vallies fhow,
And look with fcorn on the defcent below, 600
So do thefe view the mountains where they grow,
So much above their humbler tops they rife :
So ftood the giants that befieg'd the fkies,
The terror of the gods! they having thrown
Huge Offa on the leafy Pelion,   605
The Fir, with the proud Pine, thus threat'ning ftands,
Lifting to Heav'n two hundred warring hands ;
In this vaft profpect they with eafe furvey
The various figur'd land and boundlefs fea ;
With joy behold the fhips their timber builds, 610
How they 'are with cities ftor'd once fpacious fields.

 This grove of Englifh nymphs, this noble train,
In a large circle compafs in their queen,
The fceptre-bearing Dryas——
Her throne a rifing hillock, where fhe fate 615
With all the charms of majefty and ftate,
With awful grace the numbers fhe furvey'd,
Dealing around the favours of her fhade.

C ij

If I the voice of the loud winds could take,
Which the re-echoing Oaks do agitate,   620
'Twould not suffice to celebrate thy name,
Oh! sacred Dryas! of immortal fame.
If we a faith can give Antiquity,
That sings of many miracles, from thee,
In the world's infant age, mankind broke forth, 625
From thee the noble race receiv'd their birth;
Thou then in a green tender bark waft clad,
But in Deucalion's age a rougher covert had,
More hard and warm, with crufted white all o'er,
As noble authors fung in times of yore;   630
Approv'd by fome, condemn'd and argu'd down
By the vain troop of fophifts and the gown,
The fcoffing academy, and the fchool
Of Pyrrho, who traditions over-rule: 634
But let 'em doubt, yet they muft grant this truth,
Thofe brawny men that then the earth brought forth
Did on thy acorns feed, and feaft and thrive,
And with this wholefome nourifhment furvive,
In health and ftrength an equal age with thee,
Secur'd from all the banes of luxury.   640
Oh! happy Age! oh! nymph divinely good!
That mak'ft thy fhade man's houfe, thy fruit his food.
When only apples of the wood did pafs
For noble banquets, fpread on beds of grafs,
Tables not yet by any art debauch'd,   645
And fruit that ne'er the grudger's hand reproach'd,

Thy bounties, Ceres! were of little ufe,
And thy fweet food ill manners did produce;
Unluckily they did thy virtues find .
With that of the wild boar and hunted hind;   650
With all wild beafts on which their lux'ry prey'd,
While new defires their appetites invade.;
The natures they partake of what they eat,
And falvage they become, as was their meat.

Hence the republic of the world did ceafe ;   655
Hence they might date the forfeit of their peace :
The common-good was now peculiar made,
A generous int'reft now became a trade,
And men began their neighbours' rights t'invade:
For now they meafur'd out their common ground,
And outrages commit t' enlarge their bound :   661
Their own feem'd defpicable, poor, and fmall;
Each wants more room, and would be lord of all :
The ploughman with difdain his field furveys,
Forfakes the land, and ploughs the faithlefs feas : 665
The fool in thefe deep furrows feeks his gain,
Defpifing dangers, and enduring pain :
The facred Oak her peaceful manfion leaves,
Tranfplanted to the mountains of the waves.

Oh! Dryas! patron to the induftrious kind,   670
If man were wife, and would his fafety find,
What perfect blifs thy happy fhade would give,
And houfes that their mafters would outlive?

All neceſſaries thou afford'ſt alone
For harmleſs Innocence to live upon;   675
Strong yokes for oxen, handles for the plough;
What huſbandry requires thou doſt allow;
But if the madneſs of deſiring gain,
Or wild ambition agitate the brain,
Straight to a wand'ring ſhip they thee transfer, 680
And none more fitly ſerves the mariner:
Thou cutt'ſt the air, doſt on the waves rebound,
Wild death and fury raging all around;
Diſdaining to behold the manag'd wood,
Outbrave the ſtorms, and baffle the rude flood. 685
   To ſwine, O richeſt Oak! thy acorns leave,
And ſearch for man whate'er the earth can give,
All that the ſpacious univerſe brings forth,
What land and ſea conceals of any worth;
Bring aromatics from the diſtant Eaſt,   690 ⎫
And gold, ſo dangerous, from the rifled Weſt;   ⎬
Whate'er the boundleſs appetite can feaſt.   ⎭
    With thee the utmoſt bounds of earth we' invade;
By thee the unlock'd orb is common made:
By thee——.   695
The great republic of the world revives,
And o'er the earth luxurious traffic thrives:
If Argos' ſhip were valued at that rate
Which ancient poets ſo much celebrate,
From neighb'ring Colchos only bringing home 700
The Golden Fleece from ſeas whoſe tracts were known;

If of the dangers they so much have spoke
(More worthy smiles) of the Cyanean rock,
What oceans, then, of fame shall thee suffice?
What waves of eloquence can sing thy praise?   705
O sacred Oak! that great Columbus bore,
Iö! thou bearer of a happier ore
Than celebrated Argo did before.

    And Drake's brave Oak that pass'd to worlds un-
       known,
Whose toils, O Phœbus! were so like thy own,   710
Who round the earth's vast globe triumphant rode,
Deserves the celebration of a god.
O let the Pegasean ship no more
Be worshipp'd on the too unworthy shore;
After her watry life, let her become   715
A fix'd star shining equal with the Ram:
Long since the duty of a star she'as done,
And round the earth with guiding light has shone.

    Oh! how has Nature bless'd the British land,
Who both the valu'd Indies can command!   720
What tho' thy banks the Cedars do not grace,
Those lofty beauties of fam'd Libanus,
The Pine, or Palm of Idumean plains,
Arab's rich wood, or its sweet-smelling greens,
Or lovely Plantain, whose large leafy boughs   725
A pleasant and a noble shade allows?
She has thy warlike groves and mountains bless'd
With sturdy Oaks, o'er all the world the best;

And for the happy Ifland's fure defence,
Has wall'd it with a moat of feas immenfe;   730
While to declare her fafety and thy pride,
With Oaken fhips that fea is fortify'd.
   Nor was that adoration vainly made,
Which to the Oak the ancient Druids paid,
Who reafonably believ'd a god within,   735
Where fuch vaft wonders were produc'd and feen :
Nor was it the dull piety alone,
And fuperftition of our Albion,
Nor ignorance of the future age, that paid
Honours divine to thy furprifing fhade;   740
But they forefaw the empire of the fea
Great Charles fhould hold from the triumphant Thee,
   No wonder, then, that age fhould thee adore,
Who gav'ft our facred oracles heretofore;
The hidden pleafure of the gods was then   745
In a hoarfe voice deliver'd out to men.
So vapours, from Cyrrhean caverns broke,
Infpir'd Apollo's prieftefs when fhe fpoke,
Whilft, ravifh'd, the fair enthufiaftic ftood
Upon her tripos, raging with the god;   750
So prieft infpir'd with facred fury fhook,
When the winds ruffled the Dodonean Oak,
And tofs'd their branches, till a dreadful found
Of awful horror they proclaim around,
Like frantic Bacchanals, and while they move,   755
Poffefs with trembling all the facred grove :

Their rifled leaves the tempeſt bore away,
And their torn boughs ſcatter'd on all ſides lay;
The tortur'd thicket knew not that there came
A god triumphant in the hurricane, 760
Till the wing'd wind, with an amazing cry,
Deliver'd down the preſſing deity,
Whoſe thundering voice ſtrange ſecrets did unfold,
And wondrous things of worlds to come he told:
But truths ſo veil'd in obſcure eloquence, 765
They' amuſe the adoring crowd with double ſenſe.

   But by divine decree the Oak no more
Declares ſecurity, as heretofore,
With words or voice; yet to the liſt'ning wood
Her differing murmurs ſtill are underſtood; 770
For ſacred divinations, while they ſound,
Informs all but humanity around:
Nor e'er did Dryas murmur awful truth
More clear and plain from the prophetic mouth,
Than when ſhe ſpoke to the Chaonian wood, 775
While all the groves with eager ſilence ſtood,
And with erected leaves themſelves diſpoſe
To liſten to the language of her boughs.

   " You ſee, O my Companions! that the gods
Threaten a dire deſtruction to the woods, 780
And to all humankind—The black portents
Are ſeen of many ſiniſter events;
But leſt their quick approach too much ſhould preſs
(O my aſtoniſh'd Nymphs!) your tenderneſs,

The gods command me to foretel your doom,   785
And prepoſſeſs ye with the fate to come :
With heedful rev'rence, then, their will obſerve,
And in your bark's deep chinks my words preſerve.
Believe me, Nymphs! nor is your faith in vain,   ⎫
This Oaken trunk, in which conceal'd I am,   790 ⎬
From a long honour'd ancient lineage came,   ⎭
Who in the fam'd Dodonean grove firſt ſpoke,
When with aſtoniſh'd awe the ſacred valley ſhook.
Know then that Brutus, by unlucky fate
Murd'ring his ſire, bore an immortal hate   795
To his own kingdom, who's ungrateful ſhore
He leaves with vows ne'er to reviſit more ;
Then to Epirus a ſad exile came,   ⎫
(Unhappy ſon, who haſt a father ſlain,   ⎬
But happy father of the Britiſh name.)   800 ⎭
There, by victorious arms, he did reſtore
Thoſe ſceptres, once the race of Priam bore ;
In their paternal thrones his kindred plac'd,
And by that piety his fatal crime defac'd.

   There Jupiter diſdain'd not to relate   805
Thoro' an Oaken mouth his future fate ;
Who for his grandſire's (great Æneas) ſake,
Upon the royal youth will pity take ;
Whoſe toils to his ſhall this reſemblance bear,
A long and tedious wand'ring to endure.   810
'Tis ſaid the deity-retaining Oak,
Burſting her bark, thus to the hero ſpoke,

Whofe voice the nymphs furpris'd with awful dread,
Who in Chaonian groves inhabited :''
‘ Oh ! noble Trojan! of great Sylvia's blood,   815
‘ Hafte from the covert of this threat'ning wood ;
‘ A manfion here the Fates will not permit,
‘ Vaft toils and dangers thou 'rt to conquer yet,
‘ Ere for a murder'd father thou canft be
‘ Abfolv'd, tho' innocently flain by thee,   820
‘ But much muft bear by land, and much by fea.
, Then arm thy folid mind, thy virtues raife,
‘ And thro' thy rough adventures cut new ways,
‘ Whofe end fhall crown thee with immortal bays.
‘ Tho' Hercules fo great a fame achiev'd,   825
‘ His conquefts but to th' weftern Cales arriv'd ;
‘ There finifh'd all his glories and his toils,
‘ He wifh'd no more, nor fought more diftant fpoils :
‘ But the great labours which thou haft begun
‘ Muft, fearlefs of the ocean's threats, go on :   830
‘ And this remember, at thy lanching forth,
‘ To fet thy full-fpread fails againft the North :
‘ In Charles's Wain thy fates are born above,
‘ Bright ftars, defcended from thy grandfire Jove,
‘ Of motion certain, tho' they flowly move.   835
‘ The Bear, too, fhall affift thee in thy courfe
‘ With all her conftellations' glittering force ;
‘ And as thou goeft thy right hand fhall deftroy
‘ Twice fix Gom'ritifh tyrants in thy way.

'Tho' exil'd from the world, difdain all fear,   840
'The gods another world for thee prepare,
'Which in the bofom of the deep conceal'd
'From ages paft, fhall be to thee reveal'd;
'Referv'd, O Brutus! to renown thy fame,
'And fhall be blefs'd ftill with thy race and name.
'All that the air furrounds the Fates decree 846
'To Brutus' and Æneas' progeny,
'Æneas all the land, and Brutus all the fea.'
"This faid, the god from the prophetic Oak,
Who ftretching out her branches, farther fpoke:" 850
'Here, fill thy hands with acorns from my Tree,
'Which in thy tedious toils of ufe fhall be,
'And witneffes of all I promife thee;
'And when thy painful wand'ring fhall be o'er,
'And thou arriv'd on happy Britain's fhore,   855
'Then in her fruitful foil thefe acorns fow,
'Which to vaft woods of mighty ufe fhall grow:
'Not their Chaonian mother's facred name
'Shall o'er the world be fung with greater fame.
'Then holy Druids thou fhalt confecrate,   860
'My honour and my rites to celebrate:
'Teutates in the facred Oak fhall grow,
'To give blefs'd omens to the Miffeltoe.'
"Thus fpake the Oak——with rev'rend awe be-
        liev'd,
And in no one prediction was deceiv'd.   865
        4

My Lineage from Chaonian acorns came,
I two defcents from that firſt parent am,
And now oraculous truths to you proclaim.
My grandame Oak her blooming beauties wore,
When firſt the Daniſh fleet furpris'd our ſhore;   870
When Thor and Tuiſco, and the Saxon gods,
Were angry with their once-belov'd abodes,
Her age two hundred years; a fmall account
To what our long-liv'd numbers do amount:
Such prodigies then ſhe faw as we behold,   875
And fuch our ruins as their figns foretold.
Now from the Caledonian mountains came
New-rifen clouds that cover'd all the plain;
The quiet Tweed regards her bounds no more,
But, driv'n by popular winds, ufurps the ſhore;   880
In her wild courfe a horrid murmur yields,
And frightens with her found the Engliſh fields.
Nor did they hear in vain, or vainly fear
Thofe raging prologues to approaching war;
But filver ſhowers did foon the foe fubdue,   885
Weapons the noble Engliſh never knew:
The people, who for peace fo laviſh were,
Did after buy the merchandife more dear.
Curs'd Civil war even Peace betray'd to guilt,
And made her bluſh with the firſt blood was fpilt. 890
O cruel omens of thofe future woes,
Which now fate brooding in the Senate-houfe!

That den of mifchief, where obfcur'd fhe lies,
And hides her purple face from human eyes.
The working furies there lay unreveal'd,   895
Beneath the privilege of the Houfe conceal'd;
There, by the malice of the great and proud,
And unjuft clamours of the frantic crowd,
The great, the learned, Strafford met his fate;
O facred Innocence! what can expiate   900
For guiltlefs blood but blood? and much muft flow
Both from the guilty and the faultlefs too.
O Worcefter! condemn'd by Fate to be
The mournful witnefs of our mifery,
And to bewail our firft inteftine wars   905
By thy foft Severn's murmurs and her tears;
Wars that more formidable did appear
Ev'n at their end than their beginnings were.

    Me to Kintonian hills * fome god convey,
That I the horrid valley may furvey,   910
Which like a river feem'd of human blood,
Swell'd with the num'rous bodies of the dead.
What flaughters makes fierce Rupert round the field,
Whofe con'quefts pious Charles with fighs beheld?
And had not Fate the courfe of things forbade,   915
This day an end of all our woes had made.

    But our fuccefs the angry gods control,
And ftopp'd our race of glory near the goal.

                * Keinton-fields. Edge-hill.

Where'er the Britiſh empire did extend,
The tyrant War with barb'rous rigour reign'd; 920
From the remoteſt parts it rifled Peace,
From the Belerian Horn * ev'n.to the Orcades.
The fields oppreſs'd, no joyful harveſts bear,
War ruin'd all the product of the year :
Unhappy Albion! by what fury ſtung? 925
What ſerpent of Eumenides has flung
His poiſon thro' thy veins? thou bleed'ſt all o'er,
Art all one wound; one univerſal gore.
Unhappy Newberry! (I thy fatal field,
Cover'd with mighty ſlaughters, thrice beheld,) 930
In horrors you Philippi's fields outvy'd,
Which twice the Civil gore of Romans dy'd.
Long mutual loſs, and the alternate weight
Of equal ſlaughters, pois'd each others' fate :
Uncertain Ruin waver'd to and fro, 935
And knew not where to fix the deadly blow;
At laſt in Northern fields like lightning broke,
And Naſeby doubled ev'ry fatal ſtroke.
But, O ye Gods! permit me not to tell
The woes that after this the land befel; 940
O keep 'em to yourſelves, leſt they ſhould make
Humanity your rites and ſhrines forſake :
To future ages let 'em not be known,
For wretched England's credit and your own.

* S. Burien, the uttermoſt point of Cornwall.

And take from me, ye Gods! futurity, 945
And let my oracles all filent lie,
Rather than by my voice; they fhould declare
The dire events of England's Civil war.
And yet my fight a confus'd profpect fills,
A chaos all deform'd, a heap of ills, 950
Such as no mortal eyes could e'er behold,
Such as no human language can unfold.
But now———
The conqu'ring evil Genius of the wars,
The impious victor, all before him bears; 955
And O,—behold the Sacred vanquifh'd flies,
And tho' in a plebeian's mean difguife,
I know his godlike face; the monarch, fure,
Did ne'er diffemble till this fatal hour.
But, O! he flies! diftrefs'd, forlorn he flies! 960
And feeks his fafety 'mong his enemies:
His kingdoms all he finds hoftile to be,
No place to the vanquifh'd proves a fanctu'ry.
Thus Royal Charles———
From his own people could no fafety gain; 965
Alas! the King (their gueft) implores in vain.
The pilot thus the burning veffel leaves,
And trufts what moft he fears, the threat'ning waves;
But, O! the cruel flood, with rude difdain,
Throws him all ftruggling to the flames again. 970
So did the Scots; alas! what fhould they do?
That prize of war (the foldiers' int'reft now)

By pray'rs and threat'nings back they ſtrive to bring,⎫
But the wiſe Scot will yield to no ſuch thing,⎬
And England, to retrieve him, buys her King. 975⎭
O, ſhame to future worlds! who did command,
As pow'rful lord of all the ſea and land,
Is now a captive ſlave expos'd to ſale,
And Villany o'er Virtue muſt prevail.
The ſervant his bought maſter bears away,   980
O, ſhameful purchaſe of ſo glorious prey!
But yet, O Scotland! far be it from me
To charge thee wholly with this infamy;
Thy nation's virtues ſhall reverſe that fate,
And for the criminal few ſhall expiate;   985
Yet for theſe few the inn'cent reſt muſt feel
The dire effects of the avenging ſteel.

   But now, by laws to God and man unknown,
Their ſovereign, God's anointed, they dethrone,
Who to the Iſle of Wight is priſoner ſent :   990
What tongue, what cruel hearts, do not lament?
That thee, O Scotland! with juſt anger moves,
And Kent, who valued liberty ſo loves;
And thee, O Wales! of ſtill as noble fame,
As were the ancient Britons whence ye came.   995
But why ſhould I diſtinctly here relate
All I behold, the many battles fought
Under the conduct ſtill of angry ſtars,
Their new-made wounds, and old ones turn'd to ſcars;
                         D iij

The blood that did the trembling Ribla dye,   1000
Stopping its frighted stream, that strove to fly?
Or thou, O Medway! swell'd with slaughters, borne
Above the flowr'y banks that did thee once adorn?
Or why, O Colchester! should I rehearse
Thy brave united courage and thy force,   1005
Or deaths of those illustrious men relate,
Who did, with thee, deserve a kinder fate?
Or why the miserable murders tell
Of captives who, by cooler malice, fell?
Nor to your griefs will the addition bring   1010
The sad ideas of a martyr'd King;
A King who all the wounds of Fortune bore,
Nor will his mournful funerals deplore,
Lest that celestial piety (of fame   1014
O'er all the world) should my sad accents blame;
Since death he still esteem'd, howe'er 'twas given,
The greatest good and noblest gift of Heaven.
But I deplore man's wretched wickedness,
(O horrid to be heard, or to express)
Whom even Hell can ne'er enough torment   1020
With her eternal pains and punishment.

    But, oh! what do I see? alas! they bring
Their sacred master forth, their godlike King;
There on a scaffold, rais'd in solemn state,
And plac'd before the royal palace-gate,   1025
'Midst of his empire the black deed was done,
While day, and all the world, were looking on.

By common hangman's hands."——Here ftopp'd the
When from the bottom of its root there broke [Oak,
A thouſand ſighs, which to the ſky ſhe lifts,.   1030
Burſting her ſolid bark into a thouſand clefts;
Each branch her tributary ſorrow gives,.
And tears run trickling from her mournful leaves;
Such numbers after rainy nights they ſhed,
When ſhow'ring clouds, that did ſurround her head,
Are by the riſing goddeſs of the Morn....   1036
Blown off, and fly before th' approaching ſun;
At which the troop of the green nymphs around,
Echoing her ſighs, in wailing accents groan'd,
Whoſe piercing ſounds from far were underſtood, 1040
And the loud tempeſt ſhook the wond'ring wood;
And then a diſmal ſilence did ſucceed,
As in the gloomy manſions of the dead:
But after a long awful interval.
Dryas aſſum'd her ſad prophetic tale.   1045
" Now Britanny, o'erwhelm'd with many a wound,
Her head lopt off, in her own blood lies drown'd;
A horrid carcaſe, without mind or ſoul,
A trunk not to be known, deform'd and foul:
And now who would not hope there ſhould have been,
After ſo much of death, a quiet ſcene?   1051
Or rather, with their Monarch's funeral,
Eternal ſleep ſhould not have ſeiz'd 'em all?
But nothing leſs; for in the room of one,
Who govern'd juſtly on his peaceful throne,   1055

A thousand heads sprang up, deform'd and base,
With a tumultuous and ignoble race,
The vile, the vulgar offspring of the earth ;
Insects of pois'nous kinds, of monstrous birth,
And rav'nous serpents, now the land infest,   1060
And Cromwell ! viler yet than all the rest :
That serpent ev'n upon the marrow preys,
Devouring kingdoms with insatiate jaws.
Now right and wrong (mere words) confounded lie;
Rage sets no bounds to her impiety ;   1065
And having once transgress'd the rules of shame,
Honour or justice counts an empty name.
In every street, as pastime for the crowd,
Erected scaffolds reek'd with noble blood;
Prisons were now th' apartments of the brave, 1070
Whom Tyranny commits, and only deaths retrieve;
Whose paths were crowded ere the morning-dawn,
Some to the dungeons, some to gibbets drawn.
But tir'd-out Cruelty pauses for a while,
To take new breath amidst her barbarous toil. 1075
So does not Avarice, she, unwearied still,
Ne'er stops her greedy hand from doing ill.
The warrior may a while his spear forsake,
But sequestrators will no respite take.
What a long race of kings laid up with care,   1080
The gifts of happy Peace, and spoils of War;
Whatever lib'ral Piety did present,
Or the religion (all magnificent)

Of our forefathers to the church had giv'n,
And confecrated to the Pow'rs of heav'n,   1085
Altars, or whatfoe'er could guilty be
Of tempting wealth, or fatal loyalty,
Was not enough to fatisfy the rage
Of a few earth-begotten tyrants of the age:
The impious rout thought it a trivial thing   1090
To rob the houfes of their God and King;
Their facrilege, admitting of no bound,
Rejoic'd to fee 'em levell'd with the ground ;
As if the nation (wicked and unjuft)
Had ev'n in ruin found a certain luft.   1095
On ev'ry fide the lab'ring hammers found,
And ftrokes from mighty hatchets do rebound;
On ev'ry fide the groaning earth fuftains
The pond'rous weight of ftones and wondrous beams;
Fiercely they ply their work, with fuch a noife, 1100
As if fome mighty ftructure they would raife
For the proud tyrant: no, this clam'rous din
Is not for building, but demolifhing.
——When (my Companions!) thefe fad things you fee,
And each beholds the dead beams of her parent Tree,
Long fince repos'd in palaces of kings,   1106
Torn down by furious hands, as ufelefs things,
Then know your fate is come; thofe hands that could
From houfes tear dead beams, and long-hewn wood,
Thofe cruel hands, by unrefifted force,   1110
Will for your living trunks find no remorfe.

Religion, which was great of old, commands
No wood fhould be profan'd by impious hands;
Thofe noble feminaries for the fleet,
Plantations that make towns and cities great;   1115
Thofe hopes of war, and ornaments of peace,
Should live fecure from any outrages,
Which now the barb'rous conqu'ror will invade,
Tear up your roots, and rifle all your fhade;
For gain they'll fell you to the cov'tous buy'r,   1120
A facrifice to every common fire;
They'll fpare no race of Trees of any age,
But murder infant branches in their rage:
Elms, Beeches, tender Afhes, fhall be fell'd,   1124
And even the gray and reverend bark muft yield:
The foft, the murm'ring, troop fhall be no more,
No more with mufic charm, as heretofore;
No more each little bird fhall build her houfe,
And fing in her hereditary boughs,
But only Philomel fhall celebrate,   1130
In mournful notes, a new unhappy fate:
The banifh'd Hamadryads muft be gone,
And take their flight with fad but filent moan;
For a celeftial being ne'er complains,
Whatever be her grief, in noify ftrains: 1135
The wood-gods fly, and whither fhall they go?
Not all the Britifh orb can fcarce allow
A trunk fecure for them to reft in now.

But yet thefe wild Saturnals fhall not laft,
Oppreffing Vengeance follows on too faft;   1140
She fhakes her brandifh'd fteel, and ftill denies
Length to immoderate rage and cruelties.
Do not defpond, my Nymphs! that wicked birth
Th' avenging powers will chafe from off the earth;
Let 'em hew down the wood, deftroy and burn, 1145
And all the lofty groves to afhes turn,
Yet ftill there will not want a Tree to yield
Timber enough old Tyburn to rebuild,
Where they may hang at laft; and this kind one
Shall then revenge the woods of all their wrong.1150
In the mean time (for Fate not always fhows
A fwift compliance to our wifh and vows)
The offspring of great Charles, forlorn and poor,
And exil'd from their cruel native fhore,
Wander in foreign kingdoms, where in vain   1155
They feek thofe aids, alas! they cannot gain;
For ftill their preffing Fate purfues 'em hard,
And fcarce a place of refuge will afford.
O pious fon of fuch a holy fire!
Who can enough thy fortitude admire?   1160
How often, tofs'd by ftorms of land and fea,
Yet unconcern'd, thy fate thou didft furvey,
And her fatigues ftill underwent with joy?
O royal Youth! purfue thy juft difdain,
Let Fortune and her Furies frown in vain,   1165

Till, tir'd with her injuſtice, ſhe give out,
And leaves her giddy wheel for thee to turn about.
   Then that great ſceptre, which no human hand
From the tenacious tyrant can command,
Scorning the bold Uſurper to adorn,   1170
Shall, ripe and falling, to thy hand be borne.
   But, O! he rouſes now before his time!
Illuſtrious Youth! whoſe brav'ry is a crime,
Alas! what wilt thou do? Ah! why ſo faſt?
The dice of Fate, alas! not yet are caſt.   1175
While thou, all fire, fearleſs of future harms,
And prodigal of life, aſſum'dſt thy arms,
And even provoking Fame, he cuts his way
Thro' hoſtile fleets and a rude winter's ſea:
But neither ſhall his daring courſe oppoſe;   1180
Ev'n to thoſe ſhores, ſo very late his foes,
And ſtill to be ſuſpected; but, mean-while,
The Oliverian demons of the iſle,
With all Hell's deities, with fury burn,
To ſee great Charles preparing to return;   1185
They call up all their winds of dreadful force,
In vain, to ſtop his ſacred veſſel's courſe:
In vain their ſtorms a ruin do prepare
For what Fate means to take peculiar care,
And, trembling, find great Cæſar ſafe at land, 1190
By Heav'n conducted, not by Fortune's hand.
   But, Scotland! you your King recall in vain,
While you your unchang'd principles retain;

But yet the time fhall come when fome fmall fhare
Of glory that great honour fhall confer ;   1195
When you a conqu'ring hero forth fhall guide,
While Heav'n and all the ftars are on his fide,
Who fhall the exil'd King in peace recall,
And England's Genius be efteem'd by all :
But this, not yet, my Nymphs!——But now's the time
When the illuftrious heir of Fergus' line,   1201
From full a hundred kings fhall mount the throne, ⎫
Who now the temple enters, and at Scone,   ⎬
After the ancient manner, he receives the crown ; ⎭
But, oh! with no aufpicious omens done ;   1205
The left hand of the kingdom put it on.

    But now th' infulting conqueror draws nigh,
Difturbing the auguft folemnity;
When with revenge and indignation fir'd,
And by a father's murder well infpir'd,   1210
The brave, the royal, youth for war prepares;
O heir moft worthy of thy hundred-fceptred ance-
With thoughts all glorious now he fallies forth, [ftors.
Nor will he truft his fortune in the North,
That corner of his realms, nor will his hafte   1215
Lazily wait till coming winter's paft;
He fcorns that aid, nor will he hope t' oppofe
High mountains 'gainft the fury of his foes,
Nor their furrounding force will here engage,
Or ftay the preffures of a fhameful fiege;   1220

But boldly farther on refolves t' advance,
And give a gen'rous loofe to Fortune's chance,
And fhut from diftant Tay, he does effay
To Thames even with his death to force his way;
Behind he leaves his trembling enemies   1225
Amaz'd at his ftupendous enterprife.

   And now the wifh'd-for happy day appears,
Sought for fo long by Britain's pray'rs and tears;
The King returns, and, with a mighty hand,
Avow'd revenger of his native land,   1230
And thro' a thoufand dangers and extremes,
Marches a conqu'ror to Sabrina's ftreams;
(Ah! would to Heav'n Sabrina had been Thames.)
So wifh'd the King, but the perfuafive force
Of kind miftaken councils ftopp'd his courfe.   1235

   Now, warlike England! rouze at thefe alarms,
Provide your horfes, and affume your arms,
And fall on the Ufurper: now for fhame,
If piety be not pretence and name,
Advance the work Heav'n has fo well begun,   1240
Revenge the father, and reftore the fon:
No more let that old cant deftructive be,
Religion, Liberty, and Property:
No longer let that dear-bought cheat delude,
(O you too credulous fenfelefs multitude!)   1245
Words only form'd more eas'ly to enflave,
By every popular and pretending knave:

But now your bleeding land expects you should
Be wife at the expenfe of fo much blood:
Rouze then! and with awaken'd fenfe prepare
To reap the glory of this holy war,   1251
In which your King and Heav'n have equal fhare:
His right divine let ev'ry voice proclaim,
And a juft ardour every foul inflame,

  But England's evil Genius, watchful ftill   1255
To ruin Virtue, and encourage ill,
Induftrious, ev'n as Cromwell, to fubvert
Honour and loyalty in every heart,
A baneful drug of fourfold poifon makes,
And an infernal fleepy afp he takes   1260
Of cold and fearful nature, adds to this
Opium, that binds the nerves with lazinefs,
Mix'd with the venom of vile avarice;
Which all the fpirits benumb, as when ye' approach
The chilling wonderful torpedo's touch: 1265
Next drops from Lethe's ftream he does infufe,
And ev'ry breaft befprinkles with the juice,
Till a deep lethargy o'er all Britain came,
Who now forget their fafety and their fame.
Yet ftill great Charles's valour ftood the teft,   1270
By Fortune tho' forfaken and opprefs'd,
Witnefs the purple-dy'd Sabrina's ftream,
And the Red Hill, not call'd fo now in vain;
And, Worc'fter! thou, who didft the mifery bear,
And faw'ft the end of a long fatal war.   1275

The King, tho' vanquish'd, still his fate outbraves,
And was the last the captiv'd city leaves;
Which from the neighb'ring hills he does survey,
Where round about his bleeding numbers lay:
He saw 'em rifled by th' insulting foe,   1280
And sighs for those he cannot rescue now;
But yet his troops will rally once again,
Those few escap'd, all scatter'd o'er the plain;
Disdain and Anger now resolves to try
How to repair this day's fatality.   1285
The King has sworn to conquer or to die.
Darby and Wilmot, chiefs of mighty fame,
With that bold lovely youth, great Buckingham!
Fiercer than lightning, to his monarch dear,
That brave Achates, worth Æneas' care;   1290
Applaud his great resolve! there's no delay,
But toward the foe in haste they take their way,
Not by vain hopes of a new vict'ry fir'd,
But by a kind despair alone inspir'd: 1294
This was the King's resolve, and those great few
Whom glory taught to die, as well as to subdue;
Who knew that death and the reposing grave
No foes were to the wretched or the brave.

But, oh! this noble courage did not rest
In each ungen'rous unconsidering breast;   1300
They fearfully forsake their general,
Who now in vain the flying cowards call;

Deaf to his voice, will no obedience yield,
But in their hafty flight fcour o'er the dreadful field.

    O vainly gallant Youth! what pitying god   1305
Shall free thee from this foul-oppreffing load
Of grief and fhame? abandon'd and betray'd
By perjur'd flaves, whom thou haft fed and paid;
Prefs'd with more woes than mortal force could bear,
And Fortune ftill refolv'd to be fevere: 1310
But yet that God——
To whom no wonders are impoffible,
Will, to preferve thee, work a miracle,
And for the facred father's martyrdom
Will, with a crown, reward the injur'd fon;   1315
While thou, great Charles! with a prevailing pray'r
Doft to the gods commend the fafety of thy heir,
And the celeftial court of pow'rs divine,
With one confent, do in the chorus join.

    But why, O why, muft I reveal the doom   1320
(O my Companions!) of the years to come?
And why divulge the myfteries that lie
Enroll'd long fince in heav'n's vaft treafury,
In characters which no dreamer can unfold,
Nor ever yet prophetic rapture told;   1325
Nor the fmall fibres of the victim'd beaft,
Or birds which facred aug'ries have exprefs'd;
No ftars, or any divination fhows,
Made myftic by the murmurs of the boughs?

                     E iij

Yet I muft on, with a divine prefage,   1330
And tell the wonders of the coming age.
In that far part where the rich Salop gains
An ample view o'er all the weftern plains,
A grove appears, which Bofcobel they name,
Not known to maps, a grove of fcanty fame,   1335
Scarce any human thing does there intrude,
But it enjoys itfelf in its own folitude;
And yet henceforth no celebrated fhade,
Of all the Britifh groves, fhall be more glorious made.

    Near this obfcure and deftin'd happy wood,   1340
A facred houfe of lucky omen ftood,
White-Lady call'd; and old records relate
' Twas once——
To men of holy orders confecrate;
But to a king a refuge now is made,   1345
The firft that gives a wearied monarch bread;
O, prefent of a wondrous excellence!
That can relieve the hunger of a prince:
Fortune fhall here a better face put on,
And here the King fhall firft the king lay down; 1350
Here he difmiffes all his mourning friends,
Whom to their kinder ftars he recommends;
With eyes all drown'd in tears their fate to fee,
But unconcern'd at his own deftiny:
Here he puts off thofe ornaments he wore   1355
Thro' all the fplendour of his life before;

Ev'n his Blue Garter now he will difcharge,
Nor keep the warlike figure of St. George;
That holy champion now is vanquifh'd quite;
Alas! the Dragon has fubdu'd the Knight;   1360
His crown, that toilfome weight of glory, now
Divefts a while from his more eafy brow;
And all thofe charming curls that did adorn
His royal head——thofe jetty curls, are fhorn:
Himfelf he clothes in a coarfe ruffet weed;   1365
Nor was the poor man feign'd, but fo indeed:
And now the greateft king the world e'er faw
Is fubject to the houfe's ancient law;
(A convent once, which poverty did profefs,
Here he puts off all worldly pomp and drefs).   1370
And, like a Monk, a fad adieu he takes
Of all his friends, and the falfe world forfakes:
But yet, ere long, even this humble ftate,
Alas! fhall be deny'd him by his Fate;   1374
She drives him forth even from this mean abode, ⎫
Who wanders now a hermit in the wood,   ⎬
Hungry and tir'd, to reft and feek his food.   ⎭
The dark and lonely fhade conceals the King,
Who feeds on flow'rs, and drinks the murm'ring
          fpring;
More happy here than on a reftlefs throne,   1380
Could he but call thofe fhades and fprings his own:
No longer Fate will that repofe allow,
Who even of earth itfelf deprives him now;

A Tree will hardly here a feat afford,
Amidft her boughs, to her abandon'd lord.   1385
    Then (O my Nymphs!) you who your monarch love,
To fave your darling haften to that grove;
(Nor think I vain prophetics do exprefs)
In filence let each nymph her trunk poffefs;
O'er all the woods and plains let not a Tree   1390
Be uninhabited by a deity,
While I the largeft foreft Oak infpire,
And with you to this leafy court retire;
There keep a faithful watch each night and day,⎫
And with erected heads the fields furvey,   1395 ⎬
Left any impious foldier pafs that way,   ⎭
And fhould profanely touch that pledge of Heav'n,
Which to our guarding fhade in charge was given.
Here then, my Nymphs! your King you fhall receive,
And fafety in your darkeft coverts give.   1400
    But, ha! what ruftic fwain is that I fee
Sleeping beneath the fhade of yonder Tree,
Upon whofe knotty root he leans his head,
And on the moffy ground has made his bed?
And why alone? alas! fome fpy, I fear,   1405
For only fuch a wretch would wander here;
Who even the winds and fhow'rs of rain defies,
Outdaring all the anger of the fkies.
Obferve his face, fee his diforder'd hair
Is ruffled by the tempeft-beaten air;   1410
Yet look what tracks of grief have ag'd his face,
Where hardly twenty years have run their race,

Worn out with num'rous toils; and even in sleep
Sighs seem to heave his breast, his eyes to weep.
Nor is that colour of his face his own,   1415
That sooty veil, for some disguise put on,
To keep the nobler part from being known;
For, 'midst of all—something of sacred light
Beams forth, and does inform my wond'ring sight,
And now—arises to my view more bright. 1420
Ha!—can my eyes deceive me, or am I
At last no true presaging deity?
Yet if I am, that wretched rustic thing,
O Heav'ns, and all your Powers! must be the King.
—Yes, 'tis the King! his image all divine   1425
Breaks thro' that cloud of darkness, and a shine
Gilds all the sooty visor!—but, alas!
Who is it approaches him with such a pace?
O—'tis no traitor; the just gods, I find,
Have still a pitying care of humankind.   1430
This is the gallant, loyal Careless! thrown
(By the same wreck by which the King's undone)
Beneath our shades; he comes in pious care,
(O happy Man! than Cromwell happier far
On whom ill Fate this honour does confer) 1435
He tells the King the woods are overspread
With villains arm'd, to search that prize, his head,
Now poorly set to sale.—The foe is nigh,
What shall they do? ah! whither shall they fly?

They from the danger hafty counfel took,   1440
And, by fome god infpir'd, afcend my Oak;
My Oak, the largeft in the faithful wood,
Whom to receive I my glad branches bow'd,
And for the King a throne prepar'd, and fpread
My thickeft leaves a canopy o'er his head;   1445
The Miffeltoe commanded to afcend,
Around his facred perfon to attend,
(Oh, happy omen!) ftraight it did obey,
The facred Miffeltoe attends with joy:
Here without fear their proftrate heads they bow,
The King is fafe beneath my fhelter now;   1451
And you, my Nymphs! with awful filence may
Your adorations to your fovereign pay,
And cry, All hail! thou moft belov'd of Heav'n,
To whom its chiefeft attributes are giv'n;   1455
But, above all, that godlike fortitude
That has the malice of thy Fate fubdu'd:
All hail!
Thou greateft now of kings indeed, while yet
With all the miferies of life befet,   1460
Thy mighty mind could death nor danger fear,
Nor yet even then of fafety could defpair.
This is the virtue of a monarch's foul,
Who above Fortune's reach can all her turns control;
Thus, if Fate rob you of your empire's fway,   1465
You by this fortitude take lier's away;

O brave reprifal! which the gods prefer,
That makes you triumph o'er the conqueror:
The gods, who one day will this juftice do,
Both make you victor and triumpher too!   1470
That day's at hand, O let that day come on,
Wherein that wondrous miracle fhall be fhown;
May its gay morn be more than ufual bright,
And rife upon the world with new-created light:
Or let that ftar, whofe dazzling beams were hurl'd
Upon his birth-day, now inform the world;   1476
That brave bold conftellation, which in fight
Of mid-day's fun durft lift its lamp of light:
Now, happy Star! again at mid-day rife,
And with new prodigies adorn the fkies;   1480
Great Charles again is born; Monk's valiant hand
At laft delivers the long lab'ring land.
This is the month, great Prince! muft bring you forth;
May pays her fragrant tributes at your birth;
This is the month that's due to you by Fate;   1485
O month moft glorious! month moft fortunate!
When you between your royal brothers rode,
Amidft your fhining train, attended like fome god,
One would believe that all the world were met
To pay their homage at your facred feet;   1490
The wand'ring gazers numberlefs as thefe,
Or as the leaves on the vaft foreft Trees:
He comes! he comes! they cry, while the loud din
Refounds to heav'n; and then, Long live the King,

And fure the fhouts of their re-echo'd joys   1495
Reach'd to the utmoft bounds of diftant feas,
Borne by the flying winds thro' yielding air,
And ftrike the foreign fhores with awful fear.
O 'tis a wondrous pleafure to be mad;
Such frantic turns our nation oft' has had :   1500
Permit it now, ye Stoics! ne'er till now
The frenzy you more juftly might allow,
Since 'tis a joyful fit that ends the fears,
And wretched fury of fo many years.
Nor will the Night her fable wings difplay   1505
T' obfcure the luftre of fo bright a day ;
At leaft the much-tranfported multitude
Permits not the dark goddefs to intrude ;
The whole ifle feem'd to burn with joyful flames,
Whofe rays gilt all the face of neighb'ring Thames.

But how fhall I exprefs the vulgar's joys,   1511
Their fongs, their feafts, their laughter, and their cries?
How fountains run with the Vine's precious juice,
And fuch the flowing rivers fhould produce !
Their ftreams the richeft nectar fhould afford ;   1515
The Golden Age feems now again reftor'd.
See——fmiling Peace does her bright face difplay, ⎫
Down thro' the air ferene fhe cuts her way,   ⎬
Expels the clouds, and rifes on the day :   ⎭
Long exil'd from our fhores, new joy fhe brings,
Embracing Albion with her fnowy wings ;   1521

Nor comes fhe unattended, but a throng
Of noble British matrons brings along;
Plenty, fair Fame, and charming Modefty,
Religion, long fince fled with Loyalty, 1525
And in a decent garb the lovely Piety;
Juftice, from Fraud and Perj'ry forc'd to fly,
Learning, fine Arts, and generous Liberty:
Blefs'd Liberty! thou faireft in the train,
And moft efteem'd in a juft prince's reign. 1530

With thefe, as lov'd, great Mary, too, return'd,
In her own country who long exile mourn'd.
You, royal Mother! you, whofe only crime
Was loving Charles, and fharing woes with him;
Now Heav'n repays, tho' flow, yet juft and true,
For him revenge, and juft rewards for you. 1536

Hail, mighty Queen! form'd by the pow'rs divine,
The fhame of our weak fex, and pride of thine;
How well have you in either fortune fhown?
In either, ftill your mind was all your own: 1540
The giddy world roll'd round you long in vain,
Who fix'd in virtue's centre ftill remain.

And now, juft Prince! thou thy great mind fhalt
To the true weighty office of a king. ⌐bring
The gaping wounds of War thy hand fhall cure, 1545
Thy royal hand, gentle alike, and fure!
And by infenfible degrees efface
Of foregone ills the very fcars and trace;

Force to the injur'd law thou fhalt reftore,
And all that majefty in Majefty it own'd before.
Thou long-corrupted manners fhalt reclaim,   1551
And faith and honour of the Englifh name.
Thus long-neglected gardens entertain
Their banifh'd mafter when return'd again :
All over-run with weeds he finds, but foon   1555
Luxuriant branches carefully will prune;
The weaken'd arms of the fick Vine he'll raife,
And with kind bands fuftain the loofen'd fprays.
Much does he plant, and much extirpate too,
And with his art and fkill make all things new;
A work immenfe, yet fweet, and which in future
        days,   1561
When the fair Trees their blooming glories raife,
The happy gard'ner's labour overpays.
Cities and towns, great Prince! thy gardens, be
With labour cultivated worthy thee.   1565
In decent order thou doft all difpofe ;
Nor are the woods nor rural groves difdain'd ;
He who our wants, who all our breaches knows,
He all our drooping fortunes has fuftain'd.
As young colonies of Trees thou doft replace
I' th' empty realms of our arboreal race,   1571
Nay, doft our reign extend to future days,
And blefs'd Pofterity, fupinely laid,
Shall feaft and revel underneath thy fhade,

.Cool fummer arbours then thy gift fhall be,   1575
And their bright winter-fires they'll owe to thee :
To thee thofe beams their palaces fuftain,
And all their floting caftles on the main.
Who knows, great Prince ! but thou this happy
    .day   1579
For towns and navies may'ft foundations lay,
After a thoufand years are roll'd away ?
Reap thou thofe mighty triumphs, then, which for
    thee grow,
And mighty triumphs for fucceeding ages fow :
Thou Glory's craggy top fhalt firft effay,
Divide the clouds, and mark the fhining way ; 1585
To Fame's bright temples fhalt thy fubjects guide,
Thy Britons bold, almoft of night deny'd :
The foaming waves thy dread commands fhall ftay,
Thy dread commands the foaming waves obey :
The watry world no Neptune owns but thee,   1590
And thy three kingdoms fhall thy trident be.
    What madnefs, O Batavians ! you poffefs'd,
That the fea's fceptre you'd from Britain wreft,
Which Nature gave, whom fhe with floods has crown'd,
And fruitful Amphitrite embraces round :   1595
The reft o' th' world's juft kifs'd by Amphitrite ;
Albion fhe' embraces, all her dear delight.
You fcarce th' infulting ocean can reftrain,
Nor bear th' affaults of the befieging main, 1599
Your grafts, and mounds, and trenches, all in vain :

And yet what fond ambition spurs you on?
You dare attempt to make the seas your own;
O'er the vast ocean, which no limit knows,
The narrow laws of ponds and fens impose:
But Charles his lively valour this defies,   1605
And this the sturdy British Oak denies.
O'er empty seas the fierce Batavian fleet
Sings triumphs, while there was no foe to meet.
But fear not, Belgian! he'll not tarry long,
He'll soon be here, and interrupt thy song;   1610
Too late thou'lt of thy hasty joys complain,
And to thy native shores look back in vain.
Great James, as soon as the first whisper came,
Prodigal of his life, and greedy but of fame,
With eager haste returns, as fast as they,   1615
After the dreadful fight, will run away.

   And now the joyful English from afar,
Approaching saw the floting Belgian war.
Hark, what a shout they give! like those who come
From long East-India voyage rich laden home,   1620
When first they make the happy British land,
The dear white rocks, and Albion's chalky strand.

   The way to all the rest brave Rupert show'd,
And thro' their fleet cuts out his flaming road;
Rupert! who now had stubborn Fate inclin'd,   1625
Heav'n on his side engaging and the wind,
Famous by land and sea, whose valour soon
Blunts both the Horns of the Batavian Moon.

Next comes illuſtrious James, and, where he goes,
To cowards leaves the crowd of vulgar foes :   1630
To th' Royal Sovereign's deck he ſeems to grow,
Shakes his broad ſword, and ſeeks an equal foe :
Nor did bold Opadm's mighty mind refuſe
The dreadful honour which 'twas death to chuſe :
Both Admirals with haſte for fight prepare,   1635
The reſt might ſtand and gaze, themſelves a war.

   O whither, whither, Opdam! doſt thou fly ?
Can this raſh valour pleaſe the Pow'rs on high ?
It can't, it won't—or wouldſt thou proudly die
By ſuch a mighty hand? No, Opdam! no :   1640
Thy fate is to periſh by a nobler foe.
Heav'n only, Opdam! ſhall thy conqu'ror be,
A labour worth its while to conquer thee :
Heav'n ſhall be there, to guard its beſt lov'd houſe,
And juſt revenge inflict on all your broken vows.
The mighty ſhip a hundred cannons bore,   1646
A hundred cannons which like thunder roar ;
Six times as many men in ſhivers torn,
Ere one broad-ſide or ſingle ſhot it had borne,
Is with a horrid crack blown up to the ſky   1650
In ſmoke and flames o'er all the ocean nigh ;
Torn half-brunt limbs of ſhips, and ſeamen, ſcat-
     ter'd lie.
Whether a real bolt from Heav'n was thrown
Among the guilty wretches is not known,

Tho' likely 'tis ; Amboyna's wickednefs,   1655
And broken peace and oaths, deferv'd no lefs;
Or whether fatal gunpowder it were,
By fome unlucky fpark enkindled there;
Ev'n Chance, by Heav'n directed, is the rod,
The fiery fhaft of an avenging God.   1660
The flaming wreck the hiffing deep flotes o'er,
Far, far away, almoft to either fhore,
Which ev'n from pious foes would pity draw,
A trembling pity, mix'd with dreadful awe;
But pity yet fcarce any room can find;   1665
What noife, what horror, ftill remains behind ?
On either fide does wild Confufion reign,
Ship grapples fhip, and fink into the main.
The Orange, carelefs of loft Opdam's fate,
Worthy to perifh at the felf-fame rate,   1670
Will next t' attack victorious James prepare,
But Englifh guns fufficient thunder bear;
By Englifh guns, and human fire o'erpow'r'd,
'Tis quickly in the hiffing waves devour'd.   1674
Three fhips befides are burnt, if Fame fays true,
None of whofe bafer names the goddefs knew,
As many more the Dolphin did fubdue.
Their decks in fhow'rs of kindled fulphur fteep,
And fend 'em flaming to th' affrighted deep.
So burns a city, ftorm'd and fir'd by night,   1680
The fhades are pierc'd with fuch a dreadful light;

Such dufky globes of flame around 'em broke,
Thro' the dark fhadow of the guns and fmoke.

    Can fire in water then fuch licenfe claim?
Juftly the water hides itfelf for fhame;   1685
The dreadful wreck outftretching far away,
Vaft ruins o'er its trembling bofom lay :
Here mafts and rudders from their veffels torn,
There fails and flags acrofs the waves are borne;
A thoufand floting bodies there appear,   1690
As many half-dead men lie groaning here.
If any where the fea itfelf is reveal'd,
With horrid purple tracts the azure wave's conceal'd.
All funk or took, 'twere tedious to relate,
And all the fad variety of Fate   1695
One day produces——With what art and fkill
Ev'n Chance, ingenious, feems to fave or kill,
To fpare or to torment whoe'er fhe will!
The vulgar deaths, below the Mufe to heed,
Not only faith, but number, too, exceed.   1700
Three noble youths, by the fame fudden death,
A brave example to the world bequeath;
Fam'd for high birth, but merits yet more high;
All at one fatal moment's warning die,
Torn by one fhot; almoft one body they,   1705
Three brothers in one death confounded lay.
Who would not Fortune harfh and barbarous call?
Yet Fortune was benign and kind withal;

For next to thefe——I tremble ftill with fear,
My joy's difturb'd while fuch a danger near ;   1710
Fearlefs, unhurt, the Royal Adm'ral ftood,
Stunn'd with the blow, and fprinkled with their blood.
Fiercer he preffes on, while they retir'd ;
He preffes on, with grief and anger fir'd.
Nor longer can the Belgian force engage   1715
The Englifh valour, warm'd with double rage ;
Breaks with their loffes and a caufe fo ill ;
Their fhatter'd fleet all the wide ocean fill,
Till trembling Rhine opens his harbours wide,
Seeing the wretches from our thunder fly ;   1720
From our hot chafe their fhatter'd fleet he'd hide,
And bends his conquer'd Horns as we go by."
In facred rage the Dryad this reveal'd,
Yet many future wondrous things conceal'd :
But this to grace fome future bard will ferve,
For better poets this the gods referve.   1726

End of the Sixth Book.

DAVIDEIS:

A SACRED POEM OF THE

TROUBLES OF DAVID.

IN FOUR BOOKS.

Me vero primum dulces ante omnia Mufae,
Quarum facra fero ingenti percuffus amore,
Accipiant, Coeliq; vias ac fidera monftrent. VIRG. Georg. II.

BOOK I.

The Contents.

THE propofition. The invocation. The entrance into the hiftory, from a new agreement between Saul and David. A defcription of Hell. The Devil's fpeech. Envy's reply to him. Her appearing to Saul in the fhape of Benjamin. Her fpeech, and Saul's to himfelf, after fhe was vanifhed. A defcription of Heaven. God's fpeech. He fends an angel to David. The angel's meffage to him. David fent for to play before Saul. A digreffion concerning mufic. David's Pfalm. Saul attempts to kill him. His efcape to his own houfe, from whence, being purfued by the King's guard, by the artifice of his wife Michol he efcapes, and flies to Naioh, the Prophet's College at Ramah. Saul's fpeech and rage at his efcape. A long digreffion, defcribing the Prophet's College, and their manner of life there, and the ordinary fubjects of their poetry. Saul's guards purfue David thither, and prophefy. Saul among the prophets. He is compared to Balaam, whofe fong concludes the Book.

I SING the Man who Judah's fceptre bore
In that right hand which held the crook before;
Who from beft poet beft of kings did grow,
The two chief gifts Heav'n could on man beftow.

Much danger firſt, much toil, did he ſuſtain,   5
Whilſt Saul and Hell croſs'd his ſtrong fate in vain ;
Nor did his crown leſs painful work afford,
Leſs exerciſe his patience or his ſword;
So long her conqu'ror Fortune's ſpight purſu'd,
Till with unwearied virtue he ſubdu'd   10
All homebred malice and all foreign boaſts;
Their ſtrength was armies, his the Lord of Hoſts.

   Thou who didſt David's-royal ſtem adorn (*a*),
And gav'ſt him birth from whom thyſelf waſt born;
Who didſt in triumph at Death's court appear, 15
And ſlew'ſt him with thy nails, thy croſs, and ſpear,
Whilſt Hell's black tyrant trembled to behold
The glorious light he forfeited of old;
Who, Heav'n's glad burden now, and juſteſt pride,
Sitt'ſt high enthron'd next thy great Father's ſide, 20
(Where hallowed flames help to adorn that head
Which once the bluſhing thorns environed,
Till crimſon drops of precious blood hung down,
Like rubies, to enrich thine humble crown)
Ev'n thou my breaſt with ſuch bleſs'd rage inſpire, 25
As mov'd the tuneful ſtrings of David's lyre;
Guide my bold ſteps with thine old travell'ing flame(*b*),
In theſe untrodden paths to ſacred fame;
Lo! with pure hands thy heav'nly fires to take,
My well-chang'd Muſe I a chaſte Veſtal make! 30
From earth's vain joys, and love's ſoft witchcraft free,
I conſecrate my Magdalane to thee!

    (*a*) John. viii. 58.   (*b*) Exod. xiii. 21.

Lo! this great work, a temple to thy praiſe,
On poliſh'd pillars of ſtrong verſe I raiſe!
A temple where, if thou vouchſafe to dwell,   35
It Solomon's and Herod's ſhall excel.
Too long the Muſes' land hath Heathen been;
Their gods too long were devils, and virtues ſin;
But thou, Eternal Word, haſt call'd forth me,
Th' apoſtle to convert that world to thee;   40
T' unbind the charms that in ſlight fables lie,
And teach that truth is trueſt poeſy.

    The malice now of jealous Saul grew leſs,
O'ercome by conſtant virtue and ſucceſs;
He grew at laſt more weary to command   45
New dangers, than young David to withſtand,
Or conquer them; he fear'd his maſt'ring fate,
And envy'd him a king's unpow'rful hate.
Well did he know how palms by' oppreſſion ſpeed,
Victorious, and the victor's ſacred meed;   50
The burden lifts them higher: well did he know
How a tame ſtream does wild and dangerous grow
By unjuſt force: he now with wanton play
Kiſſes the ſmiling banks and glides away;
But his known channel ſtopt, begins to roar,   55
And ſwell with rage, and buffet the dull ſhore:
His mutinous waters hurry to the war,
And troops of waves come rolling from afar:
Then ſcorns he ſuch weak ſtops to his free ſource,
And over-runs the neighb'ring fields with violent
     courſe.   60

This knew the tyrant, and this useful thought
His wounded mind to health and temper brought :
He old kind vows to David did renew,
Swore constancy, and meant his oath for true.
A general joy at this glad news appear'd,   65
For David all men lov'd, and Saul they fear'd.
Angels and men did peace and David love,
But Hell did neither him nor that approve :
From man's agreement fierce alarms they take,
And quiet here does there new business make.   70.

Beneath the silent chambers of the earth,
Where the sun's fruitful beams give metals birth,
Where he the growth of fatal gold does see,
Gold, which above more influence has than he ;
Beneath the dens where unfletcht tempests lie,   75
And infant winds their tender voices try ;
Beneath the mighty ocean's wealthy caves,
Beneath th' eternal fountain of all waves,
Where their vast court the mother-waters keep,
And, undisturb'd by moons, in silence sleep,   80
There is a place deep, wondrous deep, below,
Which genuine night and horror does o'erflow ;
No bound controls th' unwearied space, but Hell
Endless, as those dire pains that in it dwell.
Here no dear glimpse of the sun's lovely face   85
Strikes thro' the solid darkness of the place ;
No dawning morn does her kind reds display ;
One slight weak beam would here be thought the day ;

2

No gentle ſtars, with their fair gems of light,
Offend the ty'rannous and unqueſtion'd Night; 90
Here Lucifer the mighty captive reigns,
Proud 'midſt his woes, and tyrant in his chains;
Once general of a gilded hoſt of ſprights,
Like Heſper, leading forth the ſpangled Nights;
But down like lightning, which him ſtruck, he came,
And roar'd at his firſt plunge into the flame : 96
Myriads of ſp'rits fell wounded round him there;
With dropping lights thick ſhone the ſinged air;
Since when the diſmal ſolace of their woe
Has only been weak mankind to undo; 100
Themſelves at firſt againſt themſelves they' excite,
(Their deareſt conqueſt, and moſt proud delight)
And if thoſe mines of ſecret treaſon fail,
With open force man's virtue they aſſail;
Unable to corrupt, ſeek to deſtroy, 105
And where their poiſons miſs the ſword employ.
Thus ſought the tyrant fiend young David's fall,
And 'gainſt him arm'd the pow'rful rage of Saul:
He ſaw the beauties of his ſhape and face,
His female ſweetneſs, and his manly grace *(c)*, 110
He ſaw the nobler wonders of his mind,
Great gifts, which for great works he knew deſign'd;
He ſaw (t' aſhame the ſtrength of man and hell *(d)*,
How by his young hands their Gathite champion fell;

(c) 1 Sam xvi. 12.   *(d)* 1 Sam. xvii.

He faw the reverend prophet boldly fhed   .   115
The royal drops round his enlarged head *(e)*,
And well he knew what legacy did place
The facred fceptre in blefs'd Judah's race *(f)*,
From which th' Eternal Shilo was to fpring,
A knowledge which new hells to Hell did bring; 120
And tho' no lefs he knew himfelf too weak
The fmalleft link of ftrong-wrought Fate to break,
Yet would he rage and ftruggle with the chain,
Lov'd to rebel, tho' fure that it was in vain.
And now it broke his form'd defign, to find   125
The gentle change of Saul's recov'ring mind :
He trufted much in Saul, and rag'd and griev'd
(The great deceiver) to be himfelf deceiv'd.
Thrice did he knock his iron teeth, thrice howl,
And into frowns his wrathful forehead roll :   130
His eyes dart forth red flames which fcare the night,
And with worfe fires the trembling ghofts affright.
A troop of ghaftly fiends compafs him round,
And greedily catch at his lips fear'd found.

   " Are we fuch nothings, then ?" faid he; " our will
" Crofs'd by a fhepherd's boy? and you yet ftill 136
" Play with your idle ferpents here? Dares none
" Attempt what becomes furies ? are ye grown
" Benumb'd with fear, or virtue's fprightlefs cold,
" You who were once (I'm fure) fo brave and bold?
" Oh, my ill chang'd condition! oh, my fate!   141
   Did I lofe heav'n for this?"

    (e) 1 Sam, xvi. 13.   *(f)* Gen. xlix. 10.

With that, with his long tail he lafh'd his breaft,
And horribly fpoke out in looks the reft.
The quaking pow'rs of Night ftood in amaze,　145
And at each other firft could only gaze :
A dreadful filence fill'd the hollow place,
Doubling the native terror of Hell's face;
Rivers of flaming brimftone, which before
So loudly rag'd, crept foftly by the fhore;　150
No hifs of fnakes, no clank of chains, was known,
The fouls amidft their tortures durft not groan.

Envy at laft crawls forth from that dire throng,
Of all the direfull'ft; her black locks hung long,
Attir'd with curling ferpents; her pale fkin　155
Was almoft dropt from the fharp bones within,
And at her breaft ftuck vipers, which did prey
Upon her panting heart both night and day,
Sucking black blood from thence, which, to repair,
Both night and day they left frefh poifons there. 160
Her garments were deep ftain'd in human gore,
And torn by her own hands, in which fhe bore
A knotted whip and bowl, that to the brim
Did with green gall and juice of wormwood fwim;
With which when fhe was drunk fhe furious grew,
And lafh'd herfelf. Thus from the accurfed crew 166
Envy, the worft of fiends, herfelf prefents,
Envy! good only when fhe herfelf torments.

" Spend not, great King! thy precious rage,"faid fhe,
" Upon fo poor a caufe; fhall mighty we　170

G ij

" The glory of our wrath to him afford?

" Are we not furies ſtill? and you our lord?

" At thy dread anger the fix'd world ſhall ſhake,

" And frighted Nature her own laws forſake.

" Do thou but threat, loud ſtorms ſhall make reply,

" And thunder echo it to the trembling ſky,   176

" Whilſt raging ſeas ſwell to ſo bold an height,

" As ſhall the fire's proud element affright.

" Th' old drudging ſun, from his long-beaten way,

" Shall at thy voice ſtart, and miſguide the day; 180

" The jocund orbs ſhall break their meaſur'd pace,

" And ſtubborn poles change their allotted place;

" Heav'n's gilded troops ſhall flutter here and there,

" Leaving their boaſting ſongs tun'd to a ſphere;

" Nay, their God, too,—for fear he did, when we

" Took noble arms againſt his tyranny,   186

" So noble arms, and in a cauſe ſo great,

" That triumphs they deſerve for their defeat:

" There was a day! oh, might I ſee it again,

" Tho' he had fiercer flames to thruſt us in!   190

" And can ſuch pow'rs be by a child withſtood?

" Will ſlings, alas! or pebbles, do him good?

" What th' untam'd lion, whet with hunger too,

" And giants, could not, that my word ſhall do:

" I'll ſoon diſſolve this peace; were Saul's new love

" (But Saul we know) great as my hate ſhall prove,

" Before their ſun twice more be gone about,   197

" I and my faithful ſnakes would drive it out.

" By me Cain offer'd up his brother's gore (g),

" A facrifice far worfe than that before;   200

" I faw him fling the ftone, as if he meant

" At once his murder and his monument,

" And laugh'd to fee (for 'twas a goodly fhow)

" The earth by her firft tiller (h) fatt'ned fo.

" I drove proud Pharaoh to the parted fea (i);   205

" He and his hoft drank up cold death by me:

" By me rebellious arms fierce Corah took (k),

" And Mofes (curfe upon that name!) forfook:

" Hither (ye know) almoft alive he came

" Thro' the cleft earth (l); our's was his fun'ral flame.

" By me——But I lofe time, methinks, and fhould 211

" Perform new acts, whilft I relate the old;

" David's the next our fury muft enjoy;

" 'Tis not thy God himfelf fhall fave thee, Boy!

" No; if he do, may the whole world have peace; 215

" May all ill actions, all ill fortune, ceafe,

" And, banifh'd from this potent court below,

" May I a ragged contemn'd Virtue grow."

     She fpoke; all ftar'd at firft, and made a paufe;

But ftraight the general murmur of applaufe   220

Ran thro' Death's courts; fhe frown'd ftill, and begun

To envy at the praife herfelf had won.

Great Belzebub ftarts from his burning throne

To' embrace the fiend; but fhe, now furious grown

(g) Gen. iv. 8.   (h) Gen. iv. 2.   (i) Exod. xiv. 23.
(k) Num. xvi. 1.   (l) Ib. ver. 31.

G iij

To act her part, thrice bow'd, and thence she fled; 225
The snakes all hifs'd, the fiends all murmured.

    It was the time when filent Night began
To' enchain with fleep the bufy fpirits of man;
And Saul himfelf, tho' in his troubled breaft
The weight of empire lay, took gentle reft: 230
So did not Envy, but with hafte arofe,
And as thro' Ifrael's ftately towns fhe goes,
She frowns and fhakes her head; "Shine on," fays fhe,
" Ruins ere long fhall your fole mon'ments be."
The filver moon with terror paler grew,   235
And neighb'ring Hermon fweated flow'ry dew;
Swift Jordan ftarted, and ftraight backward fled,
Hiding among thick reeds his aged head:
Lo! at her entrance Saul's ftrong palace fhook,
And nimbly there the rev'rend fhape fhe took   240
Of Father Benjamin; fo long her beard,
So large her limbs, fo grave her looks appear'd;
Juft like his ftatue which beftrid Saul's gate,
And feem'd to guard the race it did create.
In this known form fhe' approach'd the tyrant's fide,
And thus her words the facred form bely'd.   246

    " Arife, loft King of Ifrael; can'ft thou lie
" Dead in this fleep, and yet thy laft fo nigh?
" If King thou be'ft, if Jeffe's race as yet
" Sit not on Ifrael's throne, and fhall he fit?   250
" Did ye for this from fruitful Egypt fly?
" From the mild brickhills' nobler flavery?

" For this did feas your pow'rful rod obey ?

" Did wonders guide and feed you on your way ?

" Could ye not there great Pharaoh's bondage bear,

' You who can ferve a boy and minftrel here ?   256

" Forbid it, God, if thou be'ft juft; this fhame

" Caft not on Saul's, on mine, and Ifrael's name.

" Why was I elfe from Canaan's famine led (*m*) ?

" Happy, thrice happy, had I there been dead,   260

" Ere my full loins difcharg'd this num'rous race,

" This lucklefs tribe, ev'n crown'd to their difgrace !

" Ah, Saul! thy fervant's vaffal muft thou live ?

" Place to his harp muft thy dread fceptre give ?

" What wants he now but that? Canft thou forget 265

" (If thou be'ft man thou canft not) how they met

" The youth with fongs? Alas! poor Monarch! you

" Your thoufand only, he ten thoufand, flew (*n*) !

" Him Ifrael loves, him neighb'ring countries fear;

" You but the name and empty title bear :   270

" And yet the traitor lives, lives in thy court

" The court that muft be his, where he fhall fport

" Himfelf with all thy concubines, thy gold,

" Thy coftly robes, thy crown. Wert thou not told

" This by proud Samuel, when at Gilgal he   275

" With bold falfe threats from God affronted thee (*o*)?

" The dotard ly'd; God faid it not, I know;

" Not Baal or Moloch would have us'd thee fo.

(*m*) Gen. xlvi. 1.   (*n*) 1 Sam. xviii. 7.   (*o*) 1. Sam. xiii. 13.

" Was not the choice his own ? did not thy worth
" Exact the royal lot (*p*), and call it forth?   280
" Haſt thou not ſince (my beſt and greateſt Son)
" To him and to his periſhing nation done
" Such laſting benefits as may juſtly claim
" A ſceptre as eternal as thy fame?   284
" PoorPrince ! whom madmen, prieſts, and boys, in-
       vade !
" By thine own fleſh, thy ingrateful ſon, betray'd !
" Unnatural fool ! who can thus cheated be
" By Friendſhip's name againſt a crown and thee !
" Betray not, too, thyſelf: take courage, call   289
" Thy enchanted virtues forth, and be whole Saul.
" Lo! this great cauſe makes thy dead fathers riſe,
" Breaks the firm ſeals of their clos'd tombs and eyes:
" Nor can their jealous aſhes, whilſt this boy
" Survives, the priv'lege of their graves enjoy.
" Riſe quickly, Saul ! and take that rebel's breath   295
" Which troubles thus thy life, and ev'n our death.
" Kill him, and thou 'rt ſecure; 'tis only he
" That has boldly interpos'd 'twixt God and thee.
" As earth's low globe robs the high moon of light,
" When this eclipſe is paſt thy fate's all bright.   300
" Truſt me, dear Son! and credit what I tell;
" I 'ave ſeen thy royal ſtars, and know them well.
" Hence fears, and dull delays. Is not thy breaſt
" (Yes, Saul! it is) with noble thoughts poſſefs'd ?

" May they beget like acts." With that she takes 305
One of her worst, her best beloved snakes;
" Softly, dear Worm! soft and unseen," said she,
" Into his bosom steal, and in it be
" My vice-roy." At that word she took her flight,
And her loose shape dissolv'd into the night. 310
   Th' infected king leap'd from his bed amaz'd,
Scarce knew himself at first, but round him gaz'd,
And started back at piec'd-up shapes, which fear
And his distracted fancy painted there.
Terror froze up his hair, and on his face 315
Show'rs of cold sweat roll'd trembling down apace;
Then knocking with his angry hands his breast,
Earth with his feet, he cries, " Oh! 'tis confess'd;
" I've been a pious fool, a woman-king;
" Wrong'd by a seer, a boy, every thing. 320
" Eight hundred years of death is not so deep,
" So unconcern'd, as my lethargic sleep;
" My patience ev'n a sacrilege becomes,
" Disturbs the dead, and opes their sacred tombs.
" Ah! Benjamin! kind Father! who for me 325
" This cursed world endur'st again to see!
" All thou hast said, great Vision! is so true,
" That all which thou command'st, and more, I'll do.
" Kill him? yes, mighty Ghost! the wretch shall die(q),
" Tho' ev'ry star in heav'n should it deny, 330
" Nor mock th' assault of our just wrath again,
" Had he ten times his fam'd ten thousand slain.

(q) 1 Sam. xviii. 11.

" Should that bold popular madman, whofe defign
" Is to revenge his own difgrace by mine,
" Should my ingrateful fon oppofe th' intent,   335
" Should mine own heart grow fcrup'lous, and relent ;
" Curfe me, juft Heav'n! (by which this truth I fwear)
" If I that feer, my fon, or felf, do fpare.
" No, gentle Ghoft! return to thy ftill home ;
" Thither this day mine and thy foe fhall come : 340
" If that curs'd object longer vex my fight,
" It muft have learn'd to appear as thou to-night."
    Whilft thus his wrath with threats the tyrant fed,
The threaten'd youth flept fearlefs on his bed.
Sleep on, reft quiet as thy confcience take,   345
For tho'. thou fleep'ft thyfelf thy God's awake.
Above the fubtle foldings of the fky,
Above the well-fet orbs' foft harmony,
Above thofe petty lamps that gild the night,
There is a place o'erflown with hallowed light,   350
Where heav'n, as if it left itfelf behind,
Is ftretch'd out far, nor its own bounds can find ;
Here peaceful flames fwell up the facred place,
Nor can the glory' contain itfelf in th' endlefs fpace :
For there no twilight of the fun's dull ray   355
Glimmers upon the pure and native day ;
No pale-fac'd moon does in ftoll'n beams appear,
Or with dim taper fcatters darknefs there :
On no fmooth fphere the reftlefs feafons flide,
No circling motion doth fwift time divide :   360

Nothing is there to come, and nothing paft,
But an eternal Now does always laft :
There fits the Almighty, Firft of all, and End,
Whom nothing but himfelf can comprehend ;
Who with his Word commanded all to be,   365
And all obey'd him, for that Word was he.
Only he fpoke, and every thing that is
From out the womb of feritle Nothing rife.
Oh! who fhall tell, who fhall defcribe thy throne,
Thou Great Three-One ?   .   370
There thou thyfelf doft in full prefence fhow,
Not abfent from thefe meaner worlds below :
No ; if thou wert, the elements' league would ceafe,
And all thy creatures break thy Nature's peace :
The fun would ftop his courfe, or gallop back,   375
The ftars drop out, the poles themfelves would crack;
Earth's ftrong foundations would be torn in twain,
And this vaft work all ravel out again
To its firft nothing; for his Spirit contains
The well-knit mafs : from him each creature gains   380
Being and motion, which he ftill beftows;
From him th' effect of our weak action flows :
Round him vaft armies of fwift angels ftand,
Which feven triumphant generals command:
They fing loud anthems of his endlefs praife,   385
And with fix'd eyes drink in immortal rays.
Of thefe he call'd out one ; all heav'n did fhake,
And filence kept whilft its Creator fpake.

Are we forgotten then fo foon? can he
Look on his crown, and not remember me   390
That gave it? can he think we did not hear
(Fond Man!) his threats? and have we made the ear
To be accounted deaf? No, Saul! we heard,
And it will coft thee dear: the ills thou'ft fear'd,
Practis'd, or thought on, I'll all double fend: 395
Have we not fpoke it? and dares man contend?
Alas! poor Duft! didft thou but know the day
When thou muft lie in blood at Gilboa (*r*),
Thou and thy fons, thou wouldft not threaten ftill,
Thy trembling tongue would ftop againft thy will. 400
Then fhall thine head fix'd in curs'd temples be,
And all their foolifh gods fhall laugh at thee.
That hand which now on David's life would prey,
Shall then turn juft, and its own mafter flay.
He whom thou hat'ft on thy lov'd throne fhall fit, 405
And expiate the difgrace thou doft to it.
Hafte, then; tell David what his King has fworn,
Tell him whofe blood muft paint this rifing morn;
Yet bid him go fecurely when he fends:
'Tis Saul that is his foe, and we his friends.   410
The man who has his God no aid can lack,
And we who bid him go will bring him back.

   He fpoke; the heav'ns feem'd decently to bow,
With all their bright inhabitants; and now

        (*r*) 1 Sam. xxxi. 8.

The jocund fpheres began again to play,   415
Again each fpirit fung Halleluia,
Only that angel was ftraight gone. Ev'n fo
(But not fo fwift) the morning glories flow
At once from the bright fun, and ftrike the ground;
So winged lightning the foft air does wound: 420
Slow Time admires, and knows not what to call
The motion, having no account fo fmall.
So flew this angel, till to David's bed
He came, and thus his facred meffage faid.

 " Awake, young Man! hear what thy King has
  " fworn;   425
" He fwore thy blood fhould paint this rifing morn;
" Yet to him go fecurely when he fends:
" 'Tis Saul that is your foe, and God your friends.
" The man who has his God no aid can lack,
" And he who bids thee go will bring thee back."   430
 Up leap'd Jeffides, and did round him ftare,
But could fee nought, for nought was left but air.
Whilft this great vifion labours in his thought,
Lo! the fhort prophefy to effect is brought.
In treach'rous hafte he's fent for to the King (s), 435
And with him bid his charmful lyre to bring.
The King, they fay, lies in a raging fit,
Which does no cure but facred tunes admit:
And true it was, foft mufic did appeafe
Th' obfcure fantaftic rage of Saul's difeafe (t).   440

  (s) 1 Sam. xvi. 19. and xix. 9. (t) 1 Sam. xvi. 23.

Tell me, oh, Mufe! (for thou or none canſt tell
The myſtic pow'rs that in bleſs'd numbers dwell;
Thou their great nature know'ſt, nor is it fit
This nobleſt gem of thine own crown t' omit)
Tell me from whence theſe heav'nly charms ariſe; 445
Teach the dull world t'admire what they deſpiſe.

As firſt a various unform'd hint we find
Riſe in ſome godlike poet's fertile mind,
Till all the parts and words their places take,
And with juſt marches verſe and muſic make;   450
Such was God's poem, this world's new eſſay,
So wild and rude in its firſt draught it lay;
Th' ungovern'd parts no correſpondence knew,
An artleſs war from thwarting motions grew,
Till they to number and fix'd rules were brought 455
By the eternal Mind's poetic thought.
Water and air he for the tenor choſe,
Earth made the baſs, the treble flame aroſe;
To th' active moon a quick briſk ſtroke he gave,
To Saturn's ſtring a touch more ſoft and grave. 460
The motions ſtraight, and round, and ſwift, and ſlow,
And ſhort, and long, were mix'd and woven ſo,
Did in ſuch artful figures ſmoothly fall,
As made this decent meaſur'd dance of all.
And this is muſic; ſounds that charm our ears 465
Are but one dreſſing that rich ſcience wears;
Tho' no man hear it, tho' no man it rehearſe,
Yet will there ſtill be muſic in my verſe.

In this great world fo much of it we fee,
The leffer, man, is all o'er harmony :   470
Storehoufe of all proportions! fingle quire !
Which firft God's breath did tunefully infpire :
From hence blefs'd mufic's heav'nly charms arife,
From fympathy which them and man allies :
Thus they our fouls, thus they our bodies, win, 475
Not by their force, but party that's within :
Thus the ftrange cure on our fpilt blood apply'd,
Sympathy to the diftant wound does guide :
Thus when two brethren ftrings are fet alike,
To move them both but one of them we ftrike : 480
Thus David's lyre did Saul's wild rage control,
And tun'd the harfh diforders of his foul.

    " When Ifrael was from bondage led (*u*),
" Led by the Almighty's hand
" From out a foreign land,   485
" The great fea beheld and fled.
" As men purfu'd, when that fear paft they find,
" Stop on fome higher ground to look behind,
" So whilft thro' wondrous ways
" The facred army went,   490
" The waves afar ftood up to gaze,
" And their own rocks did reprefent,
" Solid as waters are above the firmament.

(*u*) Pfal. cxiv.

H ij

" Old Jordan's waters to their spring
" Start back with sudden fright;   .   .   495
" The spring, amaz'd at sight,
" Asks what news from sea they bring? .
" The mountains shook; and to the mountains' side
" The little hills leap'd round, themselves to hide ;
" As young affrighted lambs,   500
" When they ought dreadful spy, .
" Run trembling to their helpless dams,
" The mighty sea and river by
" Were glad, for their excuse, to see the hills to fly.

" What ail'd the mighty sea to flee ?   505
" Or why did Jordan's tide
" Back to his fountain glide?
" Jordan's tide, what ailed thee?
" Why leap'd the hills? why did the mountains shake?
" What ail'd them their fix'd natures to forsake ?
" Fly where thou wilt, O Sea!   511
" And Jordan's current cease;
" Jordan ! there is no need of thee,
" For at God's word, whene'er he please,
" The rocks shall weep new waters (x) forth instead
          of these."   515

Thus sung the great musician to his lyre,
And Saul's black rage grew softly to retire;

(x) Exod. xvii. 6. Num. xx. 11.

But Envy's ferpent ftill with him remain'd,
And the wife charmer's healthful voice difdain'd (*y*).
Th' unthankful King, cur'd truly of his fit,   520
Seems to lie drown'd and bury'd ftill in it ;
From his paft madnefs draws this wicked ufe,
To fin difguis'd, and murder with excufe :
For whilft the fearlefs youth his cure purfues,
And the foft med'cine with kind art renews,   525
The barb'rous patient cafts at him his fpear (*z*);
(The ufual fceptre that rough hand did bear)
Cafts it with vi'lent ftrength ; but into the room
An arm more ftrong and fure than his was come ;
An angel, whofe unfeen and eafy might   530
Put by the weapon, and mifled it right.
How vain man's pow'r is! unlefs God command,
The weapon difobeys his mafter's hand!
Happy was now the error of the blow ;
At Gilboa it will not ferve him fo.   535
One would have thought, Saul's fudden rage to have
He had himfelf by David wounded been ;   [feen,
He fcorn'd to leave what he did ill begin,
And thought his honour now engag'd i' th' fin.
A bloody troop of his own guards he fends   540
(Slaves to his will, and falfely call'd his Friends)
To mend his error by a furer blow ;
So Saul ordain'd, but God ordain'd not fo.

(*y*) Pfal. lviii. 5.   (*z*) 1 Sam. xviii. 11. and xix. 20.

Home flies the prince, and to his trembling wife
Relates the new-paſt hazard of his life,   545
Which ſhe with decent paſſion hears him tell,
For not her own fair eyes ſhe lov'd ſo well.
Upon their palace top, beneath a row
Of Lemon Trees, which there did proudly grow,
And with bright ſtores of golden fruit repay   550
The light they drank from the ſun's neighb'ring ray,
(A ſmall but artful paradiſe) they walk'd,
And hand in hand ſad gentle things they talk'd.
Here Michol firſt an armed troop eſpies
(So faithful and ſo quick are loving eyes)   555
Which march'd, and often gliſter'd thro' a wood,
That on right hand of her fair palace ſtood;
She ſaw them (*a*), and cry'd out, "They 're come to kill
" My deareſt lord! Saul's ſpear purſues thee ſtill:
" Behold his wicked guards: haſte, quickly fly; 560
" For Heav'n's ſake haſte; my dear lord! do not die,
" Ah, cruel Father! whoſe ill-natur'd rage
" Neither thy worth nor marriage can aſſwage!
" Will he part thoſe he join'd ſo late before?
" Were the two hundred foreſkins (*b*) worth no more?
" He ſhall not part us; (then ſhe wept between) 566
" At yonder window thou may'ſt 'ſcape unſeen;
" This hand ſhall let thee down; ſtay not, but haſte;
" 'Tis not my uſe to ſend thee hence ſo faſt."

          (*a*) 1 Sam. xix. 11.   (*b*) 1 Sam. xviii. 27.

" Beſt of all women !" he replies——and this 570
Scarce ſpoke, ſhe ſtops his anſwer with a kiſs.
" Throw not away," ſaid ſhe "thy precious breath;
" Thou ſtay'ſt too long within the reach of death."
Timely he' obeys her wiſe advice, and ſtreight 575
To unjuſt force ſhe' oppoſes juſt deceit.
She meets the murd'rers with a virtuous lie (c),
And good-diſſembling tears. " May he not die
" In quiet then?" ſaid ſhe: " Will they not give
" That freedom who ſo fear leſt he ſhould live?
" Ev'n Fate does with your cruelty conſpire, 580
" And ſpares your guilt, yet does what you deſire.
" Muſt he not live ? for that ye need not ſin ;
" My much-wrong'd huſband ſpeechleſs lies within,
" And has too little left of vital breath
" To know his murderers, or to feel his death : 585
" One hour will do your work."————
Here her well-govern'd tears dropp'd down apace:
Beauty and ſorrow, mingled in one face,
Has ſuch reſiſtleſs charms, that they believe,
And an unwilling aptneſs find to grieve 590
At what they came for. A pale ſtatue's head,
In linen wrapp'd, appear'd on David's bed;
Two ſervants mournful ſtand, and ſilent, by,
And on the table med'cinal relics lie;
In the cloſe room a well-plac'd taper's light 595
Adds a becoming horror to the ſight;

(c) 1 Sam. xix. 14.

And for th' impreſſion God prepar'd their ſenſe;
They ſaw, believ'd all this, and parted thence.
How vain attempts Saul's unbleſs'd anger tries,
By his own hands deceiv'd, and ſervants' eyes!   6co

     " It cannot be," ſaid he ; " no, can it? ſhall
" Our great ten thouſand ſlayer idly fall?
" The ſilly rout thinks God protects him ſtill;
" But God, alas! guards not the bad from ill,
" Oh may he guard him! may his members be   605
" In as full ſtrength and well-ſet harmony,
" As the freſh body of the firſt-made man,
" Ere ſin, or ſin's juſt meed, diſeaſe began :
" He will be elſe too ſmall for our vaſt hate,
" And we muſt ſhare in our revenge with Fate. 610
" No; let us have him whole; we elſe may ſeem
" To 'ave ſnatch'd away but ſome few days from him,
" And cut that thread which would have dropt in
" Will our great anger learn to ſtoop ſo low? [two.
" I know it cannot, will not; him we prize   615
" Of our juſt wrath the ſolemn ſacrifice,
" That muſt not blemiſh'd be; let him remain
" Secure, and grow up to our ſtroke again :
" 'Twill be ſome pleaſure then to take his breath,
" When he ſhall ſtrive and wreſtle with his death.
" Go, let him live—and yet——ſhall I then ſtay 621
" So long? Good and great actions hate delay.
" Some fooliſh piety perhaps, or he
" That has been ſtill mine honour's enemy,

" Samuel, may change or crofs my juft intent,   625
" And I this formal pity foon repent.
" Befides, Fate gives him me, and whifpers this,
" That he can fly no more, if we fhould mifs.
" Mifs! can we mifs again? go, bring him ftraight,
" Tho' gafping out his foul (*d*); if the wifh'd date
" Of his accurfed life be almoft paft,   631
" Some joy 'twill be to fee him breathe his laft."
The troop return'd, of their fhort virtue afham'd,
Saul's courage prais'd, and their own weaknefs blam'd;
But when the pious fraud they underftood,   635
Scarce the refpect due to Saul's facred blood,
Due to the facred beauty in it reign'd,
From Michol's murder their wild rage reftrain'd.
She alledg'd the holieft chains that bind a wife (*e*),
Duty and love; fhe alledg'd that her own life,   640
Had fhe refus'd that fafety to her lord,
Would have incurr'd juft danger from his fword.
Now was Saul's wrath full grown; he takes no reft,
A violent flame rolls in his troubled breaft,
And in fierce lightning from his eye does break;   645
Not his own fav'rites and beft friends dare fpeak,
Or look on him; but mute and trembling all,
Fear where this cloud will burft, and thunder fall.
So when the pride and terror of the wood,
A lion, prick'd with rage and want of food,   650
Efpies out from afar fome well-fed beaft,
And bruftles up, preparing for his feaft;

(*d*) 1 Sam. xix. 15.   (*e*) 1 Sam. xix. 17.

If that by fwiftnefs 'fcape his gaping jaws,
His bloody eyes he hurls round, his fharp paws
Tear up the ground ; then runs he wild about,   655
Lafhing his angry tail, and roaring out;
Beafts creep into their dens, and tremble there;
Trees, tho' no wind be ftirring, fhake with fear;
Silence and horror fill the place around,
Echo itfelf dares fcarce repeat the found.   660
'Midft a large wood that joins fair Rama's town *(f)*,
(The neighbourhood fair Rama's chief renown)
A College ftands, where, at great Prophets' feet
The prophets' fons with filent diligence meet,
By Samuel built, and mod'rately endow'd,   665
Yet more to his lib'ral tongue than hands they ow'd:
There himfelf taught, and his blefs'd voice to hear,
Teachers themfelves lay proud beneath him there.
The houfe was a large fquare, but plain and low;
Wife Nature's ufe Art ftrove not to outgo.   670
An inward fquare by well-rang'd trees was made,
And midft the friendly cover of their fhade
A pure, well-tafted, wholefome fountain rofe,
Which no vain coft of marble did enclofe,
Nor thro' carv'd fhapes did the forc'd waters pafs,
Shapes gazing on themfelves i' the liquid glafs; 676
Yet the chafte ftream, that 'mong loofe pebbles fell,
For cleannefs, thirft, religion, ferv'd as well.
The fcholars, doctors, and companions, here,
Lodg'd all apart in neat fmall chambers were;   680

(f) 1 Sam. xix. 19.

Well-furnifh'd chambers, for in each their ftood
A narrow couch, table, and chair of wood;
More is but clog where ufe does bound delight,
And thofe are rich whofe wealth's proportion'd right
To their life's form : more goods would but become
A burden to them, and contract their room.   686
A fecond court, more facred, ftood behind,
Built fairer, and to nobler ufe defign'd;
The hall and fchools one fide of it poffefs'd,
The library and fynagogue the reft :   690
Tables of plain-cut fir adorn'd the hall,
And with beafts' fkins the beds were cover'd all.
The rev'rend doctors take their feats on high,
Th' elect companions in their bofoms lie;
The fcholars far below upon the ground,   695
On frefh-ftrew'd rufhes, place themfelves around :
With more refpect the wife and ancient lay,
But ate not choicer herbs or bread than they,
Nor purer waters drank, their conftant feaft,
But by great days and facrifice increas'd.   700
The fchools built round and higher, at the end
With their fair circle did this fide extend;
To which their fynagogue on th' other fide,
And to the hall their library reply'd.
The midft tow'rds their large gardens open lay,   705
To' admit the joys of fpring and early day.
I' the library a few choice authors ftood;
Yet 'twas well ftor'd, for that fmall ftore was good :

Writing, man's spiritual physic, was not then
Itself, as now, grown a disease of men.   710
Learning (young virgin!) but few suitors knew;
The common prostitute she lately grew,
And with her spurious brood loads now the press,
Laborious effects of idleness !
Here all the various forms one might behold   715
How letters sav'd themselves from death of old :
Some painfully engrav'd in thin wrought plates,
Some cut in wood, some lightlier trac'd on slates ;
Some drawn on fair palm-leaves, with short-liv'd toil,
Had not their friend the cedar lent his oil;   720
Some wrought in silks, some writ in tender barks;
Some the sharp style in waxen tables marks ;
Some in beasts' skins, and some in Biblos reed,
Both new rude arts, which age and growth did need.
The schools were painted well with useful skill; 725
Stars, maps, and stories, the learn'd wall did fill :
Wise wholesome proverbs mix'd around the room,
Some writ, and in Egyptian figures some.
Here all the noblest wits of men inspir'd,
From earth's slight joys and worthless toils retir'd,
Whom Samuel's fame and bounty thither lead,   731
Each day by turns their solid knowledge read.
The course and pow'r of stars great Nathan taught,
And home to man those distant wonders brought;
How toward both poles the sun's fix'd journey bends,
And how the year his crooked walk attends;   736

3

By what juſt ſteps the wand'ring light's advance,
And what eternal meaſures guide their dance:
Himſelf a prophet; but his lectures ſhew'd
How little of that art to them he ow'd.   740
Mahol th' inferior world's fantaſtic face,
Thro' all the turns of matter's maze, did trace;
Great Nature's well-ſet clock in pieces took,
On all the ſprings and ſmalleſt wheels did look
Of life and motion; and with equal art   745
Made up again the whole of ev'ry part.
The prophet Gad in learned duſt deſigns
Th' immortal ſolid rules of fancy'd lines;
Of numbers, too, th' unnumber'd wealth he ſhows,
And with them far their endleſs journey goes: 750
Numbers, which ſtill increaſe more high and wide
From one, the root of their turn'd pyramid.
Of men, and ages paſt, Seraiah read,
Embalm'd in long-liv'd Hiſtory the dead;
Show'd the ſteep falls, and ſlow aſcent, of ſtates; 755
What wiſdom and what follies make their fates.
Samuel himſelf did God's rich law diſplay,
Taught doubting men with judgment to obey;
And oft' his raviſh'd ſoul with ſudden flight
Soar'd above preſent times and human ſight.   760
Theſe arts but welcome ſtrangers might appear,
Muſic and verſe ſeem'd born and bred up here;
Scarce the bleſs'd heav'n, that rings with angels' voice,
Does with more conſtant harmony rejoice.

The sacred Muse does here each breast inspire ;   765
Heman and sweet-mouth'd Asaph rule their quire;
Both charming poets, and all strains they play'd,
By artful breath or nimble fingers made.
The synagogue was dress'd with care and cost,
(The only place where that they esteem'd not lost)
The glitt'ring roof with gold did daze the view, 771
The sides refresh'd with silks of sacred blue.
Here thrice each day they read their perfect law,
Thrice pray'rs from willing Heav'n a blessing draw;
Thrice in glad hymns swell'd with the great One's
           praise,   : 775
The pliant voice on her sev'n steps they raise,
Whilst all th' enliven'd instruments around
To the just feet with various concord found.
Such things were Muses then, contemn'd low earth,
Decently proud, and mindful of their birth. · 780
'Twas God himself that here tun'd ev'ry tongue,
And gratefully of him alone they sung:
They sung how God spoke out the world's vast ball
From nothing, and from no where call'd forth all ;
No nature yet, or place for it to possess,   785
But an unbottom'd gulf of emptiness.
Full of himself th' Almighty sate, his own
Palace, and, without solitude, alone.
But he was goodness whole, and all things will'd, ·
Which ere they were his active Word fulfill'd, 790

And their aftonifh'd heads o' the fudden rear'd.
An unfhap'd kind of fomething firft appear'd,
Confeffing its new being, and undrefs'd,
As if it ftept in hafte before the reft :
Yet buried in this matter's darkfome womb,   795
Lay the rich feeds of every thing to come.
From hence the cheerful flame leap'd up fo high,
Clofe at its heels the nimble air did fly;
Dull earth with its own weight did downwards pierce
To the fix'd navel of the univerfe,   800
And was quite loft in waters; till God faid
To the proud fea, Shrink in your ins'lent head;
See how the gaping earth has made you place!
That durft not murmur, but fhrunk in apace.
Since when his bounds are fet, at which in vain   805
He foams, and rages, and turns back again.
With richer ftuff he bade heav'n's fabric fhine,
And from him a quick fpring of light divine
Swell'd up the fun, from whence his cherifhing flame
Fills the whole world, like him from whom it came.
He fmooth'd the rough-caft moon's imperfect mould,
And comb'd her beamy locks with facred gold : 812
" Be thou," faid he, " queen of the mournful Night;"
And as he fpoke fhe' arofe, clad o'er in light,
With thoufand ftars attending on her train :   815
With her they rife, with her they fet again.
Then herbs peep'd forth, new trees admiring ftood,
And fmelling flow'rs painted the infant wood :

Then flocks of birds thro' the glad air did flee,
Joyful and safe before man's luxury,   820
Teaching their Maker in their untaught lays:
Nay, the mute fish witness no less his praise;
For those he made, and cloth'd with silver scales,
From minoes to those living islands, whales.
Beasts, too, were his command; what could he more?
Yes, man he could, the bond of all before;   826
In him he all things with strange order hurl'd;
In him, that full abridgment of the world.
This, and much more, of God's great works they told;
His mercies, and some judgments, too, of old: 830
How when all earth was deeply stain'd in sin,
With an impetuous noise the waves came rushing in :
Where birds erewhile dwelt, and securely sung,
There fish (an unknown net) entangled hung:
The face of shipwreck'd Nature naked lay ;   835
The sun peep'd forth, and beheld nought but sea.
This men forgot, and burnt in lust again,
Till show'rs, strange as their sin, of fiery rain;
And scalding brimstone, dropp'd on Sodom's head;
Alive they felt those flames they fry in dead.   840
No better end rash Pharaoh's pride befel,
When wind and sea wag'd war for Israel :
In his gilt chariots amaz'd fishes sate;
And grew with corpse of wretched princes fat.
The waves and rocks half-eaten bodies stain ;   845
Nor was it since call'd the Red Sea in vain.

Much, too, they told of faithful Abram's fame,
To whose bless'd paſſage they owe ſtill their name:
Of Moſes much, and the great ſeed of Nun,
What wonders they perform'd, what lands they won;
How many kings they ſlew, or captive brought; 851
They held the ſwords, but God and angels fought.

    Thus gain'd they the wiſe ſpending of their days,
And their whole life was their dear Maker's praiſe:
No minute's reſt, no ſwifteſt thought, they ſold 855
To that beloved plague of mankind, gold;
Gold! for which all mankind with greater pains
Labour tow'rds Hell than thoſe who dig its veins.
Their wealth was the contempt of it, which more
They valu'd than rich fools the ſhining ore.   860
The ſilk-worm's precious death they ſcorn'd to wear,
And Tyrian dye appear'd but ſordid there.
Honour, which ſince the price of ſouls became,
Seem'd to theſe great ones a low idle name.
Inſtead of down, hard beds they choſe to have, 865
Such as might bid them not forget their grave.
Their board diſpeopled no full element;
Free Nature's bounty thriftily they ſpent,
And ſpar'd the ſtock; nor could their bodies ſay,
We owe this crudeneſs t' exceſs yeſterday.   870
Thus ſouls live cleanly, and no ſoiling fear,
But entertain their welcome Maker there:
The Senſes perform nimbly what they 're bid,
And honeſtly, nor are by Reaſon chid;

And when the down of sleep does softly fall,   875
Their dreams are heav'nly then, and mystical :
With hasty wings time present they outfly,
And tread the doubtful maze of Destiny :
There walk and sport among the years to come,
And with quick eye pierce ev'ry cause's womb.   880
Thus these wise saints enjoy'd their little all,
Free from the spite of much-mistaken Saul :
For if man's life we in just balance weigh,
David deserv'd his envy less than they.
Of this retreat the hunted prince makes choice,   885
Adds to their quire his nobler lyre and voice :
But long unknown ev'n here he could not lie,
So bright his lustre, so quick Envy's eye!
Th' offended troop, whom he escap'd before,
Pursue him here, and fear mistakes no more :   890
Belov'd revenge fresh rage to them affords;
Some part of him all promise to their swords.
    They came, but a new sp'rit their hearts possess'd,
Scatt'ring a sacred calm through ev'ry breast:
The furrows of their brow, so rough erewhile,   895
Sink down into the dimples of a smile :
Their cooler veins swell with a peaceful tide,
And the chaste streams with even current glide :
A sudden day breaks gently thro' their eyes,
And morning blushes in their cheeks arise :   900
The thoughts of war, of blood, and murther, cease;
In peaceful tunes they adore the God of peace (g).

(g) 1 Sam. xix. 20.

New meſſengers twice more the tyrant ſent (*h*);
And was twice more mock'd with the ſame event.
His heighten'd rage no longer brooks delay;   905
It ſends him there himſelf (*i*); but on the way
His fooliſh anger a wiſe fury grew,
And bleſſings from his mouth unbidden flew.
His kingly robes he laid at Naioh down,
Began to underſtand and ſcorn his crown;   910
Employ'd his mounting thoughts on nobler things,
And felt more ſolid joys than empire brings;
Embrac'd his wond'ring ſon, and on his head
The balm of all paſt wounds, kind tears, he ſhed.

So cov'tous Balaam, with a fond intent   915
Of curſing the bleſs'd feed, to Moab went (*k*);
But as he went, his fatal tongue to ſell,
His aſs taught him to ſpeak, God to ſpeak well (*l*).
" How comely are thy tents, oh, Iſrael (*m*)!"
Thus he began, " what conqueſts they foretel! 920
" Leſs fair are orchards in their autumn-pride,
" Adorn'd with trees on ſome fair river's ſide;
" Leſs fair are vallies, their green mantles ſpread,
" Or mountains with tall cedars on their head!
" 'Twas God himſelf (thy God who muſt not fear?)
" Brought thee from bondage to be maſter here: 926
" Slaughter ſhall wear out theſe, new weapons get,
" And Death in triumph on thy darts ſhall ſit.

(*h*) 1 Sam. xix. 21 (*i*) Ibid. ver. 23. (*k*) Num. xxii. 15, 25.
(*l*) Ibid. ver. 28. (*m*) Num. xxiv. 5.

" When Judah's Lion ſtarts up to his prey,   929
" The beaſts ſhall hang their ears and creep away :
" When he lies down, the woods ſhall ſilence keep,
" And dreadful tigers tremble at his ſleep.
" Thy curſers, Jacob ! ſhall twice curſed be,
" And he ſhall bleſs himſelf that bleſſes thee." 934

End of the Firſt Book.

DAVIDEIS.

BOOK II.

The Contents.

THE friendſhip betwixt Jonathan and David; and, upon that occaſion, a digreſſion concerning the nature of love. A diſcourſe between Jonathan and David, upon which the latter abſents himſelf from court, and the former goes thither to inform himſelf of Saul's reſolution. The feaſt of the New-Moon; the manner of the celebration of it; and therein a digreſſion of the hiſtory of Abraham. Saul's ſpeech upon David's abſence from the feaſt, and his anger againſt Jonathan. David's reſolution to fly away. He parts with Jonathan, and falls aſleep under a tree. A deſcription of Fancy. An angel makes up a viſion in David's head. The viſion itſelf; which is a propheſy of all the ſucceſſion of his race till Chriſt's time, with their moſt remarkable actions. At his awaking Gabriel aſſumes an human ſhape, and confirms to him the truth of his viſion.

Bᴜᴛ now the early birds began to call
The morning forth; up roſe the ſun and Saul:
Both, as men thought, roſe freſh from ſweet repoſe;
But both, alas! from reſtleſs labours roſe;
For in Saul's breaſt Envy, the toilſome ſin,⸱⸱⸱⸱⸱⸱⸱⸱⸱ 5
Had all that night active and tyrannous been:
She' expell'd all forms of kindneſs, virtue, grace,
Of the paſt day no footſtep left, or trace;
The new-blown ſparks of his old rage appear,
Nor could his love dwell longer with his fear: 10
So near a ſtorm wiſe David would not ſtay,
Nor truſt the glitt'ring of a faithleſs day:
He ſaw the ſun call in his beams apace,
And angry clouds march up into their place.

The fea itfelf fmooths his rough brow a while, 15
Flattering the greedy merchant with a fmile;
But he whofe fhipwreck'd bark it drank before,
Sees the deceit, and knows it would have more.
Such is the fea, and fuch was Saul;
But Jonathan, his fon, and only good,   20
Was gentle as fair Jordan's ufeful flood;
Whofe innocent ftream, as it in filence goes,
Frefh honours and a fudden fpring beftows
On both his banks, to ev'ry flower and tree;
The manner how lies hid, th' effect we fee: 25
But more than all, more than himfelf, he lov'd
The man whofe worth his father's hatred mov'd;
For when the noble youth at Dammin ftood,
Adorn'd with fweat, and painted gay with blood,
Jonathan pierc'd him thro' with greedy eye (a), 30
And underftood the future majefty
Then deftin'd in the glories of his look;
He faw, and ftraight was with amazement ftrook,
To fee the ftrength, the feature, and the grace,
Of his young limbs; he faw his comely face, 35
Where love and rev'rence fo well mingled were,
And head, already crown'd with golden hair:
He faw what mildnefs his bold fp'rit did tame,
Gentler than light, yet pow'rful as a flame:
He faw his valour by their fafety prov'd;   40
He faw all this, and as he faw he lov'd.

(a) 1 Sam. xviii. 1.

What art thou, Love! thou great myfterious thing?
From what hid ftock does thy ftrange nature fpring?
'Tis thou that mov'ft the world thro' every part,
And hold'ft the vaft frame clofe, that nothing ftart 45
From the due place and office firft ordain'd:
By thee were all things made, and are fuftain'd.
Sometimes we fee thee fully, and can fay
From hence thou took'ft thy rife, and went'ft that way;
But oft'ner the fhort beams of Reafon's eye   50
See only there thou art, not how, nor why.
How is the loadftone, Nature's fubtle pride,
By the rude iron woo'd, and made a bride?
How was the weapon wounded? what hid flame
The ftrong and conqu'ring metal overcame?   55
Love (this world's grace) exalts his natural ftate;
He feels thee, Love! and feels no more his weight.
Ye learned Heads! whom ivy garlands grace,
Why does that twining plant the oak embrace?
The oak, for courtfhip moft of all unfit,   60
And rough as are the winds that fight with it.
How does the abfent pole the needle move?
How does his cold and ice beget hot love?
Which are the wings of lightnefs to afcend?
Or why does weight to th' centre downwards bend?
Thus creatures void of life obey thy laws,   66
And feldom we, they never, know the caufe.
In thy large ftate, life gives the next degree,
Where fenfe and good apparent places thee;

But thy chief palace is man's heart alone; 70
Here are thy triumphs and full glories fhown:
Handfome defires, and reft, about thee flee,
Union, inherence, zeal, and ecftafy,
With thoufand joys, clufter around thine head,
O'er which a gallefs dove her wings does fpread : 75
A gentle lamb, purer and whiter far
Than confciences of thine own martyrs are,
Lies at thy feet; and thy right hand does hold
The myftic fceptre of a crofs of gold.
Thus doft thou fit (like men, ere fin had fram'd 80
A guilty blufh) naked, but not afham'd.
What caufe, then, did the fab'lous Ancients find,
When firft their fuperftition made thee blind?
'Twas they, alas! 'twas they who could not fee,
When they miftook that monfter, Luft, for thee. 85
Thou art a bright, but not confuming, flame;
Such in th' amazed bufh to Mofes came (*b*),
When that, fecure, its new-crown'd head did rear,
And chid the trembling branches' needlefs fear.
Thy darts are healthful gold, and downwards fall, 90
Soft as the feathers that they 're fletch'd withal.
Such, and no other, were thofe fecret darts
Which fweetly touch'd this nobleft pair of hearts:
Still to one end they both fo juftly drew,
As courteous doves together yok'd would do: 95
No weight of birth did on one fide prevail;
Two twins lefs even lie in Nature's fcale:

(*b*) Exod. iii. 2.

They mingled fates, and both in each did fhare;
They both were fervants, they both princes were.
If any joy to one of them was fent,   100
It was moſt his to whom it leaſt was meant;
And Fortune's malice betwixt both was croſs'd,
For ſtriking one, it wounded th' other moſt.
Never did marriage ſuch true union find,
Or men's deſires with ſo glad violence bind;   105
For there is ſtill ſome tinčture left of ſin,
And ſtill the ſex will needs be ſtealing in.
Thoſe joys are full of droſs, and thicker far;
Theſe, without matter, clear and liquid are.
Such ſacred love does heav'n's bright ſpirits fill, 110
Where love is but to underſtand and will,
With ſwift, and unſeen motions ſuch as we
Somewhat expreſs in heighten'd charity.
O ye bleſs'd One! whoſe love on earth became
So pure, that ſtill in heav'n 'tis but the ſame!   115
There now ye ſit, and with mix'd ſouls embrace,
Gazing upon great Love's myſterious face,
And pity this baſe world, where friendſhip's made
A bait for ſin, or elſe at beſt a trade.
Ah! wondrous Prince! who a true friend couldſt be
When a crown flatter'd, and Saul threaten'd, thee! 121
Who held'ſt him dear whoſe ſtars thy birth did croſs,
And bought'ſt him nobly at a kingdom's loſs!
Iſrael's bright ſceptre far leſs glory brings;
There have been fewer friends on earth than kings.

To this ſtrange pitch their high affections flew, 126
Till Nature's ſelf ſcarce look'd on them as two.
Hither flies David for advice and aid *(c)*,
As ſwift as love and danger could perſuade;
As ſafe in Jonathan's truſt his thoughts remain, 130
As when himſelf but dreams them o'er again.

   " My deareſt Lord! farewell," ſaid he. "Farewell;
" Heav'n bleſs the King; may no misfortune tell
" Th' injuſtice of his hate when I am dead:
" They 're coming now; perhaps my guiltleſs head,
" Here, in your ſight, muſt then a-bleeding lie, 136
" And ſcarce your own ſtand ſafe for being nigh.
" Think me not ſcar'd with death, howe'er it appear;
" I know thou canſt not think ſo: it is a fear
" From which thy love and Dammin ſpeaks me free;
" I 'ave met him face to face, and ne'er could ſee 141
" One terror in his looks to make me fly
" When Virtue bids me ſtand; but I would die
" So as becomes my life, ſo as may prove
" Saul's malice, and at leaſt excuſe your love." 145
   He ſtopp'd, and ſpoke ſome paſſion with his eyes.
" Excellent Friend!" the gallant prince replies;
" Thou haſt ſo prov'd thy virtues, that they're known
" To all good men, more than to each his own.
" Who lives in Iſrael that can doubtful be   150
" Of thy great actions? for he lives by thee.
" Such is thy valour, and thy vaſt ſucceſs,
" That all things but thy loyalty are leſs;

        (*c*) 1 Sam. xx. 1.

" And fhould my father at thy ruin aim,

" 'Twould wound as much his fafety as his fame. 155

" Think them not coming, then, to flay thee here,

" But doubt mifhaps as little as you fear;

" For by thy loving God, whoe'er defign

" Againft thy life, muft ftrike at it thro' mine.

" But I my royal father muft acquit   160

" From fuch bafe guilt, or the low thought of it.

" Think on his foftnefs, when from death he freed

" The faithlefs king of Am'lec's curfed feed (*d*);

" Can he to a friend, to a fon, fo bloody grow,

" He who ev'n finn'd but now to fpare a foe?   165

" Admit he could; but with what ftrength or art

" Could he fo long clofe and feal up his heart?

" Such counfels jealous of themfelves become,

" And dare not fix without confent of fome.

" Few men fo boldly ill, great fins to do,   170

" Till licens'd and approv'd by others too.

" No more (believe it) could he hide this from me,

" Than I, had he difcover'd it, from thee (*e*)."

: Here they embraces join, and almoft tears,

Till gentle David thus new prov'd his fears.   175

" The praife you pleas'd, great Prince! on me to fpend,

" Was all outfpoken when you ftyl'd me Friend:

" That name alone does dang'rous glofies bring,

" And gives excufe to th' envy of a king.

(*d*) 1 Sam. xv. 9.   (*e*) 1 Sam. xv. 2.

" What did his fpear, force, and dark plots, impart,

" But fome eternal rancour in his heart?   181

" Still does he glance the fortune of that day

" When, drown'd in his own blood, Goliath lay,

" And cover'd half the plain; ftill hears the found 184

" How that vaft monfter fell, and ftrook the ground.

" The dance, and, David his ten thoufand flew,

" Still wound his fickly foul, and ftill are new.

" Great acts t' ambitious princes treafon grow,

" So much they hate that fafety which they owe.

" Tyrants dread all whom they raife high in place; 190

" From the good danger, from the bad difgrace.

" They doubt the lords', miftruft the people's hate,

" Till blood become a principle of ftate.

" Secur'd nor by their guards nor by their right,

" But ftill they fear ev'n more than they affright. 195

" Pardon me, Sir, your father's rough and ftern;

" His will too ftrong to bend, too proud to learn.

" Remember, Sir, the honey's deadly fting;

" Think on that favage juftice of the King,

" When the fame day that faw you do before   200

" Things above man, fhould fee you man no more.

" 'Tis true th' accurfed Agag mov'd his ruth;

" He pity'd his tall limbs and comely youth;

" Had feen, alas! the proof of Heav'n's fierce hate,

" And fear'd no mifchief from his pow'rlefs fate. 205

" Remember how th' old feer came raging down,

" And taught him boldly to fufpect his crown.

" Since then his pride quakes at th' Almighty's rod,
" Nor dares he love the man belov'd by God.
" Hence his deep rage and trembling envy springs;
" Nothing so wild as jealousy of kings.   211
" Whom should he counsel ask, with whom advise,
" Who reason and God's counsel does despise?
" Whose headstrong will no law or conscience daunt,
" Dares he not sin, do you think, without your grant?
" Yes, if the truth of our fix'd love he knew,   216
" He would not doubt, believe it, to kill ev'n you."
   The Prince is mov'd, and straight prepares to find
The deep resolves of his griev'd father's mind.
The danger now appears, love can soon show it, 220
And force his stubborn piety to know it.
They' agree that David should conceal'd abide (*f*),
Till his great friend had the court's temper try'd;
Till he had Saul's most sacred purpose found,
And search'd the depth and rancour of his wound. 225.
   'Twas the year's seventh-born moon; the solemn
That with most noise its sacred mirth exprefs'd. [feast
From op'ning morn, till night shuts in the day,
On trumpets and shrill horns the Levites play (*g*).
Whether by this in mystic type we see   230
The new-year's day of great eternity,
When the chang'd moon shall no more changes make,
And scatter'd deaths by trumpets' sound awake;

(*f*) 1 Sam. xx. 5, &c.   (*g*) Lev. xxiii. 24. Num. xxix. 1.

K iij

Or that the law be kept in mem'ry still,
Giv'n with like noise on Sina's shining hill (*b*);   235
Or that (as some men teach) it did arise
From faithful Abram's righteous sacrifice,
Who, whilst the Ram on Isaac's fire did fry,
His horn with joyful tunes stood sounding by;
Obscure the cause, but God his will declar'd,   240
And all nice knowledge then with ease is spar'd.
At the third hour Saul to the hallow'd tent,
'Midst a large train of priests and courtiers, went;
The sacred herd march'd proud and softly by,
Too fat and gay to think their deaths so nigh.   245
Hard fate of beasts, more innocent than we!
Prey to our lux'ry and our piety!
Whose guiltless blood, on boards and altars spilt,
Serves both to make, and expiate too, our guilt!
Three bullocks of free neck, two gilded rams,   250
Two well-wash'd goats, and fourteen spotless lambs,
With the three vital fruits, wine, oil, and bread,
(Small fees to Heav'n of all by which we 're fed)
Are offer'd up: the hallowed flames arise,
And faithful pray'rs mount with them to the skies. 255
From thence the King to th'outmost court is brought,
Where heav'nly things an inspir'd prophet taught,
And from the sacred tent to his palace gates,
With glad kind shouts th' assembly on him waits;
The cheerful horns before him loudly play,   260
And fresh-strew'd flow'rs paint his triumphant way.

(*h*) Exod. xix. 19.

Thus in flow state to the palace hall they go,
Rich drefs'd for folemn luxury and fhow :
Ten pieces of bright tap'ftry hung the room,
The nobleft work e'er ftretch'd on Syrian loom, 265
For wealthy Adriel in proud Sidon wrought,
And given to Saul when Saul's beft gift he fought,
The bright-ey'd Merab (*i*) ; for that mindful day
No ornament fo proper feem'd as they.

    There all old Abram's ftory you might fee, 270
And ftill fome angel bore him company.
His painful but well-guided travels fhow
The fate of all his fons, the church below.
Here beauteous Sara to great Pharaoh came ;
He blufh'd with fudden paffion, fhe with fhame : 275
Troubled fhe feem'd, and lab'ring in the ftrife,
'Twixt her own honour and her hufband's life (*k*).
Here on a conqu'ring hoft, that carelefs lay,
Drown'd in the joys of their new-gotten prey,
The patriarch falls (*l*) ; well mingled might you fee
The confus'd marks of death and luxury. 281
In the next piece blefs'd Salem's myftic King
Does facred prefents to the victor bring (*m*) ;
Like him whofe type he bears, his rights receives,
Strictly requires his due, yet freely gives : 285
Ev'n in his port, his habit, and his face,
The mild and great, the prieft and prince, had place.

(*i*) 1 Sam. xviii. 19.   (*k*) Gen. xx. 2, 11, 16.
(*l*) Gen. xiv. 14.   (*m*) Gen. xiv. 18.

Here all their ſtarry hoſt the heav'ns diſplay;
And, lo! an heav'nly youth! more fair than they,
Leads Abram forth; points upwards; " Such," ſaid he,
" So bright and numberleſs, thy ſeed ſhall be (*n*)." 291
Here he with God a new alliance makes,
And in his fleſh the marks of homage takes (*o*):
Here he the three myſterious perſons feaſts (*p*),
Well paid with joyful tidings by his gueſts (*q*):   295
Here for the wicked town he prays (*r*), and near,
Scarce did the wicked town thro' flames appear (*s*):
And all his fate, and all his deeds, were wrought,
Since he from Ur (*t*)to Ephron's cave(*u*)was brought.
But none 'mongſt all the forms drew then their eyes
Like faithful Abram's righteous ſacrifice (*x*).   301
The ſad old man mounts ſlowly to the place,
With Nature's power triumphant in his face
O'er the mind's courage; for, in ſpight of all,
From his ſwoln eyes reſiſtleſs waters fall.   305
The innocent boy his cruel burthen bore (*y*)
With ſmiling looks, and ſometimes walk'd before,
And ſometimes turn'd to talk : above was made
The altar's fatal pile, and on it laid
The hope of mankind : patiently he lay,   310
And did his ſire, as he his God, obey (*z*).
The mournful ſire lifts up at laſt the knife (*a*),
And on one moment's ſtring depends his life

(*n*) Gen. xv. 5.   (*o*) Gen. xvii. 5, &c.   (*p*) Gen. xviii. 2.
(*q*) ℣. 10.   (*r*) ℣. 23.   (*s*) Gen. xix. 24.   (*t*) Gen. xi. 31.
(*u*) Gen. xxv. 9.   (*x*) Gen. xxii. 3.   (*y*) ℣. 6.   (*z*) ℣. 9.
(*a*) ℣. 10.

In whofe young loins fuch brooding wonders lie.
A thoufand fp'rits peep'd from th' affrighted fky, 315
Amaz'd at this ftrange fcene, and almoft fear'd,
For all thofe joyful prophefies they 'ad heard;
Till one leap'd nimbly forth (b), by God's command,
Like lightning from a cloud, and ftopp'd his hand.
The gentle fp'rit fmil'd kindly as he fpoke ;   320
New beams of joy thro' Abram's wonder broke.
The angel points to a tuft of bufhes near,
Where an entangled Ram does half appear (c),
And ftruggles vainly with that fatal net,
Which, tho' but flightly wrought, was firmly fet ; 325
For, lo! anon, to this fad glory doom'd,
The ufeful beaft on Ifaac's pile confum'd ;
Whilft on his horns the ranfom'd couple play'd,
And the glad boy danc'd to the tunes he made.
  Near this hall's end a Shittim table ftood,   330
Yet well-wrought plate ftrove to conceal the wood ;
For from the foot a golden vine did fprout,
And caft his fruitful riches all about.
Well might that beauteous ore the grape exprefs,
Which does weak man intoxicate no lefs.   335
Of the fame wood the gilded beds were made,
And on them large embroider'd carpets laid,
From Egypt, the rich fhop of follies, brought;
But arts of pride all nations foon are taught.
Behold fev'n comely blooming youths appear,   340
And in their hands fev'n filver wafhpots bear,

(b) Gen. xxii. 11.   (c) ℣. 13.

Curl'd, and gay clad, the choiceſt ſons that be
Of Gibeon's race, and ſlaves of high degree.
Sev'n beauteous maids march'd ſoftly in behind, 344
Bright ſcarves their clothes, their hair freſh garlands
And whilſt the princes waſh they on them ſhed   [bind,
Rich ointments, which their coſtly odours ſpread
O'er the whole room; from their ſmall priſons free,
With ſuch glad haſte thro' the wide air they flee.
The King was plac'd alone (*d*), and o'er his head 350
A well-wrought heav'n of ſilk and gold was ſpread,
Azure the ground, the ſun in gold ſhone bright,
But pierc'd the wand'ring clouds with ſilver light.
The right-hand bed the King's three ſons did grace,
The third was Abner's, Adriel's, David's place : 355
And twelve large tables more were fill'd below,
With the prime men Saul's court and camp could ſhow.
The palace did with mirth and muſic ſound,
And the crown'd goblets nimbly mov'd around :
But tho' bright joy in ev'ry gueſt did ſhine,   360
The plenty, ſtate, muſic, and ſprightful wine,
Were loſt on Saul, an angry care did dwell
In his dark breaſt, and all gay forms expel.
David's unuſual abſence from the feaſt (*e*),
To his ſick ſpirit did jealous thoughts ſuggeſt : 365
Long lay he ſtill, nor drank, nor ate, nor ſpoke,
And thus at laſt his troubled ſilence broke.
   " Where can he be ?" ſaid he. " It muſt be ſo."
With that he paus'd a while. " Too well we know

(*d*) 1 Sam. xx. 25.   (*e*) 1 Sam. xx. 26, 27.

" His boundlefs pride: he grieves and hates to fee 370
" The folemn triumphs of my court and me.
" Believe me, Friends! and truft what I can fhow
" From thoufand proofs; th' ambitious David now
" Does thofe vaft things in his proud foul defign,
" That too much bufinefs give for mirth or wine. 375
" He's kindling now, perhaps, rebellious fire
" Among the Tribes, and does ev'n now confpire
" Againft my crown, and all our lives, whilft we
" Are loath ev'n to fufpect what we might fee.
" By the Great Name 'tis true."   380
With that he ftrook the board, and no man there,
But Jonathan, durft undertake to clear   [fpoke,
The blamelefs Prince (*f*); and fcarce ten words he
When thus his fpeech th' enraged tyrant broke. 384
  " Difloyal Wretch! thy gentle mother's fhame (*g*)!
" Whofe cold pale ghoft ev'n blufhes at thy name!
" Who fears left her chafte bed fhould doubted be,
" And her white fame ftain'd, by black deeds of thee!
" Canft thou be mine? A crown fometimes does hire
" Ev'n fons againft their parents to confpire,   390
" But ne'er did ftory yet, or fable, tell
" Of one fo wild who, merely to rebel,
" Quitted the unqueftion'd birthright of a throne,
" And bought his father's ruin with his own. [fence;
" Thou need'ft not plead th' ambitious youth's de-
" Thy crime clears his, and makes that innocence:

   (*f*) 1 Sam. xx. 28, 29.   (*g*) ỷ. 30, 31.

4

" Nor can his foul ingratitude appear,   397
" Whilft thy unnatural guilt is plac'd fo near.
" Is this that noble friendfhip you pretend?
" Mine, thine own foe, and thy worft en'my's friend?
" If thy low fp'rit can thy great birthright quit,
" The thing's but juft, fo ill deferv'ft thou it.   402
" I, and thy brethren here, have no fuch mind,
" Nor fuch prodigious worth in David find,
" That we to him fhould our juft rights refign,   405
" Or think God's choice not made fo well as thine.
" Shame of thy houfe and tribe! hence, from mine
" To thy falfe friend and fervile mafter fly;   [eye;
" He is, ere this time, in arms expecting thee;
" Hafte, for thofe arms are rais'd to ruin me.   410
" Thy fin that way will nobler much appear,
" Than to remain his fpy and agent here.
" When I think this, Nature, by thee forfook,
" Forfakes me too." With that his fpear he took
To ftrike at him (*h*): the mirth and mufic ceafe; 415
The guefts all rife this fudden ftorm t' appeafe (*i*).
The Prince his danger and his duty knew,
And low he bow'd, and filently withdrew.
   To David ftraight, who in a foreft nigh
Waits his advice, the royal friend does fly (*k*).   420
The fole advice, now, like the danger, clear,
Was in fome foreign land this ftorm t' outwear.
All marks of comely grief in both are feen,
And mournful kind difcourfes pafs'd between.

    (*h*) 1 Sam. xx. 33.   (*i*) v. 34.   (*k*) v. 35.

Now gen'rous tears their hafty tongues reftrain; 425
Now they begin, and talk all o'er again (*l*) :
A rev'rend oath of conftant love they take,
And God's high name their dreaded witnefs make(*m*):
Not that at all their faiths could doubtful prove,
But 'twas the tedious zeal of endlefs love.　　　430
Thus, ere they part, they the fhort time beftow
In all the pomp friendfhip and grief could fhow.
And David now, with doubtful cares opprefs'd,
Beneath a fhade borrows fome little reft ;
When by command divine thick mifts arife,　　435
And ftop the fenfe, and clofe the conquer'd eyes.
There is a place which man moft high doth rear,
The fmall world's heav'n, where reafon moves the
Here in a robe which does all colours fhow, [fphere;
(Th' envy of birds, and the clouds' gaudy bow) 440
Fancy, wild dame, with much lafcivious pride,
By twin-camelions drawn, does gaily ride :
Her coach there follows, and throngs round about,
Of fhapes and airy forms an endlefs rout.
A fea rolls on with harmlefs fury here;　　　445
Straight 'tis a field, and trees and herbs appear.
Here in a moment are vaft armies made,
And a quick fcene of war and blood difplay'd.
Here fparkling wines, and brighter maids, come in,
The bawds for Senfe, and lying baits of fin.　　450

(*l*) 1 Sam. xx. 41.　　(*m*) *ψ*. 42.

Some things arife of ftrange and quarrelling kind,
The forepart lion, and a fnake behind.
Here golden mountains fwell the cov'tous place,
And Centaurs ride themfelves, a painted race.
Of thefe flight wonders Nature fees the ftore,   455
And only then accounts herfelf but poor.

    Hither an angel comes in David's trance,
And finds them mingled in an antique dance;
Of all the num'rous forms fit choice he takes,
And joins them wifely, and this vifion makes.   460

    Firft, David there appears in kingly ftate,
Whilft the Twelve Tribes his dread commands a-
       wait (*n*) :
Straight to the wars with his join'd ftrength he goes,
Settles new friends, and frights his ancient foes.
To Solima, Canaan's old head, they came,   465
(Since high in note, then not unknown to Fame)
The blind and lame th' undoubted wall defend (*o*),
And no new wounds or dangers apprehend.
The bufy image of great Joab there
Difdains the mock, and teaches them to fear :   470
He climbs the airy walls, leaps raging down,
New-minted fhapes of flaughter fill the town.
They curfe the guards their mirth and brav'ry chofe,
All of them now are flain, or made like thofe.
Far thro' an inward fcene an army lay,   475
Which with full banners a fair Fifh difplay.

    (*n*) 2 Sam. v. 1. 1 Chro. xii. 23.   (*o*) 2 Sam. v. 6.

From Sidon plains to happy Egypt's coaſt
They ſeem all met, a vaſt and warlike hoſt.
Thither haſtes David to his deſtin'd prey,
Honour and noble Danger lead the way (*p*).   480
The conſcious trees ſhook with a rev'rend fear
Their unblown tops; God walk'd before him there (*q*).
Slaughter the weary'd Riphaims' boſom fills,
Dead corpſe imboſs the vale with little hills.
On th' other ſide Sophenes mighty king   485
Numberleſs troops of the bleſs'd Eaſt does bring (*r*):
Twice are his men cut off, and chariots ta'en;
Damaſcus and rich Adad help in vain (*s*).
Here Nabathæan troops in battle ſtand,
With all the luſty youth of Syrian land;   490
Undaunted Joab ruſhes on with ſpeed,
Gallantly mounted on his fiery ſteed;
He hews down all, and deals his deaths around;
The Syrians leave, or poſſeſs dead, the ground (*t*).
On th' other wing does brave Abiſhai ride (*u*),   495
Reeking in blood and duſt: on ev'ry ſide
The perjur'd ſons of Ammon quit the field,
Some baſely die, and ſome more baſely yield.
Thro' a thick wood the wretched Hanun flies,
And far more juſtly then fears Hebrew ſpies.   500
Moloch, their bloody god, thruſts out his head,
Grinning thro' a black cloud (*x*): him they'd long fed

(*p*) 2 Sam. v. 17,—22. 1 Chro. xiv. 8, *&c.* (*q*) 2 Sam. v. 22, 23, 24.
1 Chro. xiv. 14.   (*r*) 2 Sam. viii. 3. 1 Chro. xviii. 3.
(*s*) ℣. 5.   (*t*) 2 Sam. x. 6. 1 Chro. xix. 6, 8.   (*u*) ℣. 10.
(*x*) 2 Sam. x. 3, 4. 1 Chro. xix. 3.

In his fev'n chambers, and he ftill did eat
New-roafted babes, his dear delicious meat.
Again they' arife, more anger'd and difmay'd; 505
Euphrates and fwift Tigris fends them aid :
In vain they fend it, for again they're flain,
And feaft the greedy birds on Helay plain *(y)*.
Here Rabba with proud tow'rs affronts the fky,
And round about great Joab's trenches lie; 510
They force the walls, and fack the helplefs town ;
On David's head fhines Ammon's maffy crown.
'Midft various torments the curs'd race expires(z) ;
David himfelf his fevere wrath admires.

 Next upon Ifrael's throne does bravely fit 515
A comely youth, endow'd with wondrous wit *(a)* :
Far, from the parched line, a royal dame,
To hear his tongue and boundlefs wifdom, came *(b)* :
She carry'd back in her triumphant womb
The glorious ftock of thoufand kings to come. 520
Here brighteft forms his pomp and wealth difplay;
Here they a temple's vaft foundations lay *(c)* ;
A mighty work ; and with fit glories fill'd,
For God t' inhabit, and that King to build.
Some from the quarries hew out maffy ftone, 525
Some draw it up with cranes ; fome breathe and groan
In order o'er the anvil; fome cut down
Tall cedars, the proud mountain's ancient crown;

 (y) 1 Chron. xix 15, 18. (z) 2 Sam. xi. 1. 1 Chron. xx.
2 Sam. xii. 30. 1 Chro. xx. 2. v. 3 1. 1 Chro. xx. 3. *(a)* 1 Kings i.
1 Chro. xxiii. 1. 1 Kings iii. 12. 2 Chro. i. 12. *(b)* 1 Kings x.
Mat. xii. 42. Luke xi. 31. *(c)* 1 Kings vi. 2 Chro. iii. iv. v.

Some carve the trunks, and breathing ſhapes beſtow,
Giving the trees more life than when they grow. 530
But, oh! alas! what ſudden cloud is ſpread
About this glorious King's eclipſed head (d)?
It all his fame benights, and all his ſtore,
Wrapping him round, and now he's ſeen no more.534
  When ſtraight his ſon appears at Sichem crown'd,
With young and heedleſs council circled round (e);
Unſeemly object! but a falling ſtate
Has always its own errors join'd with Fate.
Ten Tribes at once forſake the Jeſſian throne,
And bold. Adoram at his meſſage ſtone (f);   540
" Brethren of Iſrael!"— More he fain would ſay,
But a flint ſtopp'd his mouth, and ſpeech in th' way.
Here this fond king's diſaſters but begin;
He's deſtin'd to more ſhame by' his father's ſin.
Suſac comes up, and under his command   545
A dreadful army from ſcorch'd Afric's ſand,
As numberleſs as that : all is his prey;
The temple's ſacred wealth they bear away (g);
Adrazar's ſhields and golden loſs they take;
Ev'n David in his dream does ſweat and ſhake. 550
Thus fails this wretched prince; his loins appear
Of leſs weight now than Solomon's fingers were (h).
  Abijah next ſeeks Iſrael to regain,
And waſh.in ſeas of blood his father's ſtain (i).

(d) I Kings xi. (e) I Kings xii. 2 Chro. x. (f) I Kings xii. 18.
2 Chro. x. 18.   (g) I Kings xiv. 25, 26. 2 Chro. xii. 2, 3.
(h) I Kings xii. 10. 2 Chro. x. 10.   (i) I Kings xv. 1.
2 Chro. xiii. 1, 3, &c.

L iij

Ne'er faw the aged Sun fo cruel fight;   555
Scarce faw he this, but hid his bafhful light.
Nebat's curs'd fon fled with not half his men;
Where were his gods of Dan and Bethel then (*k*)?
Yet could not this the fatal ftrife decide.;
God punifh'd one, but blefs'd not th' other fide. 560
   Afan, a juft and virtuous prince, fucceeds,
High rais'd by Fame for great and godly deeds:
He cut the folemn groves where idols ftood,
And facrific'd the gods with their own wood (*l*).
He vanquifh'd thus the proud weak pow'rs of Hell;
Before him next their doting fervants fell: 566
So huge an hoft of Zerah's men he flew,
As made ev'n that Arabia defert too (*m*).
Why fear'd he then the perjur'd Baafha's fight?
Or bought the dangerous aid of Syrian's might (*n*)?
Conqueft, Heav'n's gift, cannot by man be fold. 571
Alas! what weaknefs trufts he? man and gold.
   Next Jofaphat poffefs'd the royal ftate;
An happy prince, well worthy of his fate (*o*):
His oft' oblations on God's altar, made   575
With thoufand flocks, and thoufand herds, are paid,
Arabian tribute (*p*)! What mad troops are thofe,
Thofe mighty troops that dare to be his foes?
He prays them dead (*q*); with mutual wounds they fall;
One fury brought, one fury flays them all.   580

(*k*) 2 Chro. xiii. 17.   (*l*) 1 Kings xv. 9. 2 Chro. xiv. 1, 3, &c.
m) 2 Chr. xiv. 9.   (*n*) 2 Chr. xvi. 2, 7, &c.   (*o*) 1 Kings xv.
23. and xxii. 43. 2 Chron. xvii.   (*p*) 2 Chro. xvii. 11.
(*q*) 2 Chro. xx. 18.

Thus fits he ftill, and fees himfelf to win,
Never o'ercome but by his friend Ahab's fin (*r*)
On whofe difguife Fates then did only look,
And had almoft their God's command miftook;
Him from whofe danger Heav'n fecurely brings, 585
And for his fake two ripely wicked kings (*s*).
Their armies languifh, burnt with thirft (*t*), at Seere,
Sighs all their cold, tears all their moifture there:
They fix their greedy eyes on th' empty fky,
And fancy clouds, and fo become more dry.   590
Elifha calls for waters from afar
To come (*u*); Elifha calls, and here they are.
In helmets they quaff round the welcome flood,
And the decreafe repair with Moab's blood (*x*).
Jehoram next, and Ochoziah, throng   595
For Judah's fceptre; both fhort-liv'd too long.
A woman, too, from murther title claims (*y*);
Both with her fins and fex the crown fhe fhames.
Proud, curfed Woman! but her fall at laft
To doubting men clears Heav'n for what was paft.
Joas at firft does bright and glorious fhow (*z*);   601
In life's frefh morn his fame did early crow:
Fair was the promife of his dawning ray,
But prophet's angry blood o'ercaft his day:

(*r*) 1 Kings xxii. 30. 2 Chro. xviii. 3.   (*s*) 2 Kings iii. 14.
(*t*) 2 Kings iii. 9. (*u*) 2 Kings iii. 17. (*x*) 2 Kings iii. 24.
(*y*) 2 Kings viii. 16, 25.   2 Chron. xxi. 1. and xxii. 1.
2 Kings xi. 1. 2 Chron. xxii. 10.   (*z*) 2 Kings xii.
2 Chron. xxiv.

From thence his clouds, from thence his ftorms, begin,
It cries aloud (*a*), and twice lets Aram in (*b*).   6c6
So Amaziah lives, fo ends his reign,
Both by their trait'rous fervants juftly flain (*c*).
Edom at firft dreads his victorious hand;
Before him thoufand captives trembling ftand.   610
Down a precipice deep, down he cafts them all;
The mimic fhapes in feveral poftures fall (*d*):
But then (mad Fool!) he does thofe gods adore,
Which when pluck'd down had worfhipp'd him be-
        fore (*e*).   615
Thus all his life to come is lofs and fhame;
No help from gods, who themfelves help'd not,
        came (*f*).
    All this Uzziah's ftrength and wit repairs,
Leaving a well-built greatnefs to his heirs (*g*),
Till leprous fcurf, o'er his whole body caft (*h*),
Takes him at firft from men, from earth at laft. 620
As virtuous was his fon, and happier far;
Buildings his peace, and trophies grac'd his war (*i*);
But Achaz heaps up fins, as if he meant
To make his worft forefathers innocent. (*k*):
He burns his fon at Hinnon (*l*), whilft around   625
The roaring child drums and loud trumpets found:

(*a*) 2 Chro. xxiv. 21. 22.   2 Kings xii. 20.   (*b*) 2 Chro.
xxiv 23. 2 Kings xiv.   (*c*) 2 Chro. xxv. 27. 2 Kings
xiv 19.   (*d*) 2 Ch. o. xxv 12, 13.   (*e*) 2 Chro. xxv 14.
(*f*) 2 Kings xiv. 13. 2 Chron xxv. 23.   (*g*) 2 Kings xv. 1.
2 Chro. xxvi.   (*h*) 2 Kings xv. 5. 2 Chro. xxvi. 19.
(*i*) 2 Kings xv. 32. 2 Chro. xxvii. 4.   (*k*) 2 Kings xvi. 1.
2 Chro. xxviii.   (*l*) 2 Kings xvi. 3. 2 Chro. xxviii. 3.

This to the boy a barb'rous mercy grew,
And fnatch'd him from all mis'ries to enfue.
Here Peca comes (*m*), and hundred thoufands fall;
Here Rezin marches up, and fweeps up all,　630
Till like a fea the great Belochus' fon
Breaks upon both, and both does over-run (*n*).
The laft of Adad's ancient ftock is flain,
Ifrael captiv'd, and rich Damafcus taken (*o*);
All his wild rage to revenge Juda's wrong;　635
But woe to kingdoms that have friends too ftrong!

　Thus Hezekiah the torn empire took,
And Affur's king with his worfe gods forfook (*p*),
Who to poor Juda worlds of nations brings (*q*),
There rages, utters vain and mighty things (*r*).　640
Some dream of triumphs, and exalted names,
Some of dear gold, and fome of beauteous dames;
Whilft in the midft of their huge fleepy boaft,
An angel fcatters death thro' all the hoft (*s*).
Th' affrighted tyrant back to Babel hies,　645
There meets an end far worfe than that he flies (*t*).
Here Hezekiah's life is almoft done!
So good, and yet, alas! fo fhort 'tis fpun (*u*).
Th' end of the line was ravell'd, weak, and old;
Time muft go back, and afford better hold　650

(*m*) 2 Kings xvi. 5.　2 Chro. xxviii. 6.　(*n*) 2 Kings
xvi. 7.　(*o*) 2 Kings xvi. 9. and xv. 27. 2 Chro. xxviii. 20.
(*p*) 2 Kings xviii.　2 Chro. xxix.　(*q*) 2 Kings xviii. 9.
(*r*) 2 Kings xviii. 17.　2 Chro. xxxii.　Ifaiah xxxvi.
(*s*) 2 Kings xix. 35. 2 Chro. xxxii. 21.　(*t*) 2 Kings xix. 37.
2 Chro. xxxii. 21.　(*u*) 2 Kings xx.　2 Chro. xx. 24.

To tie a new thread to it of fifteen years.
'Tis done; th' almighty power of prayer and tears!
Backward the Sun, an unknown motion, went (x);
The stars gaz'd on, and wonder'd what he meant.
Manasses next (forgetful Man!) begins,   655
Enslav'd and sold to Ashur by his sins (y);
Till by the rod of learned Mis'ry taught,
Home to his God and country both he's brought (z).
It taught not Ammon, nor his hardness brake;
He's made th' example he refus'd to take (a).   660
  Yet from this root a goodly cion springs,
Josiah! best of men, as well as kings (b).
Down went the calves, with all their gold and cost;
The priests then truly griev'd, Osiris lost.
These mad Egyptian rites till now remain'd;   665
Fools! they their worser thraldom still retain'd!
In his own fires Moloch to ashes fell (c),
And no more flames must have besides his hell.
Like end Astartes' horned image found,
And Baal's spired stone to dust was ground.   670
No more were men in female habit seen,
Or they in men's, by the lewd Syrian queen;
No lustful maids at Benos' temple sit,
And with their body's shame their marriage get.
The double Dagon neither nature saves,   675
Nor flies she back to th' Erythræan waves.

(x) 2 Kings xx. 11. 2 Chro. xxxii. 24.   (y) 2 Kings
xxi. 2 Chro. xxxiii. 1, 11.   (z) 2 Chro. xxxiii. 12, 13.
(a) 2 Kings xxi. 19. 2 Chro. xxxiii. 21. (b) 2 Kings xxii.
2 Kings xxiii.   (c) 2 Kings xxiii. 10. Ibid. ℣. 13.

The trav'lling fun fees gladly from on high
His chariots burn (*d*), and Nergal quenched lie.
The King's impartial anger lights on all,
From fly-blown Accaron to the thund'ring Baal. 680
Here David's joy unruly grows and bold,
Nor could fleep's filken chain its vi'lence hold,
Had not the angel, to feal faft his eyes,
The humours ftirr'd, and bid more mifts arife;
When ftraight a chariot hurries fwift away,   685
And in it good Jofiah bleeding lay:
One hand is held up, one ftops the wound; in vain
They both are us'd. Alas! he's flain, he's flain.

Jehoias and Jehoiakim next appear' (*e*);
Both urge that vengeance which before was near.
He in Egyptian fetters captive dies,   691
This by more courteous Anger murther'd lies (*f*)..
His fon and brother next do bonds fuftain,
Ifrael's now folemn and imperial chain.
Here's the laft fcene of this proud city's ftate;   695
All ills are met, ty'd in one knot of Fate (*g*).
Their endlefs flav'ry in this trial lay;
Great God had heap'd up ages in one day:
Strong works around the wall the Chaldees build(*h*),
The town with grief and dreadful bus'nefs fill'd:
To their carv'd gods the frantic women pray,   701
Gods which as near their ruin were as they:

(*d*) 2 Kings xxiii. 11.   (*e*) 2 Kings xxiii. 31. Ibid. ⅴ. 36.
2 Chro. xxxvi. 1, 5.   (*f*) 2 Kings xxiii. 34. 2 Chr. xxxvi. 4.
Jer. xxxvi. 30.   (*g*) 2 Kings xxiv. 8.   2 Chro. xxxvi.
(*h*) 2 Kings xxv. 1. Jer. lii. 4.

At laſt in ruſhes the prevailing foe,
Does all the miſchief of proud conqueſt ſhow.
The wond'ring babes from mothers' breaſts are rent,
And ſuffer ills they neither fear'd nor meant (*i*). 706
No ſilver rev'rence guards the ſtooping.age,
No rule or method ties their boundleſs rage.
The glorious temple ſhines in flames all o'er (*k*),
Yet not ſo bright as in its gold before.   710
Nothing but fire or ſlaughter meets the eyes;
Nothing the ear but groans and diſmal cries.
The walls and towers are levell'd with the ground,
And ſcarce ought now of that vaſt city's found
But ſhards and rubbiſh, which weak ſigns might keep
Of forepaſt glory, and bid trav'llers weep.   716
Thus did triumphant Aſſur homewards paſs,
And thus Jeruſ'lem left, Jeruſalem that was!

  Thus Zedechiah ſaw, and this not all;
Before his face his friends and children fall (*l*), 720
The ſport of ins'lent victors : this he views,
A king and father once; ill Fate could uſe
His eyes no more to do their maſter's ſpight;
All to be ſeen ſhe took, and next his ſight.
Thus a long death in priſon he outwears,   725
Bereft of Grief's laſt ſolace, ev'n his tears.

  Then Jeconiah's ſon did foremoſt come (*m*),
And he who brought the captiv'd nation home;

A row of Worthies in long order pafs'd
O'er the fhort ftage ; of all old Jofeph laft.   736
Fair angels pafs'd by next in feemly bands,
All gilt, with gilded bafkets in their hands.
Some as they went the blue-ey'd violets ftrew,
Some fpotlefs lilies in loofe order threw.
Some did the way with full-blown rofes fpread,   735
Their fmell divine, and colour ftrangely red ;
Not fuch as our dull gardens proudly wear,
Whom weathers taint, and winds' rude kiffes tear.
Such, I believe, was the firft rofe's hew,
Which, at God's word, in beauteous Eden grew ;   740
Queen of the flowers, which made that orchard gay,
The morning blufhes of the Spring's new day.

  With fober pace an heav'nly Maid walks in,
Her looks all fair, no fign of native fin
Thro' her whole body writ ; Immod'rate Grace   745
Spoke things far more than human in her face :
It cafts a dufky gloom o'er all the flow'rs,
And with full beams their mingled light devours.
An angel ftraight broke from a fhining cloud,
And prefs'd his wings, and with much rev'rence bow'd ;
Again he bow'd, and grave approach he made,   751
And thus his facred meffage fweetly faid :

  " Hail ! full of grace ! thee the whole world fhall call
  " Above all Blefs'd ; thee, who fhalt blefs them all.
  " Thy virgin womb in wondrous fort fhall fhrowd
  " Jefus the God ;" (and then again he bow'd)   756

" Conception the great Spirit fhall breath on thee.
" Hail thou!who muftGod'swife,God'smotherbe(n)."
With that his feeming form to heav'n he rear'd,
(She low obeifance made) and difappear'd.   760
Lo! a new ftar three Eaftern fages fee (o);
(For why fhould only earth a gainer be?)
They faw this Phofphor's infant-light, and knew
It bravely ufher'd in a fun as new:
They hafted all this rifing fun t' adore;   765
With them rich myrrh, and early fpices, bore.
Wife Men! no fitter gift your zeal could bring;
You'll in a noifome ftable find your King.
Anon a thoufand devils ran roaring in;
Some with a dreadful fmile deform'dly grin;   770
Some ftamp their cloven paws, fome frown, and tear
The gaping fnakes from their black-knotted hair,
As if all grief, and all the rage of hell
Were doubled now, or that juft now they fell:
But when the dreaded Maid they ent'ring faw,   775
All fled with trembling fear and filent awe:
In her chafte arms th' Eternal Infant lies,
Th' Almighty Voice chang'd into feeble cries.
Heav'n contain'd virgins oft', and will do more;
Never did virgin contain Heav'n before.   780
Angels peep round to view this myftic thing,
And halleluiah round, all halleluiah, fing.
    No longer could good David quiet bear
Th' unwieldy pleafure which o'erflow'd him here;

(n) Luke i. 28.   (o) Matth. ii. 2.

It broke the fetters, and burft ope his eye;   785
Away the tim'rous Forms together fly.
Fix'd with amaze he ftood, and time muft take,
To learn if yet he were at laft awake.
Sometimes he thinks that Heav'n this vifion fent,
And order'd all the pageants as they went: 790
Sometimes that only 'twas wild Fancy's play,
The loofe and fcatter'd reliques of the day.

   When Gabriel (no blefs'd fp'rit more kind or fair)
Bodies and clothes himfelf with thicken'd air,
All like a comely youth in life's frefh bloom,   795
Rare workmanfhip, and wrought by heav'nly loom!
He took for fkin a cloud moft foft and bright
That e'er the mid-day fun pierc'd thro' with light;
Upon his cheeks a lively blufh he fpread,
Wafh'd from the morning beauty's deepeft red;   800
An harmlefs flaming meteor fhone for hair,
And fell adown his fhoulders with loofe care:
He cuts out a filk mantle from the fkies,
Where the moft fprightly azure pleas'd the eyes;
This he with ftarry vapours fpangles all,   805
Took in their prime ere they grow ripe, and fall:
Of a new rainbow ere it fret or fade,
The choiceft piece took out, a fcarf is made;
Small ftreaming clouds he does for wings difplay,
Not virtuous lovers' fighs more foft than they;   810
Thefe he gilds o'er with the fun's richeft rays,
Caught gliding o'er pure ftreams on which he plays.

Thus drefs'd, the joyful Gabriel pofts away,

And carries with him his own glorious day   814

Thro' the thick woods; the gloomy fhades a while

Put on frefh looks, and wonder why they fmile;

The trembling ferpents clofe and filent lie,

The birds obfcene far from his paffage fly;

A fudden fpring waits on him as he goes,

Sudden as that which by creation rofe.   820

Thus he appears to David; at firft fight

All earth-bred fears and forrows take their flight:

In rufhes joy divine, and hope, and reft;

A facred calm fhines thro' his peaceful breaft.   824

" Hail, Man belov'd! from higheft heav'n," faid he,

" My mighty Mafter fends thee health by me.

" The things thou faw'ft are full of truth and light,

" Shap'd in the glafs of the divine forefight.

" Ev'n now old Time is harneffing the Years   829

" To go in order thus: hence, empty fears! [fpring

" Thy fate's all white; from thy blefs'd feed fhall

" The promis'd Shilo, the great myftic King.

" Round the whole earth his dreaded Name fhall found,

" And reach to worlds that muft not yet be found:834

" The Southern clime him her fole Lord fhall ftyle,

" Him all the North, ev'n Albion's ftubborn ifle.

" My fellow-fervant, credit what I tell."

Straight into fhapelefs air unfeen he fell.   838

End of the Second Book.

DAVIDEIS.

BOOK III.

𝕿𝖍𝖊 𝕮𝖔𝖓𝖙𝖊𝖓𝖙𝖘.

Rais'd with the news he from high Heav'n receives,
Straight to his diligent God juſt thanks he gives.
To divine Nobe directs then his flight *(a)*,
A ſmall town, great in fame by Levy's right;
Is there with ſprightly wines and hallow'd bread   5
(But what's to hunger hallow'd?) largely fed *(b)*.
The good old prieſt welcomes his fatal gueſt,
And with long talk prolongs the haſty feaſt:

(a) 1 Sam. xxi. 1.   *(b)* ℣. 4, 5, 6. Mat. xii. 4.

M iij

He lends him vain Goliath's facred fword (c),
(The fitteft help juft Fortune could afford)   10
A fword whofe weight without a blow might flay,
Able unblunted to cut hofts away;
A fword fo great, that it was only fit
To take off his great head who came with it.
Thus he arms David; " I your own reftore;   15
" Take it," faid he, " and ufe it as before (d).
" I faw you then, and 'twas the braveft fight
" That ere thefe eyes ow'd the difcov'ring light.
" When you ftepp'd forth, how did the monfter rage,
" In fcorn of your foft looks and tender age!   20
" Some your high fpirit did mad prefumption call,
" Some pity'd that fuch youth fhould idly fall.
" Th' uncircumcis'd fmil'd grimly with difdain.
" I knew the day was your's; I faw it plain."
Much more the rev'rend fire prepar'd to fay,   25
Wrapp'd with his joy; how the two armies lay;
Which way th' amazed foe did wildly flee :
All that his hearer better knew than he;
But David's hafte denies all needlefs ftay :
To Gath (e), an enemy's land, he haftes away,   30
Not there fecure, but where one danger's near,
The more remote, tho' greater, difappear.
So from the hawk birds to man's fuccour flee,
So from fir'd fhips man leaps into the fea.
There in difguife he hopes unknown t' abide!   35
Alas! in vain! what can fuch greatnefs hide?

(c) 1 Sam xxi. 9.   (d) 1 Sam. xvii. 5.   (e) 1 Sam. xxi. 10.

Stones of fmall worth may lie unfeen by day,
But night itfelf does the rich gem betray.
Tagal firft fpy'd him, a Philiftian knight,
Who erft from David's wrath by fhameful flight. 40
Had fav'd the fordid remnant of his age;
Hence the deep fore of envy mix'd with rage.
Straight with a band of foldiers, tall and rough,
Trembling, for fcarce he thought that band enough,
On him he feizes, whom they all had fear'd, 45
Had the bold youth in his own fhape appear'd.
And now this wifh'd-for, but yet dreadful prey,
To Achis' court they led in hafte away,
With all unmanly rudenefs which does wait
Upon th' immod'rate vulgar's joy and hate. 50
His valour now and ftrength muft ufelefs lie,
And he himfelf muft arts unufual try (*f*).
Sometimes he rends his garments, nor does fpare
The goodly curls of his rich yellow hair:
Sometimes a violent laughter fcrew'd his face, 55
And fometimes ready tears dropp'd down apace:
Sometimes he fix'd his ftaring eyes on ground,
And fometimes in wild manner hurl'd them round.
More full revenge Philiftians could not wifh,
But call it the juftice of their mighty Fifh. 60
They now in height of anger let him live,
And freedom, too, t' increafe his fcorn, they give (*g*).
He, by wife madnefs freed, does homeward flee,
And rage makes them all that he feem'd to be.

(*f*) 1 Sam. xxi. 13.   (*g*) ℣. 15.

Near to Adullam (*h*), in an aged wood,   65
An hill, part earth, part rocky ftone, there ftood,
Hollow and vaft within, which Nature wrought,
As if by' her fcholar Art fhe had been taught:
Hither young David with his kindred came,
Servants and friends; many his fpreading fame,   70
Many their wants or difcontents (*i*), did call;
Great men in war, and almoft armies all!
Hither came wife and valiant Joab down,
One to whom David's felf muft owe his crown;
A mighty man, had not fome cunning fin   75
Amidft fo many virtues crowded in.
With him Abifhai came, by whom there fell
At once three hundred (*k*); with him Afahel (*l*);
Afahel! fwifter than the Northern wind (*m*);
Scarce could the nimble motions of his mind   80
Outgo his feet: fo ftrangely would he run,
That Time itfelf perceiv'd not what was done.
Oft' o'er the lawns and meadows would he pafs,
His weight unknown, and harmlefs to the grafs;
Oft' o'er the fands and hollow duft would trace, 85
Yet no one atom trouble or difplace.
Unhappy Youth! whofe end fo near I fee (*n*)!
There's nought but thy ill fate fo fwift as thee.
    Hither Jeffides' wrongs Benaiah drew,
He who the vaft exceeding monfter flew (*o*).   90

(*h*) 1 Sam. xxii. 1. (*i*) 1 Sam. xxii. 2. (*k*) 1 Chron. xi. 20.
(*l*) 1 Chron. xi. 26. (*m*) 2 Sam. ii. 18. (*n*) 2 Sam. ij. 23.
(*o*) 1 Chron. xi. 22.
    3

Th' Egyptian like an hill himſelf did rear; .
Like ſome tall tree upon it ſeem'd his ſpear; ..
But by Benaiah's ſtaff he fell o'erthrown (*p*);
The earth, as if worſt ſtrook, did loudeſt groan.
Such was Benaiah; in a narrow pit   *95*
He ſaw a lion, and leap'd down to it :
As eas'ly there the royal beaſt he tore (*q*), .
As that itſelf did kids or lambs before.
Him Ira follow'd (*r*); a young lovely boy,
But full of ſp'rit, and arms was all his joy :   *100*
Oft', when a child, he in his dream would fight
With the vain air, and his wak'd mother fright;
Oft' would he ſhoot young birds, and as they fall
Would laugh, and fancy them Philiſtians all :
And now at home no longer would he ſtay,   *105*
Tho' yet the face did ſcarce his ſex betray.
Dodo's great ſon came next (*s*), whoſe dreadful hand
Snatch'd ripen'd glories from a conqu'ring band,
Who knows not Dammin, and that barley-field,
Which did a ſtrange and bloody harveſt yield ?   *110*
Many beſides did this new troop increaſe;
Adan, whoſe wants made him unfit for peace;
Eliel (*t*), whoſe full quiver did always bear
As many deaths as in it arrows were;
None from his hand did vain or inn'cent flee;   *115*
Scarce Love or Fate could aim ſo well as he.

(*p*) 1 Chron. xi. 23.   (*q*) v. 22.   (*r*) 1 Chron. xi. 28.
(*s*) 1 Chron. xi. 26.   (*t*) 1 Chron. xi. 46.

Many of Judah took wrong'd David's fide (u),
And many of old Jacob's youngeſt Tribe;
But his chief ſtrength the Gadite ſoldiers are (x),
Each ſingle man able to o'ercome a war!   120
Swift as the darts they fling thro' yielding air,
And hardy all as the ſtrong ſteel they bare;
A lion's noble rage ſits in their face,
Terrible comely! arm'd with dreadful grace!

   Th' undaunted Prince, tho' thus well guarded here,
Yet his ſtout ſoul durſt for his parents' fear;   126
He ſeeks for them a ſafe and quiet ſeat (y),
Nor truſts his fortune with a pledge ſo great.
So when in hoſtile fire rich Aſia's pride
For ten years' ſiege had fully ſatisfy'd,   130
Æneas ſtole an act of higher fame,
And bore Anchiſes thro' the wand'ring flame (z);
A nobler burden, and a richer prey,
Than all the Grecian forces bore away.
Go, pious Prince! in peace, in triumph go,   135
Enjoy the conqueſt of thine overthrow;
To 'ave ſav'd thy Troy would far leſs glorious be;
By this thou overcom'ſt their victory.
Moab next Judah, an old kingdom, lies,
Jordan their touch, and his curs'd ſea, denies: 140
They ſee north-ſtars from o'er Amoreus' ground,
Edom and Petra their ſouth part does bound:

(u) 1 Chron. xii. 16.   (x) 1 Chron. xii. 8. (y) 1 Sam. xxii. 3, 4.
(z) Virg. Aen. II.

Eastwards the lands of Cush and Ammon lie,
The morning's happy beams they first espy :
The region with fat soil and plenty's bless'd,   145
A soil too good to be of old possess'd
By monstrous Emins; but Lot's offspring came
And conquer'd both the people and the name,
Till Seon drave them beyond Arnon's flood.(*a*),
And their sad bounds mark'd deep in their own blood:
In Hesbon his triumphant court he plac'd,   151
Hesbon ! by men and Nature strangely grac'd :
A glorious town, and fill'd with all delight
Which peace could yield, tho' well prepar'd for fight.
But this proud city, and her prouder lord,   155
Felt the keen rage of Israel's sacred sword (*b*),
Whilst Moab triumphed in her torn estate,
To see her own become her conqu'ror's fate.
Yet that small remnant of Lot's patted crown
Did, arm'd with Israel's sins, pluck Israel down. 160
Full thrice six years they felt fierce Eglon's yoke, (*c*)
Till Ehud's sword God's vengeful message spoke (*d*);
Since then their kings in quiet held their own;
Quiet, the good of a not-envy'd throne:
And now a wise old prince the sceptre sway'd,   165
Well by his subjects and himself obey'd :
Only before his fathers' gods he fell;
Poor wretched Man ! almost too good for hell !
Hither does David his bless'd parents bring ;
With humble greatness begs of Moab's king   170

a) Num. xxi. 26. (*b*) ℣. 24,25. (*c*) Judg. iii. 14. (*d*) ℣. 2 r.

A fafe and fair abode, where they might live
Free from thofe ftorms with which himfelf muft
     ftrive (e).
The King with cheerful grace his fuit approv'd,
By hate to Saul and love to virtue mov'd.   174
" Welcome, great Knight, and your fair troop," faid
" Your name found welcome long before with me, [he;
" That to rich Ophir's rifing morn is known,
" And ftretch'd out far to the burnt fwarthy zone;
" Swift Fame, when her round journey fhe does make,
" Scorns not fometimes us in her way to take. 180
" Are you the man did that huge giant kill ?
" Great Baal of Phegor ! and how young he is ftill !
" From Ruth we heard yon came; Ruth was born
     here (f),
" In Judah fojourn'd, and, they fay, match'd there
" To one of Bethleh'm (g), which I hope is true : 185
" Howe'er, your virtues here entitle you :
" Thofe have the beft alliance always been ;
" To gods as well as men they make us kin."
   He fpoke, and ftraight led in his thankful guefts
To a ftately room prepar'd for fhows and feafts : 190
The room with golden tap'ftry glifter'd bright,
At once to pleafe and to confound the fight,
Th' excellent work of Babylonian hands ;
In midft a table of rich iv'ry ftands,
By three fierce tigers and three lions borne, 195
Which grin, and fearfully the place adorn ;

(e) 1 Sam. xxii. 3. (f) Ruth i. 4. (g) Ruth iv. 10.

Widely they gape, and to the eye they roar,
As if they hunger'd for the food they bore.
About it beds of Lybian citron stood,
With cov'rings dy'd in Tyrian fishes blood,   200
They say th' Herculean art; but most delight
Some pictures gave to David's learned sight.
Here sev'ral ways Lot and great Abram go (*h*),
Their too much wealth vast, and unkind, does grow:
Thus each extreme to equal danger tends;   205
Plenty as well as want can sep'rate friends.
Here Sodom's tow'rs raise their proud tops on high ;
The tow'rs as well as men outbrave the sky :
By it the waves of rev'rend Jordan run,
Here green with trees, there gilded with the sun.   210
Hither Lot's houshold comes (*i*) a num'rous train,
And all with various bus'ness fill the plain :
Some drive the crowding sheep with airal hooks,
They lift up their mild heads, and bleat in looks :
Some drive the herds : here a fierce bullock scorns   215
Th' appointed way, and runs with threat'ning horns :
In vain the herdman calls him back again ;
The dogs stand off afar, and bark in vain.
Some lead the groaning waggons, loaded high
With stuff, on top of which the maidens lie :   220
Upon tall camels the fair sisters ride,
And Lot talks with them both on either side.

(*h*) Gen. xiii. 9.   (*i*) y. 10.

Another picture to curs'd Sodom brings
Elam's proud lord, with his three servant kings;
They fack the town, and bear Lot bound away (k),
Whilst in a pit the vanquifh'd Bera lay (l);   226
Bury'd almoft alive for fear of death,
But Heav'n's juft vengeance fav'd as yet his breath.
Abraham purfues, and flays the victors' hoft (m),
Scarce had their conqueft leifure for a boaft.   230
Next this was drawn the recklefs cities' flame,
When a ftrange hell pour'd down from heav'n there
          came (n).
Here the two angels from Lot's window look
With fmiling anger; the lewd wretches ftrook   234
With fudden blindnefs, feek in vain the door (o);
Their eyes, firft caufe of luft, firft veng'ance bore;
Thro' liquid air heav'n's bufy foldiers fly,
And drive on clouds where feeds of thunder lie.
Here the fad fky glows red with difmal ftreaks;
Here lightning from it with fhort trembling breaks:
Here the blue flames of fcalding brimftone fall,   241
Involving fwiftly in one ruin all:
The fire of trees and houfes mounts on high,
And meets half way new fires that fhow'r from fky.
Some in their arms fnatch their dear babes away; 245
At once drop down the fathers' arms and they:
Some into waters leap with kindled hair,
And, more to vex their fate, are burnt ev'n there.

(k) Gen. xiv. 11, 12.   (l) v. 10.   (m) v. 13. &c.
    (n) Gen. xix. &c.   (o) v. 11.

Men thought, so much a flame by art was shown,
The picture's self would fall in ashes down.   250
Afar old Lot tow'rd little Zoar hies (*p*),
And dares not move (good Man!) his weeping eyes.
Behind his wife stood ever fix'd alone (*q*),
No more a woman, not yet quite a stone:
A lasting death seiz'd on her turning head;   255
One cheek was rough and white, the other red,
And yet a cheek: in vain to speak she strove;
Her lips, tho' stone, a little seem'd to move.
One eye was clos'd, surpris'd by sudden night,
The other trembled still with parting light: 260
The wind admir'd, which her hair loosely bore,
Why it grew stiff, and now would play no more.
To Heav'n she lifted up her-freezing hands,
And to this day a suppliant pillar stands.
She try'd her heavy foot from ground to rear;   265
And rais'd the heel, but her toe's rooted there.
Ah! foolish Woman! who must always be
A sight more strange than that she turn'd to see!
   Whilst David fed with these his curious eye,
The feast is now serv'd in, and down they lie.   270
Moab a goblet takes of massy gold,
Which Zippor, and from Zippor all of old
Quaft to their gods and friends, an health goes round
In the brisk grape of Arnon's richest ground:
Whilst Melchor to his harp with wondrous skill 275
(For such were poets then, and should be still)

(*p*) Gen. xix. 20.   (*q*) ℣. 26.

His noble verfe thro' Nature's fecrets lead;
He fung what fp'rit thro' the whole mafs is fpread,
Ev'ry where all; how heav'ns God's law approve,
And think it reft eternally to move :   280
How the kind fun ufefully comes and goes;
Wants it himfelf, yet gives to man repofe:
How his round journey does for ever laft;
And how he baits at ev'ry fea in hafte.
He fung how earth blots the moon's gilded wane, 285
Whilft foolifh men beat founding brafs in vain;
Why the great waters her flight horns obey,
Her changing horns, not conftanter than they.
He fung how grifly comets hang in air;
Why fword and plagues attend their fatal hair; 290
God's beacons for the world, drawn up fo far;
To publifh ills; and raife all earth to war:
Why contraries feed thunder in the cloud;
What motions vex it till it roar fo loud :
How lambent fires become fo wondrous tame,   295
And beat fuch fhining winter in their flame :
What radiant pencil draws the watry bow;
What ties up hail; and picks the fleecy fnow:
What palfy of the earth fhakes up fix'd hills
From off her brows, and here whole rivers fpills. 300
Thus did this Heathen Nature's fecrets tell;
And fometimes mifs'd the caufe, but fought it well.
   Such was the fauce of Moab's noble feaft;
Till night far fpent invites them to their reft :

Only the good old prince ſtays Joab there,   305
And much he tells, and much deſires to hear :
He tells deeds antique ; and the new deſires ;
Of David much, and much of Saul, inquires.
" Nay, gentle Gueſt !" ſaid he, " ſince now you 're in,
" The ſtory of your gallant friend begin :   310
" His birth, his riſing, tell, and various fate,
" And how he ſlew that man of Gath of late,
" What was he call'd? that huge and monſtrous man."
With that he ſtopp'd, and Joab thus began :   314
    ' His birth, great Sir ! ſo much to mine is ty'd (*r*),
' That praiſe of that might look from me like pride:
' Yet without boaſt, his veins contain a flood
' Of th' old Judæan Lion's richeſt blood (*s*).
' From Judah Pharez, from him Eſrom came,   319
' Ram, Naſhon, Salmon (*t*), names ſpoke loud by Fame.
' A name no leſs ought Boaz to appear,
' By whoſe bleſs'd match we come no ſtrangers here.
' From him and your fair Ruth good Obed ſprung,
' From Obed Jeſſe, Jeſſe ! whom Fame's kindeſt tongue,
' Counting his birth, and high nobil'ty, ſhall   325
' Not Jeſſe of Obed, but of David, call,
' David born to him ſeventh (*u*) ; the ſix births paſt,
' Brave trials of a work more great at laſt.
' Bleſs me ! how ſwift and growing was his wit !
' The wings of Time flagg'd dully after it.   330

(*r*) 1 Chro. ii. 16.   (*s*) Gen. xlix. 9.   (*t*) 1 Chro. ii.
Matth. i.   (*u*) 1 Chro. ii. 15. 1 Sam. xvi. 11.

‘ Scarce paſt a child, all wonders would he ſing

‘ Of Nature's law, and power of Nature's King.

‘ His ſheep would ſcorn their food to hear his lay,

‘ And ſavage beaſts ſtand by as tame as they:

‘ The fighting winds would ſtop there, and admire,

‘ Learning conſent and concord from his lyre: 336

‘ Rivers, whoſe waves roll'd down aloud before,

‘ Mute as their fiſh, would liſten towards the ſhore.

 ‘ 'Twas now the time when firſt Saul God for-
  ſook (*x*),

‘ God Saul; the room in his heart wild paſſions took :

‘ Sometimes a tyrant frenzy revell'd there,   341

‘ Sometimes black ſadneſs, and deep, deep deſpair.

‘ No help from herbs or learned drugs he finds,

‘ They cure but ſometime bodies, never minds.

‘ Muſic alone thoſe ſtorms of ſoul could lay (*y*); 345

‘ Not more Saul them, than Muſic they obey.

‘ David's now ſent for, and his harp muſt bring;

‘ His harp! that magic bore on ev'ry ſtring.   348

‘ When Saul's rude paſſions did moſt tumult keep,

‘ With his ſoft notes they all dropp'd down aſleep :

‘ When his dull ſp'rits lay drown'd in death and night,

‘ He with quick ſtrains rais'd them to life and light.

‘ Thus cheer'd he Saul, thus did his fury 'ſwage,

‘ Till wars began, and times more fit for rage.

‘ To Helah plain Philiſtian troops are come (*z*), 355

‘ And War's loud noiſe ſtrikes peaceful Muſic dumb.

 (*x*) 1 Sam. xvi. 14.   (*y*) ℣. 23.   (*z*) 1 Sam. xvii.

' Back to his rural care young David goes;

' For this rough work Saul his stout brethren chose;

' He knew not what his hand in war could do,

' Nor thought his sword could cure men's madness too.

' Now Dammin's destin'd for this scene of blood; 361

' On two near hills the two proud armies stood;

' Between a fatal valley stretch'd out wide,

' And death seem'd ready now on either side;

' When, lo! their host rais'd all a joyful shout,   365

' And from the midst an huge and monstrous man

  ' stepp'd out (a).

' Aloud they shouted; at each step he took

' We and the earth itself beneath him shook:

' Vast as the hill down which he march'd he appear'd,

' Amaz'd all eyes, nor was their army fear'd.   370

' A young tall squire (tho' then he seem'd not so)

' Did from the camp at first before him go;

' At first he did, but scarce could follow straight,

' Sweating beneath a shield's unruly weight,

' On which was wrought the gods' and giants' fight,

' Rare work! all fill'd with terror and delight.   376

' Here a vast hill 'gainst thund'ring Baal was thrown,

' Trees and beasts on't fell burnt with lightning down.

' One flings a mountain, and its river too,

' Torn up with it; that rains back on him that threw.

' Some from the main to pluck whole islands try; 381

' The sea boils round with flames shot thick from sky.

  (a) 1 Sam. xvii. 4.

' This he believ'd, and on his fhield he bore,

' And prais'd their ftrength, but thought his own was

' The valley now this monfter feem'd to fill; [more.

' And we (methoughts) look'd up to him from our

' All arm'd in brafs, the richeft drefs of war,   [hill.

' (A difmal glorious fight) he fhone afar.   388

' The Sun himfelf ftarted with fudden fright,

' To fee his beams return fo difmal bright.   390

' Brafs was his helmet (*b*), his boots brafs; and o'er

' His breaft a thick plate of ftrong brafs he wore:

' His fpear the trunk was of a lofty tree,

' Which Nature meant fome tall fhip's maft fhould be;

' The huge iron head fix hundred fhekels weigh'd,

' And of whole bodies but one wound it made,   396

' Able Death's worft command to overdo,

' Deftroying life at once, and carcafs too.

' Thus arm'd he ftood, all direful, and all gay,

' And round him flung a fcornful look away.   400

' So when a Scythian tiger gazing round,

' An herd of kine in fome fair plain has found,

' Lowing fecure, he fwells with angry pride,

' And calls forth all his fpots on ev'ry fide,

' Then ftops, and hurls his haughty eyes at all, 405

' In choice of fome ftrong neck on which to fall;

' Almoft he fcorns fo weak, fo cheap a prey,

' And grieves to fee them trembling hafte away.

" Ye Men of Jury!" he cries, " if men you be,   409

" And fuch dare prove yourfelves to Fame and me,

(*b*) 1 Sam. xvii. 5, &c.

" Chufe out 'mongft all your troops the boldeft knight,
" To try his ftrength and fate with me in fight (c):
" The chance of war let us two bear for all,   413
" And they the conqu'ror ferve whofe knight fhall
At this he paus'd a while; ftraight, " I defy [fall (d)."
" Your Gods and you; dares none come down and die?
" Go back for fhame, and Egypt's flav'ry bear,
" Or yield to us, and ferve more nobly here.
" Alas! ye have no more wonders to be done,
" Your forc'rer Mofes now, and Jofua, is gone; 420
" Your magic trumpets then could cities take (e),
" And founds of triumph did your battles make :
" Spears in your hands, and manly fwords, are vain ;
" Get you your fpells and conj'ring rods again. 424
" Is there no Sampfon here? oh! that there were!
" In his full ftrength and long enchanted hair ;
" This fword fhould be in the weak razor's ftead (f);
" It fhould not cut his hair off, but his head."
:   " Thus he blafphem'd aloud; the vallies round,
' Flatt'ring his voice, reftor'd the dreadful found: 430
' We turn'd us trembling at the noife, and fear'd
' We had behind fome new Goliath heard (g).
' 'Twas Heav'n, Heav'n, fure, (which David's glory
' Thro' this whole act) fuch facred terror fent [meant
' To all our hoft; for there was Saul in place,   435
' Who ne'er faw fear but in his enemies' face;

(c) 1 Sam. xvii. 8.   (d) ỹ. 9, 10.   (e) Jofh. vj. 20.
(f) Judg. xvi. 17.   (g) 1 Sam. xvii. 11.

‘ His godlike fon there in bright armour fhone,
‘ Who fcorn'd to conquer armies not alone (*h*) :
‘ Fate her own book miftrufted at the fight;
‘ On that fide war, on this a fingle fight.　　440
‘ There ftood Benaiah; and there trembled too,
‘ He who th' Egyptian proud Goliath flew (*i*):
‘ In his pale fright rage thro' his eyes fhot flame,
‘ He faw his ftaff, and blufh'd with gen'rous fhame:
‘ Thoufands befide ftood mute and heartlefs there,
‘ Men valiant all; nor was I us'd to fear.　　446
　‘ Thus forty days he march'd down arm'd to fight;
‘ Once ev'ry morn he march'd, and once at night.
‘ Slow rofe the fun, but gallopp'd down apace,
‘ With more than evening blufhes in his face,　　450
‘ When Jeffey to the camp young David fent (*k*)
‘ His purpofe low, but high was Fate's intent:
‘ For when the monfter's pride he faw and heard,
‘ Round him he look'd, and wonder'd why they fear'd.
‘ Anger and brave difdain his heart poffefs'd,　　455
‘ Thoughts more than manly fwell'd his youthful
‘ Much the rewards propos'd his fpirit inflame, [breaft:
‘ Saul's daughter much, and much the voice of Fame(*l*).
‘ Thefe to their juft intentions ftrongly move,
‘ But chiefly God, and his dear country's love.　　460
‘ Refolv'd for combat, to Saul's tent he's brought,
‘ Where thus he fpoke as boldly as he fought:'

(*h*) 1 Sam. xiv.　　(*i*) 1 Chro. x. 23.　　(*k*) 1 Sam. xvii.
12, &c.　　(*l*) 1 Sam. xvii. 25.

2

" Henceforth no more, great Prince! your facred
     breaft

" With that huge talking wretch of Gath moleft (*m*);

" This hand alone fhall end his curfed breath ;   465

" Fear not, the wretch blafphemes himfelf to death ;

" And cheated with falfe weight of his own might,

" Has challeng'd Heav'n, not us, to fingle fight.

" Forbid it, God, that where thy right is try'd,

" The ftrength of man fhould find juft caufe for pride !

" Firm like fome rock, and vaft he feems to ftand, 471

" But rocks, we know, were op'd at thy command (*n*).

" That foul which now does fuch large members fway,

" Thro' one fmall wound will creep in hafte away ;

" And he who now dares boldly Heav'n defy,   475

" To ev'ry bird of heav'n a prey fhall lie.

" For 'tis not human force we ought to fear ;

" Did that, alas ! plant our forefathers here ?

" Twice fifteen kings did they by that fubdue (*o*)?

" By that whole nations of Goliaths flew ?   480

" The wonders they perform'd may ftill be done;

" Mofes and Jofua is, but God's not gone.

" We 'ave loft their rod and trumpets, not their fkill:

" Pray'rs and belief are as ftrong witchcraft ftill.

" Thefe are more tall, more giants far than he,   485

" Can reach to heav'n, and thence pluck victory.

" Count this, and then, Sir ! mine th' advantage is ;

" He 's ftronger far than I, my God than his."

(*m*) 1 Sam. xvii. 32.   (*n*) Exod. xvii. 6.   (*o*) Jofh. xii. 24.

" Amazement feiz'd on all, and fhame, to fee
" Their own fears fcorn'd by one fo young as he. 490
" Brave Youth (p)!" replies the King, " whofe daring
" Ere come to manhood leaves it quite behind, [mind
" Referve thy valour for more equal fight,
" And let thy body grow up to thy fpright :
" Thou 'rt yet too tender for fo rude a foe,   495
" Whofe touch would wound thee more than him thy
" Nature his limbs only for war made fit,   [blow.
" In thine, as yet, nought befide Love fhe 'as writ.
" With fome lefs foe thy unflefh'd valour try ;
" This monfter can be no firft victory.   500
" The lion's royal whelp does not at firft,
" For blood of Bafan bulls, or tigers, thirft ;
" In tim'rous deer he hanfels his young paws,
" And leaves the rugged bear for firmer claws.
" So vaft thy hopes, fo unproportion'd be,   505
" Fortune would be afham'd to fecond thee."
   ' He faid, and we all murmur'd an affent;
' But nought moves David from his high intent.
' It brave to him, and ominous, does appear,
' To be oppos'd at firft, and conquer here,   510
' Which he refolves." " Scorn not," fays he, " mine
" For vict'ry comes not like an heritage,   [age (q),
" At fet years. When my father's flock I fed,
" A bear and lion, by fierce hunger led,   514
" Broke from the wood, and fnatch'd my lambs away;
" From their grim mouths I forc'd the panting prey :

     (p) 1 Sam. xvii. 33.   (q) V. 34.

" Both bear and lion ev'n this hand did kill,
" On our great oak the bones and jaws hang ftill.
" My God's the fame, which then he was, to-day,
" And this wild wretch almoft the fame as they. 520
" Who from fuch danger fav'd my flock, will he
" Of Ifrael, his own flock, lefs careful be ?"

    " Be't fo then," Saul burfts forth, " and Thou on
     high,
" Who oft' in weaknefs doft moft ftrength defcry,
" At whofe dread beck Conqueft expecting ftands,
" And cafts no look down on the fighters' hands,
" Affift what thou infpir'ft ; and let all fee,   527
" As boys to giants, giants are to thee."

    ' Thus, and with trembling hopes of ftrange fuccefs,
' In his own arms he the bold youth does drefs (r).
' On his head an helm of well-wrought brafs is plac'd,
' The top with warlike plumes feverely grac'd : 532
' His breaft a plate cut with rare figures bore,
' A fword much practis'd in Death's art he wore;
' Yet David, us'd fo long to no defence,   535
' But thofe light arms of fpirit and innocence,
' No good in fight of that gay burden knows,
' But fears his own arms' weight more than his foe's,
' He loft himfelf in that difguife of war,
' And guarded feems, as men by prifons are.   540
' He, therefore, to exalt the wondrous fight,
' Prepares now, and difarms himfelf for fight.

        (r) 1 Sam. xvii. 38.

' 'Gainſt ſhield, helm, breaſtplate, and inſtead of
    thoſe,   [choſe (s),
' Five ſharp ſmooth ſtones from the next brook he
' And fits them to his ſling; then marches down ;
' For ſword, his enemy's he eſteem'd his own.   546
' We all with various paſſion ſtrangely gaz'd,
' Some ſad, ſome 'ſham'd, ſome angry, all amaz'd.
  ' Now in the valley he ſtands: thro' his youthful face
' Wrath checks the beauty, and ſheds manly grace;
' Both in his looks ſo join'd, that they might move 551
' Fear ev'n in friends, and from an en'my love;
' Hot as ripe Noon, ſweet as the blooming Day;
' Like July furious, but more fair than May.
' Th' accurs'd Philiſtian ſtands on th' other ſide,
' Grumbling aloud (t), and ſmiles 'twixt rage and
    pride.'   556
" The plagues of Dagon! A ſmooth boy," ſays he,
" A curſed, beardleſs foe, oppos'd to me ! [come !
" Hell! with what arms (hence, thou fond Child!) he's
" Some friend his mother call to drive him home.
" Not gone yet ? If one minute more thou ſtay, 561
" The birds of heav'n ſhall bear thee dead away.
" Gods! a curs'd boy!" The reſt then murm'ring out,
' He walks, and caſts a deadly grin about.
' David, with cheerful anger in his eyes,   565
' Advances boldly on, and thus replies;'

(s) 1 Sam. xvii. 40.   (t) ⱱ. 43.

" Thou com'ft, vain Man! all arm'd into the field (*u*),
" And truftest thofe war toys, thy fword and fhield;
" Thy pride's my fpear, thy blafphemies my fword;
" My fhield thy Maker; Fool! the mighty Lord
" Of thee and battles; who hath fent forth me, 571
" Unarm'd thus, not to fight, but conquer thee.
" In vain fhall Dagon, thy falfe hope, withftand;
" In vain thy other god, thine own right hand.
" Thy fall to man fhall Heav'n's ftrong juftice fhew;
" Wretch! 'tis the only good which thou canft do."
  ' He faid; our hoft ftood dully filent by,   577
' And durft not truft their ears againft the eye.
' As much their champion's threats to him they fear'd,
' As when the monfter's threats to them they heard.
' His flaming fword th' enrag'd Philiftian fhakes, 581
' And hafte to his ruin with loud curfes makes.
' Backward the winds his active curfes blew,
' And fatally round his own head they flew: 584
' For now from David's fling the ftone is fled (*x*),
' And ftrikes, with joyful noife, the monfter's head:
' It ftrook his forehead, and pierc'd deeply there,
' As fwiftly as it pierc'd before the air.
' Down, down he falls! and bites in vain the ground;
' Blood, brain, and foul, crowd mingled thro' the wound.
' So a ftrong oak, which many years had ftood, 591
' With fair and flourifhing boughs, itfelf a wood,
' Tho' it might long the axe's violence bear,
' And play'd with winds which other trees did tear;

     (*u*) 1 Sam. xvii. 45.   (*x*) ℣. 49.

' Yet by the thunder's ftroke from the root 'tis rent;
' So fure the blows that from high Heav'n are fent.
' What tongue the joy and wonder can exprefs, 597
' Which did that moment our whole hoft poffefs?
' Their jocund fhouts th' air like a ftorm did tear,
' Th' amazed clouds fled fwift away with fear; 600
' But far more fwift th' accurs'd Philiftians fly (*y*),
' And their ill fate to perfect, bafely die.
' With thoufand corpfe the ways around are ftrown,
' Till they, by the day's flight, fecure their own.
' Now thro' the camp founds nought but David's name;
' All joys, of feveral ftamp and colours, came   606
' From feveral paffions : fome his valour praife,
' Some his free fpeech, fome the fair pop'lar rays
' Of youth, and beauty, and his modeft guife;   609
' Gifts that mov'd all, but charm'd the female eyes.
' Some wonder; fome they thought it would be fo
' And fome faw angels flying thro' the air :   [fwear;
' The bafeft fpirits caft back a crooked glance
' On this great act, and fain would give it to Chance.
' Women our hoft with fongs and dances meet, 615
' With much joy Saul, David with more, they greet (*z*).
' Hence the King's politic rage and envy flows (*a*),
' Which firft he hides, and feeks his life to expofe
' To gen'rous dangers, that his hate might clear, 619
' And Fate or Chance the blame, nay, David, bear.
' So vain are man's defigns! for Fate and Chance,
' And Earth and Heav'n, confpir'd to his advance :

(*y*) Sam. xvii. 52   (*z*) 1 Sam. xviii. 6.   (*a*) ỳ. 8.

' His beauty, youth, courage, and wondrous wit,
' In all mankind but Saul did love beget (*b*).
' Not Saul's own houfe, not his own nearest blood,
' The noble caufe's facred force withftood.   626
' You 'ave met, no doubt, and kindly us'd the fame
' Of godlike Jonathan's illuftrious name;
' A name which ev'ry wind to heav'n would bear,
' Which men to fpeak, and angels joy to hear.   630
' No angel ere bore to his brother-mind
' A kindnefs more exalted and refin'd
' Than his to David, which look'd nobly down,
' And fcorn'd the falfe alarums of a crown.
' At Dammin field he ftood; and from his place 635
' Leap'd forth, the wondrous conqu'ror to embrace;
' On him his mantle, girdle, fword, and bow,
' On him his heart and foul, he did beftow (*c*).
' Not all that Saul could threaten or perfuade,
' In this clofe knot the fmalleft loofenefs made. 640
' Oft his wife care did the King's rage fufpend,
' His own life's danger fhelter'd oft' his friend (*d*),
' Which he expos'd, a facrifice to fall,
' By th' undifcerning rage of furious Saul.
' Nor was young David's active yirtue grown   645
' Strong and triumphant in one fex alone;
' Imperious beauty, too, it durft invade,
' And deeper prints in the foft breaft it made (*e*);

(*b*) 1 Sam. xviii. 16.   (*c*) 1 Sam. xviii. 1, 4.
(*d*) 1 Sam. xx. 33.   (*e*) 1 Sam. xviii. 20, 28.

O iij

‘ For there t’ efteem, and Friendfhip’s graver name,
‘ Paffion was pour’d like oil into the flame.   650
‘ Like two bright eyes in a fair body plac’d,
‘ Saul’s royal houfe two beauteous daughters grac’d;
‘ Merab the firft, Michol the younger nam’d,
‘ Both equally for different glories fam’d.
‘ Merab with fpacious beauty fill’d the fight,   655
‘ But too much awe chaftis’d the bold delight.
‘ Like a calm fea, which to th’ enlarged view
‘ Gives pleafure, but gives fear and rev’rence too,
‘ Michol’s fweet looks clear and free joys did move,
‘ And no lefs ftrong, tho’ much more gentle, love;
‘ Like virtuous kings, whom men rejoice t’ obey,
‘ Tyrants themfelves lefs abfolute than they.   662
‘ Merab appear’d like fome fair princely tower,
‘ Michol fome virgin queen’s delicious bower.
‘ All beauty’s ftores in little and in great;   665
‘ But the contracted beams fhot fierceft heat.
‘ A clean and lively brown was Merab’s dye,
‘ Such as the prouder colours might envy:
‘ Michol’s pure fkin fhone with fuch taintlefs white,
‘ As fcatter’d the weak rays of human fight: 670
‘ Her lips and cheeks a nobler red did fhew,
‘ Than ere on fruits or flow’rs Heav’n’s pencil drew.
‘ From Merab’s eyes fierce and quick lightnings came,
‘ From Michol’s the fun’s mild yet active flame.
‘ Merab’s long hair was gloffy chefnut brown,   675
‘ Treffes of paleft gold did Michol crown.

‘ Such was their outward form, and one might find
‘ A diff'rence not unlike it in the mind.
‘ Merab, with comely majefty and ftate,
‘ Bore high th' advantage of her worth and fate: 680
‘ Such humble fweetnefs did foft Michol fhow,
‘ That none who reach'd fo high e'er ftoop'd fo low.
‘ Merab rejoic'd in her wreck'd lover's pain,
‘ And fortify'd her virtue with difdain:
‘ The griefs fhe caus'd gave gentle Michol grief; 685
‘ She wifh'd her beauties lefs for their relief;
‘ Ev'n to her captives civil ; yet th' excefs
‘ Of naked virtue guarded her no lefs.
‘ Bus'nefs and pow'r Merab's large thoughts did vex,
‘ Her wit difdain'd the fetters of her fex :   ·690
‘ Michol no lefs difdain'd affairs and noife,
‘ Yet did it not from ignorance, but choice.
‘ In brief, both copies were more fweetly drawn,
‘ Merab of Saul, Michol of Jonathan.
   ‘ The day that David great Goliath flew,   695
‘ Not great Goliath's fword was more his due
‘ Than Merab : by Saul's public promife fhe
‘ Was fold then, and betroth'd to Victory :
‘ But haughty fhe did this juft match defpife;
‘ Her pride debauch'd her judgment and her eyes. 700
‘ An unknown youth, ne'er feen at court before,
‘ Who fhepherd's ftaff and fhepherd's habit bore,
‘ The feventh-born fon of no rich houfe, were ftill
‘ Th' unpleafant forms which her high thoughts did
     ‘ fill;

' And much averſion in her ſtubborn mind   705
' Was bred, by being promis'd and deſign'd.
' Long had the patient Adriel humbly borne
' The rougheſt ſhocks of her imperious ſcorn ;
' Adriel the rich, but riches were in vain,
' And could not ſet him free, nor her enchain.   710
' Long liv'd they thus : but as the hunted deer,
' Cloſely purſu'd, quits all her wonted fear,
' And takes the neareſt waves, which from the ſhore
' She oft' with horror had beheld before ;
' So whilſt the violent maid from David fled,   715
' She leap'd to Adriel's long-avoided bed (*f*).
' The match was nam'd, agreed, and finiſh'd ſtraight ;
' So ſoon comply'd Saul's envy with her hate.
' But Michol, in whoſe breaſt all virtues move,
' That hatch the pregnant ſeeds of ſacred love,   720
' With juſter eyes the noble object meets,
' And turns all Merab's poiſon into ſweets.
' She ſaw, and wonder'd how a youth unknown
' Should make all fame to come ſo ſoon his own :
' She ſaw, and wonder'd how a ſhepherd's crook 725
' Deſpis'd that ſword at which the ſceptre ſhook.
' Tho' he ſeventh-born, and tho' his houſe but poor,
' She knew it noble was. and would be more.
' Oft' had ſhe heard, and fancy'd oft' the ſight,
' With what a gen'rous calm he march'd to fight :
' In the great danger how exempt from fear,   731
' And after it from pride, he did appear.

' Greatnefs, and goodnefs, and an air divine,
' She faw thro' all his words and actions fhine.
' She heard his eloquent tongue, and charming lyre,
' Whofe artful founds did violent love infpire, 736
' Tho' us'd all other paffions to relieve ;
' She weigh'd all this, and well we may conceive,
' When thofe ftrong thoughts attack'd her doubtful
' His beauty no lefs active than the reft,   [breaft,
' The fire, thus kindled, foon grew fierce and great,
' When David's breaft reflected back its heat. 742
' Soon fhe perceiv'd (fcarce can love hidden lie
' From any fight, much lefs the loving eye)
' She conqu'ror was, as well as overcome, 745
' And gain'd no lefs abroad than loft at home.
' Ev'n the firft hour they met (for fuch a pair,
' Who in all mankind elfe fo matchlefs were,
' Yet their own equals, Nature's felf does wed)
' A mutual warmth thro' both their bofoms fpread.
' Fate gave the fignal; both at once began 751
' The gentle race, and with juft pace they ran.
' Ev'n fo (methinks) when two fair tapers come
' From feveral doors, ent'ring at once the room,
' With a fwift flight that leaves the eye behind, 755
' Their amorous lights into one light are join'd.
' Nature herfelf, were fhe to judge the cafe,
' Knew not which firft began the kind embrace.
' Michol her modeft flames fought to conceal,
' But love ev'n th' art to hide it does reveal. 760

‘ Her foft unpractis’d eyes betray’d the theft,

‘ Love paft thro’ them, and there fuch footfteps left.

‘ She blufh’d when he approach’d, and when he fpoke;

‘ And fuddenly her wand’ring anfwers broke,   764

‘ At his name’s found, and when fhe heard him prais’d,

‘ With concern’d hafte her thoughtful looks fhe rais’d.

‘ Uncall’d-for fighs oft’ from her bofom flew,

‘ And Adriel’s active friend fhe’ abruptly grew.

‘ Oft’ when the court’s gay youth ftood waiting by;

‘ She ftrove to act a cold indiff’rency;   770

‘ In vain fhe acted fo conftrain’d a part,

‘ For thoufand namelefs things difclos’d her heart.

‘ On th’ other fide, David, with filent pain,

‘ Did in refpectful bounds his fires contain.

‘ His humble fear t’ offend, and trembling awe, 775

‘ Impos’d on him a no lefs rig’rous law

‘ Than modefty on her; and tho’ he ftrove

‘ To make her fee it, he durft not tell his love.

‘ To tell it firft the timorous youth made choice

‘ Of Mufic’s bolder and more active voice;   780

‘ And thus beneath her window did he touch

‘ His faithful lyre, the words and numbers fuch

‘ As did well worth my memory appear,

‘ And may perhaps deferve your princely ear.’

I.

Awake, awake my Lyre!   785

And tell thy filent mafter’s humble tale,

In founds that may prevail;
Sounds that gentle thoughts infpire,
Tho' fo exalted fhe,
And I fo lowly be,.   790
Tell her fuch diff'rent notes make all thy harmony.

II.

Hark ! how the ftrings awake !
And tho' the moving hand approach not near,
Themfelves with awful fear
A kind of num'rous trembling make.   795
Now all thy forces try,
Now all thy charms apply,
Revenge upon her ear the conquefts of her eye.

III.

Weak Lyre ! thy virtue, fure,
Is ufelefs here, fince thou art only found   800
To cure, but not to wound,
And fhe to wound, but not to cure
Too weak, too, wilt thou prove
My paffion to remove;
Phyfic to other ills, thou'rt nourifhment to love. 805

IV.

Sleep, fleep again, my Lyre !
For thou canft never tell my humble tale
In founds that will prevail,
Nor gentle thoughts in her infpire ;
All thy vain mirth lay by,   810
Bid thy ftrings filent lie.
Sleep, fleep again, my Lyre ! and let thy mafter die

' She heard all this, and the prevailing found

' Touch'd with delightful pain her tender wound :

' Yet tho' fhe joy'd th' authentic news to hear, 815

' Of what fhe gueft before with jealous fear,

' She check'd her forward joy, and blufh'd for fhame,

' And did his boldnefs with forc'd anger blame.

' The fenfelefs rules which firft falfe honour taught,

' And into laws the tyrant cuftom brought, 820

' Which women's pride and folly did invent,

' Their lovers and themfelves too, to torment,

' Made her next day a grave difpleafure feign,

' And all her words, and all her looks, conftrain

' Before the trembling youth : who when he faw 825

' His vital light her wonted beams withdraw,

' He curs'd his voice, his fingers, and his lyre,

' He curs'd his too-bold tongue, and bold defire :

' In vain he curs'd the laft, for that ftill grew ;

' From all things food its ftrong complexion drew: 830

' His joy and hope their cheerful motions ceas'd,

' His life decay'd, but ftill his love increas'd ;

' Whilft fhe whofe heart approv'd not her difdain,

' Saw and endur'd his pains with greater pain.

' But Jonathan, to whom both hearts were known,

' With a concernment equal to their own, 835

' Joyful that Heav'n with his fworn love comply'd,

' To draw that knot more faft which he had ty'd,

' With well-tim'd zeal, and with an artful care,

' Reftor'd, and better'd foon the nice affair: 840

' With eafe a brother's lawful pow'r o'ercame
' The formal decencies of virgin-fhame.
' She firft with all her heart forgave the paft,
' Heard David tell his flames, and told her own at laft.
' Lo! here the happy point of profp'rous love, 845
' Which ev'n enjoyment feldom can improve!
' Themfelves agreed, which fcarce could fail alone,
' All Ifrael's wifh concurrent with their own,
' A brother's pow'rful aid firm to the fide,
' By folemn vow the King and father ty'd; 850
' All jealous fears, all nice difguifes paft,
' All that in lefs-ripe love offends the tafte,
' In either's breaft their fouls both meet and wed,
'. Their heart the nuptial temple and the bed :
' And tho' the groffer cates were yet not drefs'd, 855
' By which the bodies muft fupply this feaft,
'. Bold hopes prevent flow pleafure's ling'ring birth,
' As faints affur'd of heav'n enjoy it on earth.
' All this the King obferv'd, and well he faw
' What fcandal and what danger it might draw 860
' To oppofe this juft and pop'lar match, but meant
' To out-malice all refufals by confent.
' He meant the pois'nous grant fhould mortal prove;
' He meant to infnare his virtue by his love :
' And thus he to him fpoke (g), with more of art 865
' And fraud than well became the kingly part.'
    " Your valour, David! and high worth," faid he,
  " To praife is all men's duty, mine to fee

(g) 1 Sam. xviii. 21.

" Rewarded; and we shall to our utmost powers

" Do with like care that part as you did your's. 870

" Forbid it, God! we like those kings should prove,

" Who fear the virtues which they're bound to love.

" Your piety does that tender point secure,

" Nor will my acts such humble thoughts endure.

" Your nearness to it rather supports the crown, 875

" And th' honours giv'n to you increase our own.

" All that we can we'll give: 'tis our intent,

" Both as a guard and as an ornament,

" To place thee next ourselves: Heav'n does approve;

" And my son's friendship, and my daughter's love,

" Guide fatally, methinks, my willing choice; 88r

" I see, methinks, Heav'n in it, and I rejoice.

" Blush not, my Son! that Michol's love I name,

" Nor need she blush to hear it; 'tis no shame

" Nor secret now; Fame does it loudly tell, 885

" And all men but thy rivals like it well.

" If Merab's choice could have comply'd with mine,

" Merab, my elder comfort, had been thine;

" And her's, at last, should have with mine comply'd,

" Had I not thine and Michol's heart descry'd. 890

" Take whom thou lov'st, and who loves thee; the last

" And dearest present made me by the chaste

" Ahinoam; and unless she me deceive,

" When I to Jonathan my crown shall leave,

" 'Twill be a smaller gift.   895

" If I thy generous thoughts may undertake

" To guefs, they are what jointure thou shalt make

" Fitting her birth and fortune; and since so
" Custom ordains, we mean to exact it too.
" The jointure we exact is that shall be   900
" No less advantage to thy fame than she.
" Go where Philistian troops infest the land;
" Renew the terrors of thy conqu'ring hand:
" When thine own hand, which needs must conqu'ror
" In this joint cause of honour and of love,   [prove,
" An hundred of the faithless foe shall slay,   906
" And for a dower their hundred foreskins pay (*h*),
" Be Michol thy reward. Did we not know
" Thy mighty fate, and worth that makes it so,
" We should not cheaply that dear blood expose, 910
" Which we to mingle with our own had chose;
" But thou 'rt secure; and since this match of thine
" We to the public benefit design,
" A public good shall its beginning grace,
" And give triumphant omens of thy race."   915
 ' Thus spoke the King: the happy youth bow'd low,
' Modest and graceful his great joy did show;
' The noble task well pleas'd his generous mind,
' And nought to except against it could he find,
' But that his mistress' price too cheap appear'd; 920
' No danger but her scorn of it he fear'd.
' She with much different sense the news receiv'd;
' At her high rate she trembled, blush'd, and griev'd:
' 'Twas a less work the conquest of his foes,
' Than to obtain her leave his life t' expose.   925

    (*h*) 1 Sam. xviii. 25.

‘ Their kind debate on this foft point would prove
‘ Tedious and needlefs to repeat: if love
‘ (As fure it has) e'er touch'd your princely breaft,
‘ 'Twill to your gentle thoughts at full fuggeft
‘ All that was done or faid, the grief, hope, fears, 930
‘ His troubled joys, and her obliging tears.
‘ In all the pomp of paffion's reign they part,
‘ And bright prophetic forms enlarge his heart;
‘ Vict'ry and fame, and that more quick delight
‘ Of the rich prize for which he was to fight.   935
   ‘ Tow'rds Gath he went; and in one month (fo foon
‘ A fatal and a willing work is done)
‘ A double dower. two hundred forefkins, brought,
‘ Of choice Philiftian knights with whom he fought;
‘ Men that in birth and valour did excel,   940
‘ Fit for the caufe and hand by which they fell.
‘ Now was Saul caught, nor longer could delay
‘ The two refiftlefs lovers' happy day.
‘ Tho' this day's coming long had feem'd, and flow,
‘ Yet feem'd its ftay as long and tedious now: 945
‘ For now the violent weight of eager love
‘ Did with more hafte, fo near its centre, move:
‘ He curs'd the ftops of form and ftate, which lay,
‘ In this laft ftage, like fcandals in his way.
   ‘ On a large gentle hill, crown'd with tall wood, 950
‘ Near where the regal Gabaah proudly ftood.
‘ A tent was pitch'd, of green wrought damafk made,
‘ And feem'd but the frefh foreft's nat'ral fhade,

' Various, and vaſt within, on pillars borne
' Of Shittim wood, that uſefully adorn :   955
' Hither, to grace the nuptial-feaſt, does Saul
' Of the Twelve Tribes th' Elders and Captains call,
' And all around the idle, buſy crowd,
' With ſhouts and bleſſings tell their joy aloud.
' Lo! the preſs breaks, and from their ſev'ral homes 960
' In decent pride the bride and bridegroom comes.
' Before the bride, in a long double row,
' With ſolemn pace, thirty choice virgins go,
' And make a moving Galaxy on earth ;
' All heav'nly beauties, all of higheſt birth,   965
' All clad in livelieſt colours, freſh and fair,
' As the bright flowers that crown'd their brighter hair;
' All in that new-blown age which does inſpire
' Warmth in themſelves, in their beholders fire.
' But all this, and all elſe the ſun did e'er,   970
' Or Fancy, ſee, in her leſs bounded ſphere,
' The bride herſelf outſhone ; and one would ſay
' They made but the faint dawn to her full day.
' Behind a numerous train of ladies went,
' Who on their dreſs much fruitleſs care had ſpent; 975
' Vain gems, and unregarded coſt, they bore,
' For all men's eyes were ty'd to thoſe before.
' The bridegroom's flouriſhing troop fill'd next the
' With thirty comely youths, of nobleſt race, [place,
' That march'd before, and Heav'n around his head 980
' The graceful beams of joy and beauty ſpread.

' So the glad ftar which men and angels love,
' Prince of the glorious hoft that fhines above,
' No light of heav'n fo cheerful or fo gay,
' Lifts up his facred lamp, and opens day. 985
' The King himfelf, at the tent's crowned gate,
' In all his robes of ceremony' and ftate,
' Sate to receive the train : on either hand
' Did the High Prieft and the Great Prophet ftand.
' Adriel behind, Jonathan, Abner, Jeffe, 990
' And all the chiefs, in their due order prefs.
' Firft Saul declar'd his choice, and the juft caufe
' Avow'd by a gen'ral murmur of applaufe,
' Then fign'd her dower, and in few words he pray'd,
' And blefs'd, and gave the joyful trembling maid 995
' T' her lover's hands, who with a cheerful look
' And humble gefture the vaft prefent took.
' The nuptial-hymn ftraight founds, and mufics play,
' And feafts and balls fhorten the thoughtlefs day
' To all but to the wedded ; till, at laft, 1000
' The long-wifh'd night did her kind fhadow caft :
' At laft th' ineftimable hour was come,
' To lead his conqu'ring prey in triumph home.
' To a palace near, drefs'd for the nuptial bed,
' Part of her dower) he his fair princefs led. 1005
' Saul, the High Prieft, and Samuel, here they leave,
' Who, as they part, their weighty bleffings give.
' Her vail is now put on ; and at the gate
' The thirty youths and thirty virgins wait

' With golden lamps, bright as the flames they bore,
' To light the nuptial-pomp, and march before. 1011
' The reft bring home in ftate the happy pair
' To that laft fcene of blifs, and leave them there,
' All thofe free joys infatiably to prove, 1014
' With which rich Beauty feafts the glutton Love.

  ' But fcarce, alas! the firft fev'n days were paft,
' In which the public nuptial-triumphs laft, 1017
' When Saul this new alliance did repent;
' Such fubtle cares his jealous thoughts torment,
' He envy'd the good work himfelf had done, 1020
' Fear'd David lefs his fervant than his fon.
' No longer his wild wrath could he command;
' He feeks to ftain his own imperial hand
' In his fon's blood; and that twice cheated too,
' With troops and armies does one life purfue. 1025
' Said I but one? his thirfty rage extends
' To the lives of all his kindred and his friends;
' Ev'n Jonathan had dy'd for being fo,
' Had not juft God put by th' unnat'ral blow.

  ' You fee, Sir, the true caufe which brings us here;
' No fullen difcontent or groundlefs fear; 1031
' No guilty act or end calls us from home,
' Only to breathe in peace a while we come,
' Ready to ferve, and in mean fpace to pray
' For you, who us receive, and him who drives away.'

      End of the Third Book.

DAVIDEIS.

BOOK IV.

The Contents.

Tho' ftate and kind difcourfe thus robb'd the night
Of half her nat'ral and more juft delight,
Moab, whom temp'rance did ftill vig'rous keep,
And regal cares had us'd to mod'rate fleep,
Up with the fun arofe; and having thrice   5
With lifted hands bow'd towards his fhining rife,
And thrice tow'rds Phegor, his Baal's holieft hill,
(With good and pious pray'rs directed ill)
Call'd to the chafe his friends, who for him ftay'd;
The glad dogs bark'd, the cheerful horfes neigh'd. 10

Moab his chariot mounts, drawn by four steeds,
The best and noblest that fresh Zerith breeds,
All white as snow, and sprightful as the light,
With scarlet trapp'd, and foaming gold they bite.
He into it young David with him took, 15
Did with respect and wonder on him look
Since last night's story, and with greedier ear
The man, of whom so much he heard, did hear.
The well-born youth of all his flourishing court
March gay behind, and joyful, to the sport. 20
Some arm'd with bows, some with straight jav'lins ride,
Rich swords and gilded quivers grace their side.
'Midst the fair troop David's tall brethren rode,
And Joab, comely as a fancy'd god ;
They entertain'd th' attentive Moab lords 25
With loose and various talk that chance affords,
Whilst they pac'd slowly on ; but the wise King
Did David's tongue to weightier subjects bring.
" Much," said the King, " much I to Joab owe,
" For the fair picture drawn by him of you : o
" 'Twas drawn in little, but did acts exprefs
" So great, that largest histories are less.
" I see (methinks) the Gathian monster still,
" His shape, last night, my mindful dreams did fill.
" Strange tyrant Saul, with envy to pursue 35
" The praise of deeds whence his own safety grew !
" I 'ave heard (but who can think it ?) that his son
" Has his life's hazard for your friendship run ;

" His matchlefs fon ! whofe worth (if Fame be true)

" Lifts him 'bove all his countrymen but you,   40

" With whom it makes him one." Low David bows,

But no reply Moab's fwift tongue allows.

" And pray, kind Gueft! whilft we ride thus," fays he,

" (To gameful Nebo ftill three leagues there be)

" The ftory of your royal friend relate,   45

" And his ungovern'd fire's imperious fate :

" Why your great ftate that namelefs family chofe,

" And by what fteps to Ifrael's throne they rofe."

.   He ftay'd ; and David thus. " From Egypt's land

' You 'ave heard, Sir, by what ftrong, unarmed hand

' Our fathers came ; Mofes their facred guide,   51

' But he in fight of the giv'n country dy'd (*a*).

' His fatal promis'd Canaan was on high,

' And Jofhua's fword muft th' active rod fupply.

' It did fo; and did wonders.   55

' From facred Jordan to the Weftern main,

' From well-clad Libanus to the Southern plain

' Of naked fands, his winged conquefts went (*b*),

' And thirty kings to hell uncrown'd he fent (*c*).

' Almoft four hundred years from him to Saul,   60

' In too much freedom pafs'd, or foreign thrall.

' Oft' ftrangers' iron fceptres bruis'd the land,

' (Such ftill are thofe borne by a conqu'ring hand)

' Oft' pitying God did well-form'd fpirits raife,

' Fit for the toilfome bus'nefs of their days,   65

(*a*) Deut. xxxiv. 5. (*b*) Jofh. i. 4.   (*c*) Jofh. xii.

' To free the groaning nation, and to give
' Peace firſt, and then the rules in peace to live.
' But they, whoſe ſtamp of pow'r did chiefly lie
' In characters too fine for moſt men's eye,
' Graces and gifts divine, not painted bright   70
' With ſtate, to awe dull minds, and force t' affright,
' Were ill obey'd whilſt living, and at death
' Their rules and pattern vaniſh'd with their breath.
' The hungry rich all near them did devour,
' Their judge was Appetite, and their law was Pow'r.
' Not want itſelf could luxury reſtrain,   76
' For what that empty'd, Rapine fill'd again.
' Robbery the field, Oppreſſion ſack'd the town;
' What the ſword's reaping ſpar'd was gleaned by the
' At courts and ſeats of juſtice to complain, [gown:
' Was to be robb'd more vexingly again :   81
' Nor was their luſt leſs active or leſs bold,
' Amidſt this rougher ſearch of blood and gold.
' Weak beauties they corrupt, and force the ſtrong;
' The pride of old men that, and this of young. 85
' You 'ave heard, perhaps, Sir, of lewd Gibeah's ſhame,
' Which Hebrew tongues ſtill tremble when they name;
' Alarmed all by one fair ſtranger's eyes,
' As to a ſudden war the town does riſe ;.
' Shaking and pale, half dead ere they begin   90
' The ſtrange and wanton tragedy of their ſin (*d*):
' All their wild luſts they force her to ſuſtain,
' Till by ſhame, ſorrow, wearineſs, and pain,

(*d*) Judg. xix.

' She 'midſt their loath'd and cruel kindneſs dies,

' Of monſtrous Luſt the innocent ſacrifice.   95

' This did ('tis true) a Civil war create,

' (The frequent curſe of our looſe-govern'd ſtate)

' All Gibeah's, and all Jabes' blood it coſt;

' Near a whole tribe, and future kings we loſt(*e*).

' Firm in this general earthquake of the land,   100

' How could religion, its main pillar, ſtand?

' Proud and fond man his fathers' worſhip hates,

' Himſelf, God's creature, his own god creates.

' Hence in each houſehold ſev'ral deities grew,

' And when no old one pleas'd, they fram'd a new.

' The only land which ſerv'd but one before,   106

' Did th' only then all nations' gods adore.

' They ſerv'd their gods at firſt, and ſoon their kings;

' Their choice of that this latter ſlav'ry brings;

' Till ſpecial men, arm'd with God's warrant, broke

' By juſteſt force th' unjuſtly forced yoke: 111

' All matchleſs perſons, and thrice worthy they

' Of power more great, or lands more apt t' obey.

' At laſt the prieſthood, join'd in Ithamar's ſon,

' More weight and luſtre to the ſceptre won (*f*):115

' But whilſt mild Ely and good Samuel were

' Buſy'd with age, and th' altar's ſacred care,

' To their wild ſons they their high charge commit (*g*),

' Who expoſe to ſcorn and hate both them and it.

' Ely's curs'd houſe th' exemplar vengeance bears

' Of all their blood, and all ſad Iſrael's tears.   121

(*e*) Judg. xx. & xxi. (*f*) 1 Sam. i. (*g*) 1 Sam. ii. 12. & viii.1.

4

' His fons abroad, himfelf at home, lies flain,

' Ifrael's captiv'd, God's ark and law are ta'en (*h*.)

' Thus twice are nations by ill princes vex'd;

' They fuffer by them firft, and for them next.　125

' Samuel fucceeds (*i*). Since Mofes, none, before,

' So much of God in his bright bofom bore.

' In vain our arms Philiftian tyrants feis'd;

' Heav'n's magazines he open'd when he pleas'd (*k*).

' He rains and winds for auxiliaries brought;　130

' He mufter'd flames and thunders when he fought(*l*).

' Thus thirty years, with ftrong and fteddy hand,

' He held th' unfhaken balance of the land.

' At laft his fons th' indulgent father chofe (*m*)　134

' To fhare that ftate which they were born to lofe.

' Their hateful acts that change's birth did hafte,

' Which had long growth i' th' womb of ages paft.

' To this (for ftill were fome great periods fet,

' There's a ftrong knot of fev'ral caufes met)

' The threats concurr'd of a rough neighb'ring war,

' A mighty ftorm, long gath'ring from afar:　141

' For Ammon, heighten'd with mix'd nations' aid,

' Like torrents fwoln with rain prepar'd the land
　　　　　t' invade.

' Samuel was old, and by his fons' ill choice,

' Turn'd dotard in th' unfkilful vulgar's voice:　145

(*h*) 1 Sam. iv. 10, 11.　　(*i*) 1 Sam. iv. 1. (*k*) 1 Sam. vii.
(*l*) 1 Sam. vii. 10.　　(*m*) 1 Sam. viii. 1.

‘ His fons, fo fcorn’d and hated, that the land
‘ Nor hop’d nor wifh’d a vict’ry from their hand.
‘ Thefe were the juft and faultlefs caufes why
‘ The general voice did for a Monarch cry.
‘ But God ill grains did in this incenfe fmell ;   150
‘ Wrapp’d in fair leaves he faw the canker dwell.
‘ A mutinous itch of change, a dull defpair
‘ Of helps divine oft’ prov’d; a faithlefs care
‘ Of common means; the pride of heart, and fcorn
‘ Of th’ humble yoke under low Judges borne;   155
‘ They faw the ftate and glitt’ring pomp, which blefs’d,
‘ In vulgar fenfe, the fceptres of the Eaft :
‘ They faw not pow’r’s true fource, and fcorn’d t’ obey
‘ Perfons that look’d no dreadfuller than they;   159
‘ They mifs’d courts, guards, a gay and num’rous train;
‘ Our Judges, like their laws, were rude and plain.
‘ On an old bench of wood, her feat of ftate,
‘ Beneath the well-known palm, wife Deb’rah fate(*n*):
‘ Her maids with comely diligence round her fpun,
‘ And fhe, too, when the pleadings there were done.
‘ With the fame goad Samgar his oxen drives,   166
‘ Which took, the fun before, fix hundred lives
‘ From his fham’d foes(*o*): he midft his work dealt laws,
‘ And oft’ was his plough ftopp’d to hear a caufe.
‘ Nor did great Gideon his old flail difdain (*p*), 170
‘ After won fields, fack’d towns, and princes flain;
‘ His fceptre that, and Ophra’s threfhing-floor,
‘ The feat and emblem of his juftice bore.

(*n*) Judg. iv. 5.   (*o*) Judg. iii. 31.   (*p*) Judg. vi. 1.

' What fhould I Jair (*q*), the happieft father, name?
' Or mournful Jephtha, known no lefs to Fame 175
' For the moft wretched (*r*)? both at once did keep
. ' The mighy flocks of Ifrael and their fheep:
' Oft' from the field in hafte they fummon'd were,
' Some weighty foreign embafy to hear; 179
' They called their flaves, their fons, and friends, around;
' Who all at fev'ral cares were fcatter'd found;
' They wafh'd their feet, their only gown put on,
' And this chief work of ceremony was done.
' Thefe reafons; and all elfe that could be faid,
' In a ripe hour by factious Eloquence fpread 185
' Thro" all the tribes, made all defire a King (*s*);
' And to their Judge felected deputies bring
' This harfh demand, which Nacol for the reft
' (A bold and artful mouth) thus with much grace
        exprefs'd.' 189
    " We're come, moft facred Judge, to pay th' arrears
    " Of much-ow'd thanks for the bright thirty years.
    " Of your juft reign, and at your feet to lay
    " All that our grateful hearts can weakly pay
    " In unproportion'd words; for you alone
    " The not unfit reward, who feek for none: 195
    " But when our forepaft ills we call to mind,
    " And fadly think how little's left behind,
    " Of your important life, whofe fudden date
    " Would difinherit th' unprovided ftate;

(*q*) Judg. x. 3. (*r*) Judg. xi. 34. (*s*) 1 Sam. viii. 4.
        Q ij

" When we confider how unjuft 'tis you,　　2co
" Who ne'er of pow'r more than the burden knew,
" At once the weight of that and age fhould have,
" Your ftooping days prefs'd doubly tow'rds the grave ;
" When we behold by Ammon's youthful rage,
" Proud in th' advantage of your peaceful age,　205
" And all th' united Eaft, our fall confpir'd,
" And that your fons, whom chiefly we defir'd
" As ftamps of you in your lov'd room to place,
" By unlike acts that noble ftamp deface (*t*);
" 'Midft thefe new fears and ills we 're forc'd to fly
" To a new and yet unpractis'd remedy ;　　211
" A new one, but long promis'd and foretold
" By Mofes (*u*), and to Abraham fhown of old ;
"　A prophefy long forming in the womb
" Of teeming years, and now to ripenefs come :　215
" This remedy's a King ; for this we all
" With an infpir'd and zealous union call :
" And in one found when all men's voices join,
" The mufic's tun'd, no doubt, by hand divine.
" 'Tis God alone fpeaks a whole nation's voice ; 220
" That is his public language ; but the choice
" Of what peculiar head that crown muft bear,
" From you, who his peculiar organ are,
" We' expect to hear ; the people fhall to you
" Their king, the king his crown and people owe.
" To your great name what luftre will it bring　226
" T' have been our Judge, and to have made our King !"

　　　(*t*) 1 Sam. viii. 5.　　(*u*) Deut. xvii. 14.

‘ He bow'd, and ended here; and Samuel ftraight,

‘ Paufing a while (*x*) at this great queftion's weight,

‘ With a grave figh, and with a thoughtful eye, 230

‘ That more of care than paffion did defcry,

‘ Calmly replies :' " You 're fure the firft," fays he,

" Of free-born men that begg'd for flavery.

" I fear, my Friends! with heav'nly manna fed,

" (Our old forefathers' crime) we luft for bread. 235

" Long fince by God from bondage drawn, I fear

" We build anew th' Egyptian brick-kiln here.

" Cheat not yourfelves with words; for tho' a king

" Be the mild name, a tyrant is the thing (*y*) :

" Let his power loofe, and you fhall quickly fee 240

" How mild à thing unbounded man will be :

" He'll lead you forth your hearts' cheap blood to fpill,

" Where'er his guidelefs paffion leads his will.

" Ambition, luft, or fpleen, his wars will raife, 244

" Your lives' beft price his thirft of wealth or praife.

" Your ableft fons for his proud guards he'll take,

" And by fuch hands your yoke more grievous make.

" Your daughters and dear wives he'll force away,

" His lux'ry fome, and fome his luft, t' obey. 249

" His idle friends your hungry toils fhall eat, [fweat.

" Drink your rich wines, mix'd with your blood and

" Then you'll all figh, but fighs will treafons be ;

" And not your griefs themfelves, or looks, be free.

" Robb'd even of hopes, when you thefe ills fuftain,

" Your watry eyes you'll then turn back in vain 255

(*x*) 1 Sam. viii. 6.   (*y*) 1 Sam. viii. 11.

Q

" On your old Judges, and perhaps on me,

" Nay, ev'n my fons, howe'er they' unhappy be

" In your difpleafure now; not that I'd clear

" Their guilt, or mine own innocence endear;

" Witnefs th' Unutterable Name, there's nought 260

" Of private ends into this queſtion brought :

" But why this yoke on your own necks to draw ?

" Why man your God, and paffion made your law!"

  " Methinks," (thus Moab interrupts him here)

" The good old feer 'gainſt kings was too fevere. 265

" 'Tis jeſt to tell a people that they 're free :

" Who, or how many, ſhall their maſters be

" Is the fole doubt : laws guide, but cannot reign ;

" And tho' they bind not kings, yet they reſtrain.

" I dare affirm (fo much I truſt their love)   270

" That no one Moabite would his fpeech approve.

" But, pray, go on." ' Tis true, Sir,' he replies;

' Yet men whom age and action renders wife,

' So much great changes fear, that they believe

' All evils will, which may, from them arrive.   275

' On men refolv'd thefe threats were ſpent in vain :

' All that his pow'r or eloquence could obtain

' Was to inquire God's will, ere they proceed

' To a work that would fo much his bleffing need (z).

' A folemn day for this great work is fet,   280

' And at the Anointed Tent (a) all Ifrael met

' Expect th' event. Below fair bullocks fry

' In hallow'd flames; above there mount on high

(z) 1 Sam. viii. 19,—22.   (a) Exod. xl. 9. and xxx. 26.

' The precious clouds of incenfe (*b*); and, at laft,
' The fprinkling, pray'rs, and all due honours paft;
' Lo! we the facred bells o' the fudden hear (*c*), 386
' And in mild pomp grave Samuel does appear;
' His ephod, mitre, well cut diadem, on (*d*),
' Th' oraculous ftones on his rich breaftplate fhone (*e*):
' Tow'rds the blue curtains of God's holieft place
' (The Temple's bright third heav'n) he turn'd his
   face: 291
' Thrice bow'd he, thrice the folemn mufic play'd,
' And at third reft thus the great Prophet pray'd:'
 " Almighty God! to whom all men that be
" Owe all they have, yet none fo much as we; 295
" Who tho' thou fill'ft the fpacious world alone,
" Thy too fmall court, haft made this place thy throne,
" With humble knees, and humbler hearts, lo! here
" Blefs'd Abraham's feed implores thy gracious ear:
" Hear them, great God! and thy juft will infpire; 300
" From thee, their long-known King, they a king defire:
" Some gracious figns of thy good pleafure fend,
" Which, lo! with fouls refign'd we humbly here at-
   tend."
 ' He fpoke, and thrice he bow'd, and all about
' Silence and reverend horror feiz'd the rout: 305
' The whole tent fhakes, the flames on th' altar by
' In thick dull rolls mount flow and heavily:
' The feven lamps (*f*) wink; and, what does moft dif-
' Th' orac'lous gems fhut in their nat'ral day: [may,

(*b*) Exod. xl. 5, 6. (*c*) Exod. xxxix. 25. (*d*) ỹ. 2.
(*e*) ỹ. 8,—13. (*f*) Exod. xxv. 37.

' The ruby's cheek grew pale ; the em'raud by   310
' Faded ; a cloud o'ercaft the fapphire s fky ;
' The di'mond's eye look'd fleepy, and fwift night
' Of all thofe little funs eclips'd the light :
' Sad figns of God's dread anger for our fin ;
' But ftraight a wondrous brightnefs from within 315
' Strook thro' the curtains, for no earthly cloud
' Could thofe ftrong beams of heav'nly glory fhroud :
' The altar's fire burnt pure, and every ftone
' Their radiant parent, the gay fun, outfhone :
' Beauty th' illuftrious vifion did impart   320
' To ev'ry face, and joy to ev'ry heart.
' In glad effects God's prefence thus appear'd,
' And thus in wondrous founds his voice was heard :'
This ftubborn land fins ftill ; nor is it thee, but us
(Who have been fo long their King) they feek to caft
          off thus.   325
Five hundred rolling years hath this ftiff nation ftrove
To exhauft the boundlefs ftores of our unfathom'd
          love.
Be't fo, then ; yet, once more, are we refolv'd to try
T' outweary them thro' all their fins' variety ;   329
Affemble, ten days hence, the num'rous people here,
To draw the royal lot which our hid mark fhall bear.
Difmifs them now in peace ; but their next crime
          fhall bring
Ruin without redrefs on them, and on their King.
' Th' Almighty fpoke ; th' aftonifh'd people part,
' With various ftamps imprefs'd on ev'ry heart : 335

' Some their demand repented, others prais'd;
' Some had no thoughts at all, but star'd and gaz'd.
  ' There dwelt a man, nam'd Kis, in Gibeah town,
' For wisdom much, and much for courage known;
' More for his son; his mighty son was Saul (*g*), 340
' Whom Nature, ere the lots, to a throne did call.
' He was much Prince, and when or wheresoe'er
' His birth had been, then had he reign'd, and there.
' Such beauty as great strength thinks no disgrace,
' Smil'd in the manly features of his face :   345
' His large black eyes, fill'd with a sprightful light,
' Shot forth such lively and illustrious night,
' As the sunbeams on jet reflecting show,
' His hair as black, in long curl'd waves did flow :
' His tall straight body amidst thousands stood, 350
' Like some fair pine o'erlooking all th' ignobler wood.
' Of all our rural sports he was the pride ;
' So swift, so strong, so dex'trous none beside.
' Rest was his toil, labours his lust and game;
' No nat'ral wants could his fierce diligence tame, 355
' Not thirst nor hunger; he would journies go
' Thro' raging heats, and take repose in snow.
' His soul was ne'er unbent from weighty care,
' But active as some mind that turns a sphere.
' His way once chose, he forward thrust outright, 360
' Nor stepp'd aside for dangers or delight.
' Yet was he wise all dangers to foresee;
' But born t' affright, and not to fear, was he.

    (*g*) 1 Sam. ix. 1, 2.

' His wit was ſtrong, not fine; and on his tongue

' An artleſs grace, above all eloquence, hung.   365

' Theſe virtues, too, the rich unuſual dreſs

' Of modeſty adorn'd, and humbleneſs (*h*):

' Like a clear varniſh o'er fair pictures laid,

' More freſh and laſting they the colours made:

' Till pow'r and vi'lent fortune, which did find 370

' No ſtop or bound, o'erwhelm'd no leſs his mind;

' Did, deluge-like, the nat'ral forms deface,

' And brought forth unknown monſters in their place.

' Forbid it, God! my maſter's ſpots ſhould be,

' Were they not ſeen by all, diſclos'd by me!   375

' But ſuch he was; and now to Ramah went

' (So God diſpos'd) with a ſtrange low intent,

' Great God! he went loſt aſſes to inquire,

' And a ſmall preſent, his ſmall queſtion's hire,

' Brought ſimply with him, to that man to give, 380

' From whom high Heav'n's chief gifts he muſt re-

    ceive (*i*).

' Strange play of Fate! when mightieſt human things

' Hang on ſuch ſmall imperceptible ſtrings!

' 'Twas Samuel's birth-day, a glad annual feaſt

' All Ramah kept (*k*); Samuel his wond'ring gueſt

' With ſuch reſpect leads to it, and does grace 386

' With the choice meats o' the feaſt, and higheſt

    place (*l*):

(*h*) 1 Sam. ix. 21. and x. 22.   (*i*) 1 Sam. ix. 8.

(*k*) 1 Sam. ix. 12.   (*l*) V. 22, 23, 24.

' Which done, him forth alone the Prophet brings,

' And feafts his ravifh'd ears with nobler things (*m*):

' He tells the mighty fate to him affign'd,   390

' And with great rules fills his capacious mind:

' Then takes the facred vial, and does fhed

' A crown of myftic drops around his head (*n*);

' Drops of that royal moifture which does know

' No mixture, and difdains the place below.   395

' Soon comes the kingly day (*o*), and with it brings

' A new account of time upon his wings.

' The people met, the rites and pray'rs all paft,

' Behold! the Heav'n-inftructed lot is caft:

' 'Tis taught by Heav'n its way, and cannot mifs; 400

' Forth Benjamin, forth leaps the Houfe of Kis.

' As glimm'ring ftars juft at th' approach of day,

' Cafheer'd by troops, at laft drop all away,

' By fuch degrees all men's bright hopes are gone,

' And, like the fun, Saul's lot fhines all alone.   405

' Ev'n here, perhaps, the people's fhout was heard,

' The loud long fhout when God's fair choice appear'd.

' Above the whole vaft throng he' appear'd fo tall,

' As if by Nature made for the head of all;

' So full of grace and ftate, that one might know 410

' 'Twas fome wife eye the blind lot guided fo:

' But blind unguided lots have more of choice

' And conftancy than the flight vulgar's voice.

(*m*) 1 Sam. ix. 26.   (*n*) 1 Sam. x. 1.   (*o*) ℣. 17.

‘ Ere yet the crown of facred oil is dry,

‘ Whilft echoes yet preferve the joyful cry,   415

‘ Some grow enrag’d their own vain hopes to mifs,

‘ Some envy Saul, fome fcorn the Houfe of Kis :

‘ Some their firft mutinous wifh, a king, repent,

‘ As if, fince that, quite fpoil’d by God’s confent.

‘ Few to this prince their firft juft duties pay;   420

‘ All leave the old, but few the new obey.

‘ Thus changes man, but God is conftant ftill

‘ To thofe eternal grounds that mov’d his will;

‘ And tho’ he yielded firft to them, ’tis fit

‘ That ftubborn men at laft to him fubmit.   425

‘ As midft the main a low fmall ifland lies,

‘ Affaulted round with ftormy feas and fkies,

‘ Whilft the poor heartlefs natives ev’ry hour

‘ Darknefs and noife feems ready to devour;

‘ Such Ifrael’s ftate appear’d, whilft o’er the Weft 430

‘ Philiftian clouds hung threat’ning, and from th’Eaft

‘ All nations’ wrath into one tempeft joins,

‘ Thro’ which proud Nahas like fierce lightning fhines.

‘ Tigris and Nile to his affiftance fend;

‘ And waters to fwoll’n Jaboc’s torrent lend;   435

‘ Seir, Edom, Soba, Amalec, add their force,

‘ Up with them march the Three Arabias’ horfe;

‘ And ’mongft all thefe none more their hope or pride

‘ Than thofe few troops your warlike land fupply’d.

‘ Around weak Jabes this vaft hoft does lie (*p*),   440

‘ Difdains a dry and bloodlefs victory.

(*p*) 1 Sam. xi. 1.

' The hopelefs town for flav'ry does entreat,
' But barb'rous Nahas thinks that grace too great.
' He (his firft tribute) their right eyes demands (*q*);
' And with their faces' fhame difarms their hands. 445
' If unreliev'd feven days by Ifrael's aid,
' This bargain for o'er-rated life is made (*r*).
' Ah! mighty God! let thine own Ifrael be
' Quite blind itfelf ere this reproach it fee!
　' By his wanton people the new King forfook, 450
' To homely rural cares himfelf betook (*s*):
' In private plenty liv'd, without the ftate,
' Luftre, and noife, due to a public fate.
' Whilft he his flaves and cattle follows home,
' Lo! the fad meffengers from Jabes come, 455
' Implore his help (*t*), and weep, as if they meant
' That way, at leaft, proud Nahas to prevent.
' Mov'd with a kingly wrath, his ftrict command
' He iffues forth t' affemble all the land (*u*).
' He threatens high, and difobedient they, 460
' Wak'd by fuch princely terrors, learnt t' obey.
' A mighty hoft is rais'd (*x*); th' important caufe
' Age from their reft, youth from their pleafure, draws;
' Arm'd as unfurnifh'd hafte could them provide;
' But conduct, courage, anger, that fupply'd. 465
' All night they march, and are at th' early dawn
' On Jabes' heath in three fair bodies drawn (*y*).

(*q*) I Sam. xi. 2. 　(*r*) ℣. 3. 　(*s*) ℣. 5. 　(*t*) ℣. 4.
(*u*) ℣. 7. 　(*x*) ℣. 8. 　(*y*) ℣. 11.

' Saul did himfelf the firft and ftrongeft band,

' His fon the next, Abner the third, command:

' But pardon, Sir, if naming Saul's great fon,   470

' I ftop with him a while ere I go on.

   ' This is that Jonathan, the joy and grace,

' The beautifull'ft and beft of human race;

' That Jonathan, in whom does mix'd remain,

' All that kind mothers' wifhes can contain.   475

' His courage fuch, as it no ftop can know,

' And vict'ry gains by' aftonifhing the foe:

' With lightning's force his enemies it confounds,

' And melts their hearts e'er it the bofom wounds:

' Yet he the conquer'd with fuch fweetnefs gains,

' As captive lovers find in beauty's chains.   481

' In war the adverfe troops he does affail

' Like an impetuous ftorm of wind and hail:

' In peace, like gentleft dew that does affwage

' The burning months, and temper Syrius' rage. 485

' Kind as the fun's blefs'd influence: and where'er

' He comes, plenty and joy attend him there.

' To help feems all his power; his wealth to give;

' To do much good his fole prerogative:

' And yet this gen'ral bounty of his mind,   490

' That with wide arms embraces all mankind,

' Such artful prudence does to each divide,

' With diff'rent meafures all are fatisfy'd:

' Juft as wife God his plenteous manna dealt,

' Some gather'd more, but want by none was felt (z).

       (z) Exod. xvi. 17.

‘ To all relations their juſt rights he pays,   496
‘ And worth's reward above its claim does raiſe.
‘ The tend'reſt huſband, maſter, father, ſon,
‘ And thoſe parts by his friendſhip far outdone.
‘ His love to friends no bound or rule does know;
‘ What he to Heav'n, all that to him they owe.   501
‘ Keen as his ſword, and pointed, is his wit;
‘ His judgment, like beſt armour, ſtrong and fit:
‘ And ſuch an eloquence to both theſe does join,
‘ As makes in both beauty and uſe combine,   505
‘ Thro' which a noble tincture does appear
‘ By learning and choice books imprinted there.
‘ As well he knows all times and perſons gone,
‘ As he himſelf to the future ſhall be known :
‘ But his chief ſtudy is God's ſacred law,   510
‘ And all his life does comments on it draw.
‘ As never more by Heav'n to man was giv'n,
‘ So never more was paid by man to Heav'n :
‘ And all theſe virtues were to ripeneſs grown,
‘ Ere yet his flower of youth was fully blown.   515
‘ All autumn's ſtore did his rich ſpring adorn;
‘ Like trees in Paradiſe, he with fruit was born.
‘ Such is his ſoul; and if, as ſome men tell,
‘ Souls form and build thoſe manſions where they
‘ Whoe'er but ſees his body muſt confeſs   [dwell,
‘ The architect, no doubt, could be no leſs.   521
‘ From Saul his growth and manly ſtrength he took;
‘ Chaſtis'd by bright Ahinoam's gentler look (*a*).

(*a*) 1 Sam. xiv. 50.

' Not bright Ahinoam, Beauty's loudeſt name, 524
' Till ſhe to' her children loſt, with joy, her fame,
' Had ſweeter ſtrokes, colours more freſh and fair,
' More darting eyes, or lovelier auburne hair.
' Forgive me that I thus your patience wrong,
' And on this boundleſs ſubject ſtay ſo long,
' Where too much haſte e'er to end it would be, 530
' Did not his acts ſpeak what is untold by me.
' Tho' from the time his hands a ſword could wield,
' He ne'er miſs'd fame and danger in the field,
' Yet this was the firſt day that call'd him forth,
' Since Saul's bright crown gave luſtre to his worth;
' 'Twas the laſt morning whoſe uncheerful riſe 536
' Sad Jabes was to view with both their eyes.
' Secure proud Nahas ſlept, as in his court,
' And dream'd, vain Man! of that day's barb'rous
' Till noiſe and dreadful tumults him awoke, [ſport,
' Till into' his camp our vi'lent army broke. 541
' The careleſs guards, with ſmall reſiſtance kill'd,
' Slaughter the camp, and wild confuſion, fill'd.
' Nahas his fatal duty does perform,
' And marches boldly up to outface the ſtorm : 545
' Fierce Jonathan he meets, as he purſues
' Th' Arabian horſe, and a hot fight renews.
' 'Twas here your troops behav'd themſelves ſo well,
' Till Uz and Jathan, their ſtout colonels, fell :
' 'Twas here our vict'ry ſtopp'd, and gave us cauſe
 Much to ſuſpect th' intention of her pauſe : 551

‘ But when òur thund'ring prince Nahas efpy'd,
‘ Who with a courage equal to his pride
‘ Broke thro'our troops,and tow'rdshimboldlyprefs'd,
‘ A gen'rous joy leap'd in his youthful breaft.   555
‘ As when a wrathful dragon's difmal light
‘ Strikes fuddenly fome warlike eagle's fight,
‘ The mighty foe pleafes his fearlefs eyes,
‘ He claps his joyful wings, and at him flies.
‘ With vain, tho' vi'lent force, their darts they flung;
‘ In Ammon's plated belt Jonathan's hung,   561
‘ And ftopp'd there; Ammon did his helmet hit,
‘ And gliding off, bore the proud creft from it. [came,
‘ Straight with their fwords to the fierce fhock they
‘ Their fwords,their armour,and their eyes,fhot flame:
‘ Blows ftrong as thunder,thick as rain,they dealt, 566
‘ Which more than they th' engag'd fpectators felt.
‘ In Ammon force, in Jonathan addrefs,
‘ (Tho' both were great in both to an excefs)
‘ To the well-judging eye did moft appear;   570
‘ Honour and anger in both equal were.
‘ Two wounds our Prince receiv'd, and Ammon three,
‘ Which he enrag'd to feel, and 'fham'd to fee,
‘ Did his whole ftrength into one blow collect;
‘ And as a fpaniel, when we our aim direct   575
‘ To fhoot fome bird, impatiently ftands by,
‘ Shaking his tail, ready with joy to fly,
‘ Juft as it drops upon the wounded prey,
‘ So waited Death itfelf to bear away

' The threaten'd life; did glad and greedy ſtand 580
' At ſight of mighty Ammon's lifted hand.
' Our watchful Prince by bending ſav'd the wound,
' But Death in other coin his reck'ning found;
' For whilſt th' immod'rate ſtroke's miſcarrying force
' Had almoſt borne the ſtriker from his horſe,   585
' A nimble thruſt his active en'my made;
' 'Twixt his right ribs deep pierc'd the furious blade,
' And open'd wide thoſe ſecret veſſels, where
' Life's light goes out when firſt they let in air.
' He falls, his armour clanks againſt the ground; 590
' From his faint tongue imperfect curſes found.
' His amaz'd troops ſtraight caſt their arms away;
' Scarce fled his ſoul from thence more ſwift than they.
' As when two kings of neighbour hives (whom rage
' And thirſt of empire in fierce wars engage,   595
' Whilſt each lays claim to th' garden as his own,
' And ſeeks to uſurp the bord'ring flowers alone)
' Their well-arm'd troops drawn boldly forth to fight,
' I' th' air's wide plain diſpute their doubtful right,
' If by ſad chance of battle either king   600
' Fall wounded down, ſtrook with ſome fatal ſting,
' His army's hopes and courage with him die,
' They ſheath up their faint ſwords, and routed fly:
' On th' other's ſides at once, with like ſucceſs,
' Into the camp great Saul and Abner preſs;   605
' From Jonathan's part a wild mix'd noiſe they hear,
' And, whatſoe'er it mean, long to be there.

' At the fame inftant from glad Jabes' town
' The hafty troops march loud and cheerful down.
' Some few at firft with vain refiftance fall,   610
' The reft is flaughter, and vaft conqueft all.
' The fate by which our hoft thus far had gone,
' Our hoft with noble heat drove farther on;
' Victorious arms thro' Ammon's land it bore,
' Ruin behind, and Terror march'd before.   615
' Where'er from Rabba's tow'rs they caft their fight,
' Smoke clouds the day, and flames make clear the
          night.
' This bright fuccefs did Saül's firft action bring;
' The oil, the lot, and crown, lefs crown'd him king.
' The happy all men judge for empire fit,   620
' And none withftands where Fortune does fubmit.
' Thofe who before did God's fair choice withftand,
' The exceffive vulgar now to death demand *(b)*;
' But wifer Saul repeal'd their hafty doom *(c)*,
' Conqueft abroad with mercy crown'd at home;   625
' Nor ftain'd with civil flaughter that day's pride,
' Which foreign blood in nobler purple dy'd.
' Again the crown th' affembled people give *(d)*,
' With greater joy than Saul could it receive :   629
' Again th' old Judge refigns his facred place *(e)*,
' God glorify'd with wonders his difgrace.
' With decent pride, fuch as did well befit
' The name he kept, and that which he did quit,

(*b*) 1 Sam. xi. 12.   (*c*) ℣. 13.   (*d*) ℣. 15.
(*e*) 1 Sam. xii. 1. &c.

' The long-paſt row of happy years he ſhow'd,
' Which to his heav'nly government they ow'd; 635
' How the torn ſtate his juſt and prudent reign
' Reſtor'd to order, plenty, power, again;
' In war what conqu'ring miracles he wrought; 638
' God, then their King, was gen'ral when they fought,
' Whom they depos'd with him.' " And that," ſaid he,
" You may ſee God concern'd in it more than me,
" Behold how ſtorms his angry preſence ſhrowd,
" Hark! how his wrath in thunder threats aloud!"
' 'Twas now the ripen'd ſummer's higheſt rage, 644
' Which no faint cloud durſt mediate to aſſwage:
' Th' earth, hot with thirſt, and hot with luſt for rain,
' Gap'd and breath'd feeble vapours up in vain,
' Which ſtraight were ſcatter'd, or devour'd by th' ſun,
' When, lo! ere ſcarce the active ſpeech was done,
' A vi'lent wind roſe from his ſecret cave, 650
' And troops of frighted clouds before it drave:
' Whilſt with rude haſte the confuſ'd tempeſt crowds,
' Swift dreadful flames ſhot thro' th' encount'ring clouds;
' From whoſe torn womb th' impriſon'd thunder broke,
' And in dire ſounds the Prophet's ſenſe it ſpoke. 655
' Such an impetuous ſhower it downwards ſent,
' As if the waters 'bove the firmament
' Were all let looſe; horror and fearful noiſe
' Fill'd the black ſcene, till the great Prophet's voice,
' Swift as the wings of Morn, reduc'd the day; 660
' Wind, thunder, rain, and clouds, fled all at once away.'

" Fear not,"ſaid he,"Godhis fierce wrath removes(*f*);
" And tho' this ſtate my ſervice diſapproves,
" My prayers ſhall ſerve it conſtantly. No more,
" I hope a pardon for paſt ſins to implore,   665
" But juſt rewards from gracious Heav'n to bring
" On the good deeds of you and of our King.
" Behold him there! and as you ſee, rejoice
" In the kind care of God's impartial choice.   669
" Behold his beauty, courage, ſtrength, and wit!
" The honour Heav'n has cloath'd him with ſits fit
" And comely on him. Since you needs muſt be
" Rul'd by a king, you 're happy that 'tis he.
" Obey him gladly, and let him, too, know
" You were not made for him, but he for you,   675
" And both for God,
" Whoſe gentleſt yoke, if once you caſt away,
" In vain ſhall he command, and you obey;
" To foreign tyrauts both ſhall ſlaves become (*g*),
" Inſtead of King and ſubjects here at home."   680
   ' The crown thus ſev'ral ways confirm'd to Saul,
' One way was wanting yet to crown them all;
' And that was force, which only can maintain
' The power thatFortune gives, orWorth does gain.684
' Three thouſand guards of big bold men he took (*h*),
' Tall, terrible, and guards ev'n with their look;
' His ſacred perſon two, and throne, defend,
' The third on matchleſs Jonathan attend,

(*f*) 1 Sam. xii. 20.   (*g*) ℣. 25.   (*h*) 1 Sam. xiii. 2.

' O'er whofe full thoughts honour and youthful heat
' Sate brooding to hatch actions good and great. 690
' On Geba firft, where a Philiftian band
' Lies (*i*), and around torments the fetter'd land,
' He falls, and flaughters all; his noble rage
' Mix'd with defign, his nation to engage   694
' In that juft war, which from them long in vain
' Honour and Freedom's voice had ftrove t' obtain.
' Th' accurs'd Philiftian rous'd with this bold blow,
' All the proud marks of enrag'd power does fhow (*k*);
' Raifes a vaft, well-arm'd, and glitt'ring hoft;
' If human ftrength might authorize a boaft,   700
' Their threats had reafon here; for ne'er did we
' Ourfelves fo weak, our foe fo potent, fee.
' Here we vaft bodies of their foot efpy,
' The rear outreaches far th' extended eye :   704
' Like fields of corn their armed fquadrons ftand;
' As thick and numberlefs they hide the land.
' Here with fharp neighs the warlike horfes found,
' And with proud prancings beat the putrid ground.
' Here with worfe noife three thoufand chariots pafs,
' With plates of iron bound, or louder brafs :   710
' About it forks, axes, and fithes, and fpears,
' Whole magazines of death each chariot bears.
' Where it breaks in, there a whole troop it mows,
' And with lopp'd panting limbs the field beftrows.
' Alike the valiant and the cowards die ;   715
' Neither can they refift, nor can thefe fly.

(*i*) 1 Sam. xiii. 3.   (*k*) ⅴ. 5.

' In this proud equipage at Micmas they (*l*),
' Saul in much different ſtate at Gilgal, lay (*m*):
' His forces ſeem'd no army, but a crowd,
' Heartleſs, unarm'd, diſorderly, and loud :   720
' The quick contagion, fear, ran ſwift thro' all,
' And into trembling fits th' infected fall.
' Saul and his ſon (for no ſuch faint diſeaſe
' Could on their ſtrong-complexion'd valour ſeize)
' In vain all parts of virtuous conduct ſhow'd,   725
' And on deaf Terror gen'rous words beſtow'd.
' Thouſands from thence fly ſcatter'd ev'ry day,
' Thick as the leaves that ſhake and drop away
' When they th'approach of ſtormy winter find,
' The noble tree all bare, expos'd to the wind.   730
' Some to ſad Jordan fly, and ſwim it for haſte,
' And from his farther bank look back at laſt :
' Some into woods and caves their cattle drive,
' There with their beaſts on equal terms they live,
' Nor deſerve better ; ſome in rocks on high,   735
' The old retreats of ſtorks and ravens, lie ;
' And, were they wing'd like them, ſcarce would they
' To ſtay, or truſt their frighted ſafety there. [dare
' As th' hoſt with fear, ſo Saul, diſturb'd with care,
' T' avert theſe ills by ſacrifice and pray'r (*n*),   740
' And God's bleſs'd will t' inquire, for Samuel ſends,
' Whom he ſix days with troubled haſte attends,
' But ere the ſeventh unlucky day (the laſt
' By Samuel ſet for this great work) was paſt,   744

     (*l*) 1 Sam. xiii. 5.   (*m*) ℣. 7.   (*n*) ℣. 9.

' Saul, alarm'd hourly from the neighb'ring foe,

' Impatient, ere God's time, God's mind to know,

' 'Sham'd and enrag'd to see his troops decay,

' Jealous of an affront in Samuel's stay,

' Scorning that any's presence should appear

' Needful besides, when he himself was there,   750

' And, with a pride too nat'ral, thinking Heav'n

' Had giv'n him all, because much pow'r it had giv'n,

' Himself the sacrifice and off'rings made,

' Himself did the high selected charge invade,   754

' Himself inquir'd of God, who then spake nought,

' But Samuel straight his dreadful answer brought;

' For straight he came, and with a virtue bold,

' As was Saul's sin, the fatal message told:

' His foul ingratitude to Heav'n he chid,

' To pluck that fruit which was alone forbid   760

' To kingly power, in all that plenteous land,

' Where all things else submit to his command:

' And as fair Eden's violated tree

' To' immortal man brought in mortality,   764

" So shall that crown, which God eternal meant,

" From thee," said he, " and thy great house, be
        rent (*o*).

" Thy crime shall death to all thine honours send,

" And give thy immortal royalty an end."   768

' Thus spoke the Prophet; but kind Heav'n, we hope,

' (Whose threats and anger know no other scope

(*o*) I. Sam. xiii. xiv

5

' But man's amendment) does long fince relent,
' And with repentant Saul itfelf repent.
' Howe'er (tho' none more pray for this than we,
' Whofe wrongs and fuff'rings might fome colour be
' To do it lefs) this fpeech we fadly find   775
' Still extant, and ftill active in his mind;
' But then a worfe effect of it appear'd ;
' Our army, which before modeftly fear'd,
' Which did by ftealth and by degrees decay,
' Difbanded now, and fled in troops away ;   780
' Bafe fear fo bold and impudent does grow,
' When an excufe and colour it can fhow.
' Six hundred only (fcarce a princely train)
' Of all his hoft, with diftrefs'd Saul remain (*p*) :
' Of his whole hoft fix hundred ; and ev'n thofe 785
' (So did wife Heav'n for mighty ends difpofe,
' Nor would that ufelefs multitudes fhould fhare
' In that great gift it did for one prepare)
' Arm'd not like foldiers marching in a war,
' But country-hinds alarmed from afar   790
' By wolves' loud hunger, when the well-known found
' Raifes the affrighted villages around.
' Some goads, flails, ploughfhares, forks, or axes, bore,
' Made for life's ufe and better ends before (*q*) ; 794
' Some knotted clubs, and darts, or arrows dry'd
' I' th' fire, the firft rude arts that Malice try'd,

(*p*) 1 Sam. xiii. 15.   (*q*) ℣. 19, 20, 21.

' Ere man the fins of too much knowledge knew,
' And Death by long experience witty grew.
' Such were the numbers, fuch the arms, which we
' Had by Fate left us for a victory   800
' O'er well-arm'd millions ; nor will this appear
' Ufeful itfelf, when Jonathan was there.
　' 'Twas juft the time when the new ebb of night
' Did the moift world unveil to human fight :
' The Prince, who all that night the field had beat
' With a fmall party, and no en'my met,   806
' (So proud and fo fecure the en'my lay,
' And drench'd in fleep th' exceffes of the day)
' With joy this good occafion did embrace,
' With better leifure, and at nearer fpace,   810
' The ftrength and order of their camp to view ;
' Abdon alone his gen'rous purpofe knew ;
' Abdon ! a bold, a brave, and comely youth,
' Well-born, well-bred, with honour fill'd, and truth;
' Abdon ! his faithful fquire, whom much he lov'd,815
' And oft' with grief his worth in dangers prov'd ;
' Abdon ! whofe love to his mafter did exceed
' What Nature's law or Paffion's pow'r could breed;
' Abdon alone did on him now attend,
' His humbleft fervant, and his deareft friend. 820
　' They went, but facred fury as they went
' Chang'd fwiftly, and exalted his intent (r).
" What may this be ? (the Prince breaks forth) I find
" God or fome pow'rful fpirit invades my mind.

(r) 1 Sam. xiv. 1.

" From ought but Heav'n can never, fure, be brought

" So high, fo glorious, and fo vaſt a thought :   826

" Nor would ill Fate, that meant me to furprife,

" Come cloath'd in fo unlikely a difguife.

" Yon' hoſt, which its proud Fifhes fpreads fo wide

" O'er the whole land, like fome fwoll'n river's tide,

" Which terrible and numberlefs appears,   831

" As the thick waves which their rough ocean bears,

" Which lies fo ſtrongly encamp'd, that one would

" The hill might be remov'd as foon as they,   [ſay

" We two alone muſt fight with, and defeat :   835

" Thou'rt ſtrook, and ſtarteſt at a found fo great;

" Yet we muſt do it; God our weak hands has chofe

" T' aſhame the boaſted numbers of our foes,

" Which to his ſtrength no more proportion'd be

" Than millions are of hours to his eternity.   840

" If when their carelefs guards efpy us here,

" With fportful fcorn they call to us to come near(s),

" We'll boldly climb the hill, and charge them all;

" Not they, but Ifrael's angel gives the call."

' He fpoke, and as he fpoke a light divine   845

' Did from his eyes, and round his temples, ſhine;

' Louder his voice, larger his limbs appear'd ;

' Lefs feem'd the num'rous army to be fear'd.

' This faw, and heard with joy, the brave efquire,

' As he with God's, fill'd with his maſter's fire : 850

" Forbid it, Heav'n," faid he, " I fhould decline,

" Or wiſh, Sir, not to make your danger mine (*t*);

(s) 1 Sam, xiv. 9.   (t) ℣. 7.

" The great example which I daily fee,
" Of your high worth, is not fo loft on me :
" If wonder-ftrook I at your words appear,   855
" My wonder yet is innocent of fear :
" Th' honour which does your princely breaft inflame,
" Warms mine too, and joins there with duty's name.
" If in this act ill Fate our tempter be,
" May all the ill it means be aim'd at me.   860
" But fure, I think, God leads, nor could you bring
" So high thoughts from a lefs exalted fpring.
" Bright figns thro' all your words and looks are
" A rifing vict'ry dawns around your head." [fpread,
' With fuch difcourfe blowing their facred flame,
' Lo, to the fatal place and work they came.   866
    ' Strongly encamp'd on a fteep hill's large head,
' Like fome vaft wood the mighty hoft was fpread (*u*),
' Th' only accefs on neighb'ring Gabaa's fide,
' An hard and narrow way, which did divide   870
' Two cliffy rocks, Bofes and Senes nam'd,
' Much for themfelves and their big ftrangenefs fam'd,
' More for their fortune, and this ftranger day ;
' On both their points Philiftian out-guards lay,
' From whence the two bold fpies they firft efpy'd ;'
" And, lo ! the Hebrews !" proud Elcanor cry'd, 876
" From Senes' top : lo ! from their hungry caves
" A quicker fate here fends them to their graves.
" Come up, (aloud he cries to them below)
" Ye Egyptian Slaves ! and to our mercy owe   880

(*u*) I Sam. xiv. 4.

" The rebel lives long fince to our juftice due."
' Scarce from his lips the fatal omen flew,
' When th' infpir'd Prince did nimbly underftand
' God, and his godlike virtues' high command.
' It call'd him up, and up the fteep afcent   885
' With pain and labour, hafte and joy, they went.
' Eleanor laugh'd to fee them climb, and thought
' His mighty words th' affrighted fupplants brought,
' Did new affronts to the great Hebrew name,
' (The barbarous!) in his wanton fancy frame.   890
' Short was his fport; for fwift as thunder's ftroke
' Rives the frail trunk of fome heav'n-threat'ning oak,
' The Prince's fword did his proud head divide;
' The parted fcull hung down on either fide.
' Juft as he fell, his vengeful fteel he drew   895
' Half way; no more the trembling joints could do,
' Which Abdon fnatch'd, and dy'd it in the blood
' Of an amazed wretch that next him ftood.
' Some clofe to earth fhaking and grov'lling lie,
' Like larks when they the tyrant hobby fpy;   900
' Some, wonder-ftrook, ftand fix'd; fome fly, fome arm
' Wildly, at th' unintelligible alarm,
' Like the main channel of an high-fwoll'n flood,
' In vain by dikes and broken works withftood:
' So Jonathan, once climb'd th' oppofing hill,   905
' Does all around with noife and ruin fill;
' Like fome large arm of which, another way
' Abdon o'erflows; him, too, no bank can ftay:

S iij

' With cries th' affrighted country flies before,
' Behind the following waters loudly roar :   910
' Twenty at leaft flain on this out-guard lie (x),
' To th' adjoin'd camp the reft diftracted fly,
' And ill mix'd wonders tell, and into it bear
' Blind Terror, deaf Diforder, helplefs Fear.
' The conqu'rors, too, prefs boldly in behind,   915
' Doubling the wild confufions which they find.
' Hamgar at firft, the Prince of Afhdod Town (y),
' Chief 'mongft the Five in riches and renown,
' And General then by courfe, oppos'd their way,
' Till drown'd in death at Jonathan's feet he lay,920
' And curs'd the heav'ns for rage, and bit the ground ;
' His life for ever fpilt ftain'd all the grafs around.
' His brother, too, who virtuous hafte did make
' His fortune to revenge or to partake,   924
' Falls grov'lling o'er his trunk on mother Earth ;
' Death mix'd no lefs their bloods than did their birth.
' Mean-while the well-pleas'd Abdon's reftlefs fword
' Difpatch'd the following train t' attend their lord.
' On ftill o'er panting corpfe great Jonathan led,
' Hundreds before him fell, and thoufands fled. 930
' Prodigious Prince ! which does moft wondrous fhow,
' Thy attempt, or thy fuccefs ? thy Fate, or thou ?
' Who durft alone that dreadful hoft affail,
' With purpofe not die, but to prevail !
' Infinite numbers thee no more affright   935
' Than God, whofe unity is infinite.

(x) 1 Sam. xiv. 14.   (y) 1 Sam. v. 6.

' If Heav'n to men'fuch mighty thoughts would give,
' What breaft but thine capacious to receive
' The vaft infufion ? or what foul but thine
' Durft have believ'd that thought to be divine ? 940
' Thou follow'dft Heav'n in the defign, and we
' Find in the act 'twas Heav'n that follow'd thee (z).
' Thou ledd'ft on angels, and that facred band
' (The Deity's great Lieutenant) didft command.
' 'Tis true, Sir, and no figure, when I fay   945
' Angels themfelves fought under him that day.
' Clouds with ripe thunder charg'd fome thither drew,
' And fome the dire materials brought for new. 948
' Hot drops of fouthern fhowers (the fweats of death)
' The voice of ftorms and winged whirlwinds' breath,
' The flames fhot forth from fighting dragons' eyes,
' The fmokes that from fcorch'd fevers' ovens rife,
' The reddeft fires with which fad comets glow,
' And Sodom's neighb'ring lake did fp'rits beftow
' Of fineft fulphur, amongft which they put   955
' Wrath, fury, horror, and all mingled fhut
' Into a cold moift cloud, t'enflame it more,
' And make th' enraged prifoner louder roar.
' Th' affembled clouds burft o'er their army's head ;
' Noife, darknefs, difmal lightnings, round them fpread.
' Another fpirit, with a more potent wand   661
' Than that which Nature fear'd in Mofes' hand,
' And went the way that pleas'd, the mountain ftrook ;
' The mountain felt it ; the vaft mountain fhook.

(z) 1 Sam. xiv. 15.

' Thro' the wide air another angel flew   965
' About their hoft, and thick amongft them threw
' Difcord, defpair, confufion, fear, miftake,
' And all th' ingredients that fwift ruin make.
' The fertile glebe requires no time to breed,
' It quickens and receives at once the feed.   970
' One would have thought, this difmal day t' have feen,
' That Nature's felf in her death-pangs had been:
' Such will the face of that great hour appear,
' Such the diftracted finner's confcious fear.
' In vain fome few ftrive the wild flight to ftay; 975
' In vain they threaten, and in vain they pray:
' Unheard, unheeded, trodden down they lie,
' Beneath the wretched feet of crowds that fly.
' O'er their own foot trampled the vi'lent horfe;
' The guidelefs chariots with impetuous courfe   980
' Cut wide thro' both; and all their bloody way
' Horfes and men, torn, bruis'd, and mangled, lay.
' Some from the rocks caft themfelves down headlong;
' The faint weak paffion grows fo bold and ftrong,
' To almoft certain prefent death they fly,   985
' From a remote and caufelefs fear to die.
' Much diff'rent error did fome troops poffefs,
' And madnefs that look'd better, tho' no lefs:
' Their fellow troops for th' enter'd foe they take(*a*),
' And Ifrael's war with mutual flaughter make. 990
' Mean-while the king from Gabaa's hill did view (*b*),
' And hear the thick'ning tumult as it grew

(*a*) 1 Sam. xiv. 20.   (*b*) ỿ. 16.

' Still great and loud; and tho' he knows not why

' They fled, no more than they themfelves that fly,

' Yet by the ftorms and terrors of the air　　995

' Gueffes fome vengeful fpirits working there,

' Obeys the loud occafion's facred call,

' And fiercely on the trembling hoft does fall.

' At the fame time their flaves and prifoners rife (c),

' Nor does their much-wifh'd liberty fuffice　　1000

' Without revenge: the fcatter'd arms they feize,

' And their proud vengeance with the memory pleafe

' Of who fo lately bore them. All about

' From rocks and caves the Hebrews iffue out (d)

' At the glad noife, joy'd that their foes had fhown

' A fear that drowns the fcandal of their own.　1006

' Still did the Prince 'midft all this ftorm appear,

' Still fcatter'd deaths and terrors every where;

' Still did he break, ftill blunt his wearied fword;

' Still flaughter new fupplies to his hands afford.　1010

' Where troops yet ftood, there ftill he hotly flew,

' And till at laft all fled, fcorn'd to purfue.

' All fled at laft, but many in vain; for ftill

' Th' infatiate conqu'ror was more fwift to kill

' Than they to fave their lives; till, lo! at laft　1015

' Nature, whofe power he had fo long furpafs'd,

' Would yield no more, but to him ftronger foes,

' Drought, faintnefs, and fierce hunger, did oppofe.

' Reeking all o'er in duft, and blood, and fweat,

' Burnt with the fun's and violent action's heat,1020

(c) 1 Sam. xiv. 21.　　(d) ℣. 22.

‘ 'Gainſt an old oak his trembling limbs he ſtaid
‘ For ſome ſhort eaſe; Fate in th' old oak had laid
‘ Proviſions up for his relief; and, lo!
‘ The hollow trunk did with bright honey flow (c).
‘ With timely food his decay'd ſpirits recruit,   1025
‘ Strong he returns, and freſh to the purſuit;
‘ His ſtrength and ſpirits the honey did reſtore,
‘ But, oh! the bitter-ſweet ſtrange poiſon bore!
‘ Behold, Sir! and mark well the treach'rous fate
‘ That does ſo cloſe on human glories wait;   1030
‘ Behold the ſtrong and yet fantaſtic net
‘ T' enſnare triumphant virtue darkly ſet!
‘ Could it before (ſcarce can it ſince) be thought
‘ The Prince, who had alone that morning fought
‘ A duel with an hoſt, had th' hoſt o'erthrown, 1035
‘ And threeſcore thouſand hands diſarm'd with one,
‘ Waſh'd off his country's ſhame, and doubly dy'd
‘ In blood and bluſhes the Philiſtian pride;   1038
‘ Had ſav'd and fix'd his father's tott'ring crown,
‘ And the bright gold new burniſh'd with renown,
‘ Should be ere night, by's king and father's breath,
‘ Without a fault, vow'd and condemn'd to death?
‘ Deſtin'd the bloody ſacrifice to be
‘ Of thanks himſelf for his own victory?
‘ Alone with various fate like to become   1045
‘ Fighting an hoſt, dying an hecatomb?
‘ Yet ſuch, Sir, was his caſe:

(e) 1 Sam. xiv. 27.

' For Saul, who fear'd left the full plenty might
' (In the abandon'd camp expos'd to fight)
' His hungry men from the purfuit diffuade,   1050
' A rafh but folemn vow to Heav'n had made (f);
" Curs'd be the wretch, thrice curfed let him be,
" Who fhall touch food this bufy day," faid he
" Whilft the blefs'd fun does with his fav'ring light
" Affift our vengeful fwords againft their flight. 1055
" Be he thrice curs'd; and if his life we fpare,
" On us thofe curfes fall that he fhould bear."
' Such was the King's rafh vow, who little thought
' How near to him Fate th' application brought.
' The two-edg'd oath wounds deep; perform'd or
' Ev'n perjury its leaft and bluntelt ftroke.   [broke,
' 'Twas his own fon, whom God and mankind lov'd,
' His own victorious fon, that he devov'd,
' On whofe bright head the baleful curfes light;
' But Providence, his helmet in the fight,   1065
' Forbids their entrance or their fettling there;
' They with brute found diffolv'd into the air.
' Him what religion or what vow could bind,
' Unknown, unheard-of, till he his life did find
' Entangled in it? Whilft wonders he did do,   1070
' Muft he die now for not being prophet too?
' To all but him this oath was meant and faid;
' He, afar off, the ends for which 'twas made
' Was acting then, till faint and out of breath,
' He grew half dead with toil of giving death. 1075

(f) 1 Sam. xiv. 24.

' What could his crime in this condition be,

' Excus'd by ignorance and neceffity?

' Yet the remorfelefs King, who did difdain

' That man fhould hear him fwear or threat in vain,

' Tho' 'gainft himfelf, or Fate a way fhould fee 1080

' By which attack'd and conquer'd he might be;

' Who thought compaffion female weaknefs here,

' And equity injuftice would appear,

' In his own caufe; who falfely fear'd, befide,

' The folemn curfe on Jon'than did abide,   1085

' And the infected limb not cut away,

' Would like a gangreen o'er all Ifrael ftray,

' Prepar'd this godlike facrifice to kill,

' And his rafh vow more rafhly to fulfil.

' What tongue can th' horror and amazement tell

' Which on all Ifrael that fad moment fell?   1091

' Tamer had been their grief, fewer their tears,

' Had the Philiftian fate that day been theirs.

' Not Saul's proud heart could mafter his fwoll'n eye;

' The Prince alone ftood mild and patient by;   1095

' So bright his fuff'rings, fo triumphant fhow'd,

' Lefs to the beft than worft of fates he ow'd.

' A vict'ry now he o'er himfelf might boaft;

' He conquer'd now that conqu'ror of an hoft:

' It charm'd thro' tears the fad fpectators' fight,

' Did rev'rence, love, and gratitude, excite,   1101

' And pious rage; with which infpir'd, they now

' Oppofe to Saul's a better public vow:

2

' They all confent all Ifrael ought to be   1104
' Accurs'd, and kill'd themfelves, rather than he.
' Thus with kind force they the glad King withftood,
' And fav'd their wondrous faviour's facred blood(*g*).'
    Thus David fpoke, and much did yet remain
Behind, th' attentive Prince to entertain ;
Edom and Zoba's war, for what befel   1110
In that of Moab (*h*) was known there too well;
The boundlefs quarrel with curs'd Amalec's land (*i*),
Where Heav'n itfelf did cruelty command,
And practis'd on Saul's mercy, nor did e'er
More punifh innocent blood, than pity there (*k*).
But, lo ! they arriv'd now at the appointed place,
Well chofen and well furnifh'd for the chafe.   1117

(*g*) 1 Sam. xiv. 45.   (*h*) ℣. 47.   (*i*) 1 Sam. xv. 3.
(*k*) 1 Sam. xv. 23.

End of the Fourth Book.

IMITATIONS.

IN IMITATION OF MARTIAL'S EPIGRAM.

MARTIAL, LIB. V. EP. XXI.

Si tecum mihi chare Martialis, &c.

If, deareſt Friend! it my good fate might be
T' enjoy at once a quiet life and thee;
If we for happineſs could leiſure find
And wand'ring Time into a method bind,
We ſhould not, ſure, the great men's favour need, 5
Nor on long hopes, the Court's thin diet, feed;
We ſhould not patience find daily to hear
The calumnies and flatt'ries ſpoken there;
We ſhould not the lords' tables humbly uſe,
Or talk in ladies' chambers love and news; 10
But books and wiſe diſcourſe, gardens and fields,
And all the joys that unmix'd Nature yields,
Thick ſummer-ſhades, where winter ſtill does lie,
Bright winter-fires, that ſummer's part ſupply,
Sleep not controll'd by cares, confin'd to night, 15
Or bound in any rule but appetite;
Free, but not ſavage or ungracious mirth,
Rich wines to give it quick and eaſy birth;
A few companions, which ourſelves ſhould chuſe,
A gentle miſtreſs, and a gentler Muſe; 20
Such, deareſt Friend! ſuch, without doubt, ſhould be
Our place, our buſ'neſs, and our company:

Now to himfelf, alas! does neither live,
But fees good funs, of which we are to give
A ftrict account, fet and march thick away;
Knows a man how to live, and does he ftay?   26

MARTIAL, LIB. II.

Vota tui breviter, &c.

Well, then, Sir, you fhall know how far extend
The pray'rs and hopes of your poetic friend:
He does not palaces nor manors crave,
Would be no lord, but lefs a lord would have:
The ground he holds, if he his own can call,   5
He quarrels not with Heaven becaufe 'tis fmall:
Let gay and toilfome greatnefs others pleafe,
He loves of homely littlenefs the eafe:
Can any man in gilded rooms attend,
And his dear hours in humble vifits fpend,   10
When in the frefh and beauteous fields he may
With various healthful pleafures fill the day?
If there be man, ye Gods! I ought to hate,
Dependence and attendance be his fate;
Still let him bufy be, and in a crowd,   15
And very much a flave, and very proud:
Thus he, perhaps, pow'rful and rich may grow;
No matter, O ye Gods! that I'll allow;
But let him peace and freedom never fee;
Let him not love this life who loves not me.   20

T ij

MARTIAL, LIB. II.

Vis fieri liber? &c.

WOULD you be free? 'Tis your chief wish, you say:
Come on; I'll shew thee, Friend! the certain way.
If to no feasts abroad thou lov'st to go,
Whilst bounteous God does bread at home bestow;
If thou the goodness of thy clothes dost prize,   5
By thine own use, and not by others' eyes;
(If, only safe from weathers) thou canst dwell
In a small house, but a convenient shell;
If thou, without a sigh, or golden wish,
Canst look upon thy beachen bowl and dish;   10
If in thy mind such pow'r and greatness be,
The Persian king's a slave compar'd with thee.   12

MARTIAL, LIB. II.

Quod te nomine? &c.

THAT I do you with humble bows no more,
And danger of my naked head, adore;
That I, who lord and master cry'd erewhile,
Salute you in a new and different style,
By your own name, a scandal to you now,   5
Think not that I forgot myself or you;
By loss of all things by all others fought,
This freedom, and the freeman's hat, is bought.

A lord and mafter no man wants, but he
Who o'er himfelf has no authority·   10
Who does for honours and for riches ftrive,
And follies, without which lords cannot live.
If thou from Fortune doft no fervant crave,
Believe it thou no mafter need'ft to have.   14

MARTIAL, LIB. II. EP. XC.

Wonder not, Sir, (you who inftruct the town
In the true wifdom of the facred gown)
That I make hafte to live, and cannot hold
Patiently out till I grow rich and old:
Life for delays and doubts no time does give;   5
None ever yet made hafte enough to live:
Let him defer it whofe prepoft'rous care
Omits himfelf and reaches to his heir;
Who does his father's bounded ftores defpife,
And whom his own, too, never can fuffice.   10
My humble thoughts no glitt'ring roofs require,
Or rooms that fhine with ought but conftant fire:
I well content the av'rice of my fight
With the fair gildings of reflected light:
Pleafures abroad the fport of Nature yields,   15
Her living fountains and her fmiling fields;
And then at home what pleafure is it to fee
A little cleanly cheerful family?
Which, if a chafte wife crown, no lefs in her
Than Fortune I the the golden mean prefer: 20

Too noble nor too wife she should not be;
No, nor too rich, too fair, too fond of me.
Thus let my life slide silently away,
With sleep all night, and quiet all the day.   24

MARTIAL, LIB. V. EP. LIX.

To-morrow you will live, you always cry;
In what far country does this morrow lie,
That 'tis so mighty long ere it arrive?
Beyond the Indies does this morrow live?   4
'Tis so far-fetch'd this morrow, that I fear
'Twill be both very old and very dear.
To-morrow I will live, the fool does say;
To-day itself's too late; the wise liv'd yesterday.   8

MARTIAL, LIB. X. EP. XLVII.

Vitam quæ faciunt beatiorem, &c.

Since, dearest Friend! 'tis your desire to see
A true receipt of happiness from me,
These are the chief ingredients, if not all:
Take an estate neither too great nor small,
Which *quantum sufficit* the doctors call: 5
Let this estate from parents' care descend;
The getting it too much of life does spend.
Take such a ground whose gratitude may be
A fair encouragement for industry:
Let constant fires the winter's fury tame,   10
And let thy kitchens be a Vestal flame;

Thee to the Town let never fuit at law,
And rarely, very rarely, bufinefs, draw:
Thy active mind in equal temper keep,
In undifturbed peace, yet not in fleep: 15
Let exercife a vigorous health maintain,
Without which all the compofition's vain.
In the fame weight prudence and innocence take;
Ana of each does the juft mixture make:
But a few friendfhips wear, and let them be   20
By Nature and by Fortune fit for thee:
Inftead of art and luxury in food,
Let mirth and freedom make thy table good:
If any cares into thy day-time creep,
At night, without wine's opium, let them fleep: 25
Let reft, which Nature does to Darknefs wed,
And not luft, recommend to thee thy bed.
Be fatisfy'd and pleas'd with what thou art;
Act cheerfully and well th' allotted part:
Enjoy the prefent hour, be thankful for the paft, 30
And neither fear nor wifh th' approaches of the laft.

MARTIAL, LIB. X. EP. XCVI.

Me who have liv'd fo long among the great,
You wonder to hear talk of a retreat,
And a retreat fo diftant, as may fhow
No thoughts of a return when once I go.
Give me a country, how remote foe'er,   5
Where happinefs a mod'rate rate does bear,

Where poverty itfelf in plenty flows,
And all the folid ufe of riches knows:
The ground about the houfe maintains it there;
The houfe maintains the ground about it here.   10
Here even hunger's dear, and a full board
Devours the vital fubftance of the lord.
The land itfelf does there the feaft beftow,
The land itfelf muft here to market go.
Three or four fuits one winter here does wafte,   15
One fuit does there three or four winters laft.
Here ev'ry frugal man muft oft' be cold,
And little luke warm fires are to you fold.
There fire's an element, as cheap and free
Almoft as any other of the three.   20
Stay you then here, and live among the great,
Attend their fports, and at their tables eat:
When all the bounties here of men you fcore,
The place's bounty there fhall give me more.   24

HORAT. EPODON.

Beatus ille qui procul, &c.

HAPPY the man whom bounteous gods allow
With his own hands paternal grounds to plough!
Like the firft golden mortals, happy he,
From bufinefs and the cares of money free!
No human ftorms break off at land his fleep,   5
No loud alarms of Nature on the deep;

From all the cheats of law he lives fecure,
Nor does th' affronts of palaces endure,
Sometimes the beauteous marriageable Vine
He to the lufty bridegroom Elm does join;   10
Sometimes he lops the barren trees around,
And grafts new life into the fruitful wound;
Sometimes he fhears his flock, and fometimes he
Stores up the golden treafures of the bee:
He fees his lowing herds walk o'er the plain;   15
Whilft neighb'ring hills low back to them again;
And when the feafon rich, as well as gay,
All her autumnal bounty does difplay,
How is he pleas'd th' increafing ufe to fee
Of his well-trufted labours bend the tree?   20
Of which large fhares, on the glad facred days,
He gives to friends, and to the gods repays:
With how much joy does he beneath fome fhade,
By aged trees' rev'rend embraces made,
His carelefs head on the frefh green recline,   25
His head, uncharg'd with fear or with defign?
By him a river conftantly complains,
The birds above rejoice with various ftrains,
And in the folemn fcene their orgies keep,
Like dreams mix'd with the gravity of fleep;   30
Sleep, which does always there for entrance wait,
And nought within againft it fhuts the gate.
     Nor does the rougheft feafon of the fky,
Or fullen Jove, all fports to him deny;

He runs the mazes of the nimble hare,   35

His well-mouth'd dogs' glad concert rends the air ;

Or with game bolder, and rewarded more,

He drives into a toil the foaming boar :

Here flies the hawk t' affault, and there the net

To intercept the travelling fowl is fet :   40

And all his malice, all his craft, is fhown

In innocent wars on beafts and birds alone.

This is the life from all misfortunes free,

From thee the great one, tyrant Love ! from thee;

And if a chafte and clean, tho' homely wife,   45

Be added to the bleffings of this life,

Such as the ancient fun-burnt Sabines were,

Such as Apulia, frugal ftill, does bear,

Who makes her children and the houfe her care,

And joyfully the work of life does fhare,   50

Nor thinks herfelf too noble, or too fine,

To pin the fheepfold, or to milch the kine,

Who waits at door againft her bufband come,

From rural duties, late, and weary'd home,

Where fhe receives him with a kind embrace,   55

A cheerful fire, and a more cheerful face,

And fills the bowl up to her homely lord,

And with domeftic plenty loads the board;

Not all the luftful fhellfifh of the fea,

Drefs'd by the wanton hand of Luxury,   60

Nor ortolans, nor godwits, nor the reft

Of coftly names that glorify a feaft,

Are at the princely tables better cheer
Than lamb and kid, lettuce and olives, here. 64

A paraphrase upon the

TENTH EPISTLE OF HORACE, BOOK I.

Horace to Fuscus Aristius.

HEALTH from the lover of the country, me;
Health to the lover of the city, thee:
A diff'rence in our souls this only proves;
In all things else we agree like marry'd doves.
But the warm nest, and crowded dovehouse, thou 5
Dost like; I loosely fly from bough to bough,
And rivers drink, and all the shining day
Upon fair trees or mossy rocks I play:
In fine, I live and reign, when I retire
From all that you equal with Heav'n admire. 10
Like one at last from the priest's service fled,
Loathing the honey'd cakes, I long for bread.
Would I a house for happiness erect,
Nature alone should be the architect:
She'd build it more convenient than great, 15
And, doubtless, in the country chuse her seat.
Is there a place doth better helps supply
Against the wounds of Winter's cruelty?
Is there an air that gentler does asswage
The mad celestial Dog's or Lion's rage? 20
Is it not there that sleep (and only there)
Nor noise without, nor cares within, does fear?

Does art thro' pipes a purer water bring,
Than that which Nature ftrains into a fpring?
Can all your tap'ftries, or your pictures, fhow   25
More beauties than in herbs and flow'rs do grow?
Fountains and trees our weary'd pride do pleafe,
Ev'n in the midft of gilded palaces;
And in your towns that profpect gives delight,
Which opens round the country to our fight.   30
Men to the good from which they rafhly fly
Return at laft, and their wild luxury
Does but in vain with thofe true joys contend,
Which Nature did to mankind recommend.
The man who changes gold for burnifh'd brafs,   35
Or fmall right gems for larger ones of glafs,
Is not, at length, more certain to be made
Ridiculous, and wretched by the trade,
Than he who fells a folid good, to buy
The painted goods of pride and vanity.   40
If thou be wife, no glorious fortune chufe,
Which 'tis but pain to keep, yet grief to lofe;
For when we place ev'n trifles in the heart,
With trifles, too, unwillingly we part.
An humble roof, plain bed, and homely board,   45
More clear untainted pleafures do afford
Than all the tumult of vain greatnefs brings
To kings, or to the favourites of kings.
The horned deer, by Nature arm'd fo well,
Did with the horfe in common pafture dwell,   50

And when they fought the field it always wan,
Till the ambitious horfe begg'd help of man,
And took the bridle, and thenceforth did reign
Bravely alone, as lord of all the plain;
But never after could the rider get   55
From off his back, or from his mouth the bit.
So they, who poverty too much do fear,
T' avoid that weight, a greater burden bear:
That they might pow'r above their equals have,
To cruel mafters they themfelves enflave;   60
For gold their liberty exchang'd we fee,
That faireft flow'r which crowns humanity;
And all this mifchief does upon them light,
Only becaufe they know not how, aright,
That great but fecret happinefs to prize,   65
That's laid up in a little for the wife.
That is the beft and eafieft eftate
Which to a man fits clofe, but not too ftrait:
'Tis like a fhoe; it pinches and it burns
Too narrow, and too large it overturns.   70
My deareft Friend! ftop thy defires at laft,
And cheerfully enjoy the wealth thou haft;
And if me ftill feeking for more you fee,
Chide and reproach, defpife and laugh at me.
Money was made not to command our will,   75
But all our lawful pleafures to fulfil.
Shame and woe to us if we our wealth obey;
The horfe does with the horfeman run away.   78

VIRG. GEORG. LIB. II.

O fortunatos nimium, &c.

A tranſlation out of Virgil.

Oh happy (if his happineſs he knows)
The country ſwain on whom kind Heav'n beſtows
At home all riches that wiſe Nature needs,
Whom the juſt earth with eaſy plenty feeds.
'Tis true, no morning-tide of clients comes,   5
And fills the painted channels of his rooms,
Adoring the rich figures, as they paſs,
In tap'ſtry wrought, or cut in living braſs;
Nor is his wool ſuperfluouſly dy'd
With the dear poiſon of Aſſyrian pride;   10
Nor do Arabian perfumes vainly ſpoil
The native uſe and ſweetneſs of his oil:
Inſtead of theſe, his calm and harmleſs life,
Free from th' alarms of fear and ſtorms of ſtrife,
Does with ſubſtantial bleſſedneſs abound,   15
And the ſoft wings of peace cover him round:
'Thro' artleſs grots the murm'ring waters glide,
Thick trees both againſt heat and cold provide,
From whence the birds ſalute him, and his ground
With lowing herds and bleating ſheep does ſound; 20
And all the rivers and the foreſts nigh,
Both food, and game, and exerciſe, ſupply.

Here a well-harden'd active youth we see,
Taught the great art of cheerful poverty;
Here, in this place alone, there still do shine   25
Some streaks of love both human and divine:
From hence Astræa took her flight, and here
Still her last footsteps upon earth appear.
'Tis true, the first desire which does control
All the inferior wheels that move my soul,   30
Is that the Muse me her high priest would make,
Into her holiest scenes of myst'ry take,
And open there, to my mind's purged eye,
Those wonders which to sense the gods deny;
How in the moon such change of shapes is found, 35
The moon, the changing world's eternal bound:
What shakes the solid earth, what strong disease
Dares trouble the firm centre's ancient ease;
What makes the sea retreat, and what advance,
Varieties too regular for Chance;   40
What drives the chariot on of winter's light,
And stops the lazy waggon of the Night:
But if my dull and frozen blood deny
To send forth spirits that raise a soul so high,
In the next place let woods and rivers be   45
My quiet tho' inglorious destiny:
In life's cool vale let my low scene be laid,
Cover me, gods! with Tempe' thickest shade.
Happy the man, I grant thrice happy he
Who can thro' gross effects their causes see,   50

Whofe courage from the deeps of knowledge fprings,
Nor vainly fears inevitable things,
But does his walk of virtue calmly go,
Thro' all the alarms of death and hell below.
Happy! but next fuch conqu'rors happy they,   55
Whofe humble life lies not in Fortune's way;
They, unconcern'd, from their fafe diftant feat,
Behold the rods and fceptres of the great;
The quarrels of the mighty, without fear,
And the defcent of foreign troops, they hear;   60
Nor can ev'n Rome their fteddy courfe mifguide,
With all the luftre of her perifhing pride.
Them never yet did Strife or Av'rice draw
Into the noify markets of the law,
The camps of gowned war; nor do they live   65
By rules or forms that many madmen give:
Duty for Nature's bounty they repay,
And her fole laws religioufly obey.
    Some with bold labour plough the faithlefs main,
Some rougher ftorms in princes' courts fuftain   70
Some fwell up their flight fails with pop'lar fame,
Charm'd with the foolifh whiftlings of a name:
Some their vain wealth to earth again commit;
With endlefs cares fome brooding o'er it fit:
Country and friends are by fome wretches fold,   75
To lie on Tyrian beds, and drink in gold;
No price too high for profit can be fhown;
Not brothers' blood, nor hazards of their own:

Around the world in fearch of it they roam,
It makes ev'n their antipodes their home :   80
Mean-while the prudent hufbandman is found
In mutual duties ftriving with his ground,
And half the year he care of that does take,
That half the year grateful returns does make :
Each fertile month does fome new gifts prefent,   85
And with new work his induftry content :
This the young lamb, that the foft fleece, doth yield;
This loads with hay, and that with corn, the field :
All forts of fruit crown the rich Autumn's pride,
And on a fwelling hill's warm ftony fide,   90
The pow'rful princely purple of the vine,
Twice dy'd with the redoubled fun, does fhine :
In th' evening to a fair enfuing day,
With joy he fees his flocks and kids to play,
And loaded kine about his cottage ftand,   95
Inviting with known found the milker's hand;
And when from wholefome labour he doth come,
With wifhes to be there, and wifh'd-for home,
He meets at door the fofteft human blifles,
His chafte wife's welcome, and dear children's kifles.
When any rural holydays invite   101
His genius forth to innocent delight,
On earth's fair bed, beneath fome facred fhade,
Amidft his equal friends carelefsly laid,
He fings thee, Bacchus! patron of the vine,   105
The beechen bowl foams with a flood of wine,

Not to the lofs of reafon or of ftrength:
To active games and manly fport, at length,
Their mirth afcends, and with fill'd veins they fee
Who can the beft at better trials be.   110
Such was the life the prudent Sabines chofe;
From fuch the old Hetrurian virtue rofe;
Such Remus and the god his brother led;
From fuch firm footing Rome grew the world's head:
Such was the life that ev'n till now does raife   115
The honour of poor Saturn's golden days,
Before men born of earth, and bury'd there,
Let in the fea their mortal fate to fhare,
Before new ways of perifhing were fought,
Before unfkilful Death on anvils wrought,   120
Before thofe beafts which human life fuftain,
By men, unlefs to the gods' ufe, were flain.   122

SENECA, EX THYESTE, ACT. II. CHOR.

Stet quicunque volet, potens
Aulæ culmine lubrico, &c.

Upon the flippery tops of human ftate,
The gilded pinnacles of Fate,
Let others proudly ftand, and, for a while,
The giddy danger to beguile,
With joy and with difdain look down on all,   5
Till their heads turn, and down they fall;
Me, O ye Gods! on earth, or elfe fo near
That I no fall to earth may fear,

And, O ye Gods ! at a good diftance, feat
From the long ruins of the great :   10
Here wrapt in th' arms of Quiet let me lie ;
Quiet ! companion of Obfcurity :
Here let my life with as much filence flide,
As Time, that meafures it, does glide :
Nor let the breath of Infamy or Fame,   15
From town to town echo about my name :
Nor let my homely death embroider'd be
With fcutcheon or with elegy.
An old plebeian let me die,
Alas ! all then are fuch as well as I.   20
To him, alas ! to him, I fear,
The face of Death will terrible appear,
Who in his life flatt'ring his fenfelefs pride,
By being known to all the world befide,
Does not himfelf, when he his dying, know,
Nor what he is, nor whither he is to go.   26

CLAUDIAN'S OLD MAN OF VERONA.

Happy the man who his whole time doth bound
Within th' inclofure of his little ground :
Happy the man whom the fame humble place
(Th' hereditary cottage of his race)
From his firft rifing infancy has known,   5
And by degrees fees gently bending down,
With natural propenfion to that earth
Which both preferv'd his life and gave him birth :

Him no falfe diftant lights, by Fortune fet,
Could ever into foolifh wand'rings get;   10
He never dangers either faw or fear'd;
The dreadful ftorms at fea he never heard :
He never heard the fhrill alarms of war,
Or the worfe noifes of the lawyers' bar :
No change of Confuls marks to him the year;   15
The change of feafons is his calendar :
The cold and heat winter and fummer fhows,
Autumn by fruits, and fpring by flow'rs, he knows :
He meafures time by landmarks, and has found
For the whole day the dial of his ground :   20
A neighb'ring wood, born with himfelf, he fees,
And loves his old contemporary trees :
He 'as only heard of near Verona's name,
And knows it, like the Indies, but by fame :
Does with a like concernment notice take   25
Of the Red fea, and of Benacus' lake :
Thus health and ftrength he to' a third age enjoys,
And fees a long pofterity of boys.
About the fpacious world let others roam,
The voyage life is longeft made at home.   30

FRAGMENTS.

*In the Difcourfe, by way of vifion, concerning the govern-
ment of Oliver Cromwell.*

I.

Ah! happy Ifle! how art thou chang'd and curs'd
Since I was born, and knew thee firft!
When Peace, which had forfook the world around,
(Frighted with noife, and the fhrill trumpet's found)
Thee for a private place of reft,   5
And a fecure retirement, chofe
Wherein to build her halycon neft;
No wind durft ftir abroad the air to difcompofe.

II.

When all the riches of the globe befide
Flow'd in to thee with ev'ry tide;   10
When all that Nature did thy foil deny,
The growth was of thy fruitful induftry,
When all the proud and dreadful fea
And all his tributary ftreams,
A conftant tribute paid to thee;   15
When all the liquid world was one extended Thames.

III.

When Plenty in each village did appear,
And Bounty was its fteward there;
When Gold walk'd free about in open view,
Ere it one conqu'ring party's pris'ner grew;   20

When the religion of our ſtate
Had face and ſubſtance with her voice,
Ere ſhe by' her fooliſh loves of late
Like Echo (once a nymph) turn'd only into noiſe.

IV.

When men to men reſpect and friendſhip bore,   25
And God with reverence did adore;
When upon earth no kingdom could have ſhown
A happier Monarch to us than our own,
And yet his ſubjects by him were
(Which is a truth will hardly be   30
Receiv'd by any vulgar ear,
A ſecret known to few) made happier ev'n than he.

V.

Thou doſt a chaos and confuſion now,
A Babel, and a Bedlam grow,
And like a frantic perſon thou doſt tear   35
The ornaments and clothes which thou ſhouldſt wear
And cut thy limbs; and if we ſee
(Juſt as thy barb'rous Britons did)
Thy body with hyporciſy
Painted all o'er, thou think'ſt thy naked ſhame is hid.

VI.

The nations which envy'd thee erewhile   41
Now laugh, (too little 'tis to ſmile)
They laugh, and would have pity'd thee, alas!
But that thy faults all pity do ſurpaſs.

Art thou the country which didſt hate,   45
And mock the French inconſtancy ?
And have we, have we ſeen of late
Leſs change of habits there than governments in thee?
VII.

Unhappy Iſle! no ſhip of thine at ſea
Was ever toſs'd and torn like thee ;   50
Thy naked hulk looſe on the waves does beat,
The rocks and banks around her ruin threat ;
What did thy fooliſh pilots ail,
To lay the compaſs quite aſide?
Without a law or rule to ſail,   55
And rather take the winds than heav'ns to be their
VIII.   [guide?

Yet, mighty God! yet, yet, we humbly crave,
This floting Iſle from ſhipwreck ſave;
And tho' to waſh that blood which does it ſtain,
It well deſerves to ſink into the main,   60
Yet for the Royal Martyr's prayer
(The Royal Martyr prays, we know)
This guilty, periſhing, veſſel ſpare;
Hear but his ſoul above, and not his blood below. 64

'Ουχ' ὅσιον ν.Ἰαμήνοσιν ἐπ' ἄνδρασιν εὐχεταάσϑαι.

'Tis wicked, with inſulting feet to tread
Upon the monuments of the dead.

I.

Curs'd be the man (what do I wish ? as tho'
The wretch already were not so.;
But curs'd on let him be) who thinks it brave
And great his country to enslave;
Who seeks to over-poise alone   5
The balance of a nation :
Against the whole, but naked state,
Who in his own light scale makes up with arms the
                            II.   [weight.
Who of his nation loves to be the first,
Tho' at the rate of being worst;   10
Who would be rather a great monster, than
A well-proportion'd man,
The son of Earth, with hundred hands,
Upon his three-pil'd mountain stands,
Till thunder strikes him from the sky ;   15
The son of Earth again in his earth's womb does lie.

III.

What blood, confusion, ruin, to obtain
A short and miserable reign?
In what oblique and humble creeping wise
Does the mischievous serpent rise?   20
But ev'n his forked tongue strikes dead,
When he 'as rear'd up his wicked head;
He murders with his mortal frown;
A basilisk he grows if once he get a crown

3

IV.

But no guards can oppofe affaulting ears,   25
Or undermining tears;
No more than doors or clofe-drawn curtains keep
The fwarming dreams out when we fleep:
That bloody confcience, too, of his,
(For, oh! a rebel red-coat 'tis)   30
Does here his early hell begin;
He fees his flaves without, his tyrant feels within.

V.

Let, gracious God! let never more thine hand
Lift up this rod againft our land:
A tyrant is a rod and ferpent too,   35
And brings worfe plagues than Egypt knew.
What rivers ftain'd with blood have been?
What ftorm and hailfhot have we feen?
What fores deform'd the ulcerous ftate?
What darknefs to be felt has bury'd us of late?   40

VI.

How has it fnatch'd our flocks and herds away!
And made even of our fons a prey!
What croaking fects and vermin has it fent
The reftlefs nation to torment!
What greedy troops, what armed power   45
Of flies and locufts, to devour
The land, which ev'ry where they fill!
Nor fly they, Lord! away; no, they devour it ftill.

Volume II.   X

VII.

Come the eleventh plague rather than this fhould be;
Come fink us rather in the fea :   50
Come rather Peſtilence, and reap us down;
Come God's fword rather than our own :
Let rather Roman come again,
Or Saxon, Norman, or the Dane:
In all the bonds we ever bore   55
We griev'd, we figh'd, we wept; we never bluſh'd before.

VIII.

If by our fins the divine vengeance be
Call'd to this laſt extremity,
Let fome denouncing Jonas firſt be fent
To try if England can repent :   60
Methinks at leaſt fome prodigy,
Some dreadful comet from on high,
Should terribly forewarn the earth,
As of good princes' deaths, fo of a tyrant's birth. 64

THE Chartreux wants the warning of a bell
To call him to the duties of his cell :
There needs no noife at all to awaken fin ;
Th' adult'rer and the thief his larum has within.   4

IT is a truth fo certain and fo clear,
That to the firſt-born man it did appear:
Did not the mighty heir, the noble Cain,
By the freſh laws of Nature taught, difdain

That (tho' a brother) any one should be   5
A greater favourite to God than he?
He strook him down, and so, said he, so fell
The sheep which thou didst sacrifice so well.
Since all the fullest sheaves which I could bring,
Since all were blasted in the offering,   10
Left God should my next victim, too, despise,
The acceptable priest I'll sacrifice.
Hence coward Fears; for the first blood so spilt,
As a reward, he the first city built.
'Twas a beginning generous and high,   15
Fit for a grandchild of the Deity :
So well advanc'd, 'twas pity there he staid ;
One step of glory more he should have made,
And to the utmost bounds of greatness gone; [alone.
Had Adam, too, been kill'd, he might have reign'd
One brother's death what do I mean to name,   21
A small oblation to Revenge and Fame ?
The mighty-soul'd Abimelec, to shew
What for high place a higher sp'rit can do,
A hecatomb almost of brethren slew,   25
And seventy times in nearest blood he dy'd
(To make it hold) his royal purple pride.
Why do I name the lordly creature man?
The weak, the mild, the coward woman, can,
When to a crown she cuts her sacred way,   30
All that oppose with manlike courage slay.

X ij

So Athaliah, when she saw her son,
And with his life her dearer greatness gone,
With a majestic fury slaughter'd all
Whom high birth might to high pretences call: 35
Since he was dead who all her power sustain'd,
Resolv'd to reign alone; resolv'd, and reign'd.
In vain her sex, in vain the laws, withstood,
In vain the sacred plea of David's blood.
A noble and a bold contention she   40
(One woman) undertook with Destiny :
She to pluck down, Destiny to uphold,
(Oblig'd by holy oracles of old).
The great Jessæan race on Juda's throne,
Till 'twas at last an equal wager grown;   45
Scarce Fate, with much ado, the better got by one.
Tell me not she herself at last was slain;
Did she not first sev'n years (a lifetime) reign?
Sev'n royal years, to a public spirit, will seem
More than the private life of a Methusalem.   50
'Tis godlike to be great; and as they say
A thousand years to God are but a day,
So to a man, when once a crown he wears,
The coronation-day is more than a thousand years. 54

WHEN, lo! ere the last words were fully spoke,
From a fair cloud, which rather op'd than broke,
A flash of light, rather than lightning, came
So swift, and yet so gentle was the flame :

Upon it rode, and in his full career   5
Seem'd to my eyes no fooner there than here,
The comelieft youth of all th' angelic race,
Lovely his fhape, ineffable his face.
The frowns with which he ftrook the trembling fiend,
All fmiles of human beauty did tranfcend;   10
His beams of locks fell part difhevell'd down,
Part upwards curl'd, and form'd a nat'ral crown,
Such as the Britifh monarchs us'd to wear,
If gold might be compar'd with angels' hair :
His coat and flowing mantle were fo bright,   15
They feem'd both made of woven filver light :
Acrofs his breaft an azure ribband went,
At which a medal hung, that did prefent,
In wondrous living figures, to the fight,
The myftic Champions and old Dragon's fight;   20
And from his mantle's fide there fhone afar
A fix'd, and, I believe, a real ftar.
In his fair hand (what need was there of more ?)
No arms but th' Englifh bloody Crofs he bore,
Which when he tow'rds the affrighted tyrant bent, 25
And fome few words pronounc'd, (but what they meant,
Or were, could not, alas! by me be known,
Only I well perceiv'd Jefus was one)
He trembled, and he roar'd, and fled away,
Mad to quit thus his more than hop'd-for prey. 30
Such rage inflames the wolf's wild heart and eyes,
(Robb'd, as he thinks, unjuftly of his prize)

Whom unawares the fhepherd fpies, and draws
The bleating lamb from out his rav'nous jaws;
The fhepherd fain himfelf would he affail,   35
But fear above his hunger does prevail :
He knows his foe too ftrong, and muft be gone;
He grins as he looks back, and howls as he goes on.

In feveral difcourfes by way of effays in verfe and profe.

I. Of Liberty.

Who governs his own courfe with fteddy hand,
Who does himfelf with fov'reign pow'r command;
Whom neither death nor poverty does fright,
Who ftands not awkwardly in his own light   4
Againft the truth; who can, when pleafures knock
Loud at his door, keep firm the bolt and lock ;
Who can, tho' Honour at his gate fhould ftay
In all her mafking clothes, fend her away,
And cry, Be gone, I have no mind to play.   9

Magne Deus; quod ad has vitæ brevis attinet horas,
Da mihi, da panem libertatemque, nec ultrà
Sollicitas effundo preces, fiquid datur ultrà
Accipiam gratus ; fi non, contentus abibo.   4

For the few hours of life allotted me,
Give me, great God ! but bread and liberty,
I'll beg no more; if more thou'rt pleas'd to give,
I'll thankfully that overplus receive :
If beyond this no more be freely fent,
I'll thank for this, and go away content.   6

II. *Of Solitude.*

Sic ego fecretis poffum benè vivere filvis
Quà nulla humano fit via trita pedé,
Tu mihi curarum requies, tu nocte vel atrâ
Lumen, et in folis tu mihi turba locis.　　4

With thee for ever I in woods could reft,
Where never human foot the ground has prefs'd;
Thou from all fhades the darknefs canft exclude,
And from a defert banifh folitude.　　4

Odi et amo, quanám id faciam ratione requiris?
Nefcio, fed fieri fentio, et excrutior.

I hate, and yet I love thee too;
How can that be? I know not how;
Only that fo it is I know,
And feel with torment that 'tis fo.　　4

O vita! ftulto longa, fapienti brevis!

O life! long to the fool, fhort to the wife!

I.

Hail old Patrician Trees, fo great and good!
Hail, ye Plebeian Underwood!
Where the poetic birds rejoice,
And for their quiet nefts and plenteous food
Pay with their grateful voice.　　5

II.

Hail the poor Mufes' richeft Manor-feat!
Ye country Houfes and retreat,
Which all the happy gods fo love,
That for you oft! they quit their bright and great
Metropolis above.　　　　　　　　　　　　10

III.

Here Nature does a houfe for me erect,
Nature! the faireft architect,
Who thofe fond artifts does defpife
That can the fair and living trees neglect,
Yet the dead timber prize.　　　　　　　　15

IV.

Here let me, carelefs and unthoughtful lying,
Hear the foft winds above me flying,
With all their wanton boughs difpute,
And the more tuneful birds to both replying,
Nor be myfelf, too, mute.　　　　　　　　20

V.

A filver ftream fhall roll his waters near,
Gilt with the funbeams here and there,
On whofe enamell'd bank I'll walk,
And fee how prettily they fmile,
And hear how prettily they talk.　　　　　　25

VI.

Ah! wretched, and too folitary he,
Who loves not his own company!

He'll feel the weight of it many a day,
Unlefs he call in Sin or Vanity
To help to bear it away.   30

VII.

Oh, Solitude! firft ftate of human-kind!
Which blefs'd remain'd till man did find
Ev'n his own helper's company :
As foon as two, alas! together join'd,
The ferpent made up three.   35

VIII.

Tho' God himfelf, thro' countlefs ages, thee
His fole companion chofe to be,
Thee, facred Solitude! alone,
Before the branchy head of Number's tree
Sprang from the trunk of one;   40

IX.

Thou (tho' men think thine an unactive part)
Doft break and tame th' unruly heart,
Which elfe would know no fettled pace,
Making it move, well manag'd by thy art,
With fwiftnefs and with grace.   45

X.

Thou the faint beams of Reafon's fcatter'd light
Doft, like a burning-glafs, unite,
Doft multiply the feeble heat,
And fortify the ftrength, till thou doft bright
And noble fires beget.   50

XI.

Whilft this hard truth I teach, methinks I fee
The monfter London laugh at me;
I fhould at thee too, foolifh City!
If it were fit to laugh at mifery;
But thy eftate I pity.   55

XII.

Let but thy wicked men from out thee go,
And all the fools that crowd thee fo,
Ev'n thou, who doft thy millions boaft,
A village lefs than Iflington wilt grow,
A folitude almoft.   60

III: Of Obscurity.

Nam neque divitibus contingunt gaudia folis,
Nec vixit male, qui natus morienfque fefellit.

Hor. Epift. l. i. 18.

God made not pleafures only for the rich;
Nor have thofe men without their fhare, too, liv'd,
Who both in life and death the world deceiv'd.   3

IV. Of Agriculture.

Nescio qua natale folum dulcedine Mufas
Ducit, et immemores non finit effe fui.

The Mufes ftill love their own native place,
It has fecret charms which nothing can deface.

As well might corn as verſe in cities grow;
In vain the thankleſs glebe we plough and ſow,
Againſt the unnatural ſoil in vain we ſtrive;
'Tis not a ground in which theſe plants will thrive. 4

Νήπιοι, ὐδ᾿ ἴσασιν ὅσῳ Πλέον Ἥμισυ Παντὸς,
᾿Ουδ᾿ ὅσον ἐν μαλάχῃ τε ἣ ἀσφοδέλῳ μέγ᾿ ὄνειαρ,
Κρύψαντες γὰρ ἔχυσι Θεοὶ βίον ἀνθρώποισι.

UNHAPPY they to' whom God has not reveal'd,
By a ſtrong light which muſt their ſenſe control,
That half a great eſtate's more than the whole;
Unhappy, from whom ſtill conceal'd does lie
Of roots and herbs the wholeſome luxury.   5

———Hæc (inquit) limina victor
Alcides ſubiit, hæc illum regia cepit,
Aude, Hoſpes! contemnere opes, et te quoq; dignum
Finge Deo, rebuſque veni non aſper egenis.   4

THIS humble roof, this ruſtic court, ſaid he,
Receiv'd Alcides crown'd with victory:
Scorn not, great Gueſt! the ſteps where has he trod,
But contemn wealth, and imitate a god.   4

THE COUNTRY LIFE.

Lib. IV. Plantarum.

BLESS'D be the man (and bleſs'd he is) whom e'er
(Plac'd far out of the roads of hope or fear)

A little field and little garden feeds;
The field gives all that frugal Nature needs;
The wealthy garden lib'rally beftows   5
All fhe can afk, when fhe luxurious grows.
The fpecious inconveniencies that wait
Upon a life of bus'nefs and of ftate,
He fees (nor does the fight difturb his reft)
By fools defir'd, by wicked men poffefs'd.   10
Thus, thus (and this deferv'd great Virgil's praife
The old Corycian yeoman pafs'd his days:
Thus his wife life Abdolonymus fpent:
Th' ambaffadors, which the great emp'ror fent
To offer him a crown, with wonder found   15
The rev'rend gard'ner hoeing of his ground:
Unwillingly, and flow, and difcontent,
From his lov'd cottage to a throne he went;
And oft' he ftopp'd in his triumphant way,
And oft' look'd back, and oft' was heard to fay,   20
Not without fighs, Alas! I there forfake
A happier kingdom than I go to take.
Thus Aglaüs (a man unknown to men,
But the gods knew, and therefore lov'd him then)
Thus liv'd obfcurely then without a name,   25
Aglaüs, now confign'd t' eternal fame:
For Gyges, the rich king, wicked and great,
Prefum'd at wife Apollo's Delphic feat,
Prefum'd to afk, oh! thou, the whole world's eye,
Seeft thou a man that happier is than I?   30

4

The god, who fcorn'd to flatter man, reply'd,
Aglaüs happier is. But Gyges cry'd,
In a proud rage, Who can that Aglaüs be?
We 'ave heard as yet of no fuch king as he.
And true it was, thro' the whole earth around   35
No king of fuch a name was to be found.
Is fome old hero of that name alive,
Who his high race does from the gods derive?
Is it fome mighty gen'ral, that has done
Wonders in fight, and godlike hohours won?   40
Is it fome man of endlefs wealth? faid he.
None, none of thefe. Who can this Aglaüs be?
After long fearch and vain inquiries paft,
In an obfcure Arcadian vale at laft,
(Th' Arcadian life has always fhady been)   45
Near Sopho's town (which he but once had feen)
This Aglaüs, who monarchs' envy drew,
Whofe happinefs the gods flood witnefs to,
This mighty Aglaüs was lab'ring found,
With his own hands, in his own little ground.   50
    So, gracious God! (if it may lawful be
Among thofe foolifh gods to mention thee)
So let me act, on fuch a private ftage,
The laft dull fcenes of my declining age:
After long toils and voyages in vain,   55
This quiet port let my tofs'd veffel gain:
Of heav'nly reft this earneft to me lend;
Let my life fleep, and learn to love her end.   58

V. *The Garden.*

And there (with no defign beyond my wall) whole
  and entire to lie,
In no unactive eafe, and no unglorious poverty.

I.

Happy art thou, whom God does blefs
With the full choice of thine own happinefs;
And happier yet, becaufe thou 'rt blefs'd
With prudence how to chufe the beft.
In books and gardens thou haft plac'd aright   5
(Things which thou well doft underftand,
And both doft make with thy laborious hand)
Thy noble innocent delight;
And in thy virtuous wife, where thou again doft meet
Both pleafures more refin'd and fweet;   10
The faireft garden in her looks,
And in her mind the wifeft books.
Oh! who would change thefe foft yet folid joys
For empty fhows and fenfelefs noife,
And all which rank ambition breeds,   15
Which feem fuch beauteous flow'rs, and are fuch pois'-
      II.   [nous weeds?

When God did man to his own likenefs make,
As much as clay, tho' of the pureft kind,
By the great Potter's art refin'd,
Could the divine imprefion take,   20

He thought it fit to place him where
A kind of heav'n, too, did appear.
As far as earth could such a likeness bear,
That man no happiness might want
Which earth to her first master could afford, 25
He did a garden for him plant,
By the quick hand of his omnipotent word.
As the chief help and joy of human life,
He gave him the first gift first, ev'n before a wife.

III.

For God, the universal architect, 30
It had been as easy to erect
A Louvre, or Escurial, or a Tower,
That might with heav'n communication hold,
As Babel vainly thought to do of old:
He wanted not the skill or power; 35
In the world's fabric those were shown,
And the materials were all his own;
But well he knew what place would best agree
With innocence and with felicity;
And we elsewhere still seek for them in vain, 40
If any part of either yet remain;
If any part of either we expect,
This may our judgment in the search direct,
God the first garden made, and the first city Cain.

IV.

Oh! blessed Shades! O gentle cool retreat 45
From all th' immoderate heat
In which the frantic world does burn and sweat!

This does the Lion-ſtar, ambition's rage ;
This avarice, the Dogſtar's thriſt, aſſwage :
Ev'ry where elſe their fatal pow'r we ſee,   50
They make and rule man's wretched deſtiny :
They neither ſet nor diſappear,
But tyrannize o'er all the year,
Whilſt we ne'er feel their flame or influence here.
The birds that dance from bough to bough,   55
And ſing above in ev'ry tree,
Are not from fears and cares more free
Than we who lie, or ſit, or walk, below,
And ſhould by right be ſingers too.
What prince's quire of muſic can excel   60
That which within this ſhade does dwell ?
To which we nothing pay or give ;
They like all other poets live,
Without reward or thanks for their obliging pains;
'Tis well if they become not prey: 65
The whiſtling winds add their leſs artful ſtrains,
And a grave baſs the murm'ring fountains play;
Nature does all this harmony beſtow;
But to our plants art's muſic too,
The pipe, theorbo, and guitar, we owe;   70
The lute itſelf, which once was green and mute,
When Orpheus ſtrook th' inſpired lute,
The trees danc'd round, and underſtood,
By ſympathy, the voice of wood.

V.

These are the spells that to kind sleep invite,   75
And nothing does within resistance make,
Which yet we moderately take:
Who would not chuse to be awake
While he's encompass'd round with such delight
To th' ear, the nose, the touch, the taste, and sight?
When Venus would her dear Ascanius keep   81
A pris'ner in the downy bands of sleep,
She od'rous herbs and flow'rs beneath him spread,
As the most soft and sweetest bed;
Not her own lap would more have charm'd his head.
Who that has reason and has smell   86
Would not among roses and jasmine dwell,
Rather than all his spirits choke
With exhalations of dirt and smoke?
And all th' uncleanness which does drown,   90
In pestilential clouds, a populous town?
The earth itself breathes better perfumes here
Than all the female men or women there,
Not without cause, about them bear.

VI.

When Epicurus to the world had taught   95
That pleasure was the chiefest good,
(And was perhaps i' th' right, if rightly understood)
His life he to his doctrine brought,
And in a garden's shade that sov'reign pleasure sought.

Whoever a true epicure would be,   100
May there find cheap and virtuous luxury.
Vitellius his table, which did hold
As many creatures as the Ark of old;
That fiscal table, to which ev'ry day
All countries did a constant tribute pay,   105
Could nothing more delicious afford
Than Nature's liberality,
Help'd with a little art and industry,
Allows the meanest gard'ner's board.
The wanton taste no fish or fowl can chuse,   110
For which the grape or melon he would lose.
Tho' all th' inhabitants of sea and air
Be listed in the glutton's bill of fare,
Yet still the fruits of earth we see
Plac'd the third story high in all her luxury.   115

VII.

But with no sense the garden does comply;
None courts or flatters, as it does, the eye.
When the great Hebrew king did almost strain
The wondrous treasures of his wealth and brain,
His royal southern guest to entertain;   120
Tho' she on silver floors did tread,
With bright Assyrian carpets on them spread,
To hide the metal's poverty;
Tho' she look'd up to roofs of gold,
And nought around her could behold   125
But silk and rich embroidery,
And Babylonian tapestry,

And wealthy Hiram's princely die;
Tho' Ophir's ftarry ftones met ev'ry where her eye;
Tho' fhe herfelf, and her gay hoft, were drefs'd   130
With all the fhining glories of the Eaft;
When lavifh Art her coftly work had done,
The honour and the prize of bravery
Was by the garden from the palace won,
And ev'ry rofe and lily there did ftand,   135
Better attir'd by Nature's hand.
The cafe thus judg'd againft the king we fee,
By one that would not be fo rich, tho' wifer far than he.

VIII.

Nor does this happy place only difpenfe
Such various pleafures to the fenfe;   140
Here Health itfelf does live,
That falt of life which does to all a relifh give;
Its ftanding pleafure and intrinfic wealth,
The body's virtue, and the foul's good fortune, health.
The tree of Life, when it in Eden ftood,   145
Did its immortal head to heaven rear,
It lafted a tall cedar till the flood,
Now a fmall thorny fhrub it does appear,
Nor will it thrive, too, ev'ry where;
It always here is frefheft feen,   150
'Tis only here an ever-green.
If thro' the ftrong and beauteous fence
Of temperance and innocence,
And wholefome labours, and a quiet mind,
Any difeafes paffage find,   155

They muſt not think here to aſſail
A land unarm'd, or without a guard;
They muſt fight for it, and diſpute it hard,
Before they can prevail:
Scarce any plant is growing here   160
Which againſt death ſome weapon does not bear.
Let cities boaſt that they provide
For life the ornaments of pride;
But 'tis the country and the field
That furniſh it with ſtaff and ſhield.   165

IX.

Where does the wiſdom and the pow'r divine
In a more bright and ſweet reflection ſhine?
Where do we finer ſtrokes and colours ſee
Of the Creator's real poetry,
Than when we with attention look   170
Upon the third day's volume of the book?
If we could open and intend our eye,
We all, like Moſes, ſhould eſpy
Ev'n in a buſh, the radiant Deity:
But we deſpiſe theſe his inferior ways,   175
(Tho' no leſs full of miracle and praiſe)
Upon the flow'rs of heav'n we gaze;
The ſtars of earth no wonder in us raiſe,
Tho' theſe, perhaps, do more than they
The life of mankind ſway: 180
Altho' no part of mighty Nature be
More ſtor'd with beauty, pow'r, and myſtery,

Yet, to encourage human industry,
God has so order'd, that no other part
Such space and such dominion leaves for art.   185

X.

We no where Art do so triumphant see,
As when it grafts or buds the tree:
In other things we count it to excel,
If it a docile scholar can appear
To Nature, and but imitate her well;   190
It over-rules, and is her master here:
It imitates her Maker's power divine,
And changes her sometimes, and sometimes does re-
It does, like grace, the fallen tree restore   [fine.
To its bless'd state of Paradise before.   195
Who would not joy to see his conqu'ring hand
O'er all the vegetable world command,
And the wild giants of the wood receive
What law he is pleas'd to give?
He bids th' ill-natur'd crab produce   200
The gentler apple's winy juice,
The golden fruit that worthy is
Of Galatea's purple kiss:
He does the savage hawthorn teach
To bear the medlar and the pear;   205
He bids the rustic plum to rear
A noble trunk, and be a peach;
Ev'n Daphne's coyness he does mock,
And weds the cherry to her stock,

Tho' fhe refus'd Apollo's fuit;   210
Ev'n fhe, that chafte and virgin tree,
Now wonders at herfelf, to fee
That fhe is a mother made, and blufhes in her fruit.

XI.

Methinks I fee great Dioclefian walk
In the Salonian garden's noble fhade,   215
Which by his own imperial hands was made:
I fee him fmile, methinks, as he does talk
With the ambaffadors, who come in vain
T' entice him to a' throne again.
If I, my Friends! (faid he) fhould to you fhow   220
All the delights which in thefe gardens grow,
'Tis likelier much that you fhould with me ftay,
Than 'tis that you fhould carry me away:
And truft me not, my Friends! if ev'ry day
I walk not here with more delight   225
Than ever, after the moft happy fight,
In triumph to the Capitol I rode,
To thank the gods, and to be thought myfelf almoft a
                                                    [god.

VI. *Of Greatnefs.*

If ever I more riches did defire
Than cleanlinefs and quiet do require;
If e'er ambition did my fancy cheat,
With any wifh fo mean as to be great,
Continue, Heav'n! ftill from me to remove
The humble bleffings of that life I love.   6

WAs it for this that Rome's beft blood he fpilt,
With fo much falfehood, fo much guilt?
Was it for this that his ambition ftrove
To equal Cæfar firft, and after Jove?
Greatnefs is barren, fure, of folid joys;   5
Her merchandife, I fear, is all in toys;
She could not elfe, fure, fo uncivil be
To treat his univerfal majefty,
His new-created deity,
With nuts, and bounding-ftones, and boys.   10

———Sed quantum vertice ad auras
Ætherias, tantum radice ad Tartara tendit.

As far as up tow'rds heav'n the branches grow,
So far the root finks down to hell below.

AND what a noble plot was crofs'd,
And what a brave defign was loft!

VII. *Of Avarice.*

AND, oh! what man's condition can be worfe
Than his whom plenty ftarves and bleffings curfe?
The beggars but a common fate deplore;
The rich poor man's emphatically poor.   4

I ADMIRE, Mecænas! how it comes to pafs
That no man ever yet contented was,
Nor is, nor perhaps will be, with that ftate
In which his own choice plants him, or his Fate.

Happy the merchant, the old foldier cries :⠀⠀⠀⠀5
The merchant, beaten with tempeftuous fkies,
Happy the foldier ; one half hour to thee
Gives fpeedy death or glorious victory.
The lawyer, knock'd up early from his reft
By reftlefs clients, calls the peafant blefs'd ;⠀⠀10
The peafant, when his labours ill fucceed,
Envies the mouth which only talk does feed.
'Tis not (I think you'll fay) that I want ftore
Of inftances, if here I add no more ;
They are enough to reach at leaft a mile⠀⠀⠀⠀15
Beyond long Orator Fabius his ftyle.
But, hold, you whom no fortune e'er endears,
Gentlemen, male-contents, and mutineers,
Who bounteous Jove fo often cruel call,
Behold Jove's now refolv'd to pleafe you all.⠀⠀20
Thou, foldier, be a merchant ; merchant, thou
A foldier be ; and, lawyer, to the plough.
Change all their ftations ftraight ; why do they ftay?
The devil a man will change now when he may.
Were I in General Jove's abufed cafe,⠀⠀⠀⠀25
By Jove I'd cudgel this rebellious race :
But he's too good. Be all then as you were,
However, make the beft of what you are,
And in that ftate be cheerful and rejoice,
Which either was your fate or was your choice.⠀⠀30
No ; they muft labour yet, and fweat, and toil,
And very miferable be a while;

5

But 'tis with a defign only to gain
What may their age with plenteous eafe maintain.
The prudent pifmire does this leffon teach,   35
And induftry to lazy mankind preach :
The little drudge does trot about and fweat,
Nor does he ftraight devour all he can get,
But in his temp'rate mouth carries it home,
A ftock for winter, which he knows muft come;   40
And when the rolling world to creatures here
Turns up the deform'd wrong fide of the year,
And fhuts him in with ftorms, and cold, and wet,
He cheerfully does his paft labours eat.
O, does he fo? your wife example, th' ant,   45
Does not at all times reft and plenty want;
But weighing juftly a mortal ant's condition,
Divides his life 'twixt labour and fruition.
Thee neither heat, nor ftorms, nor wet, nor cold,
From thy unnatural diligence can with-hold :   50
To th' Indies thou wouldft run, rather than fee
Another, tho' a friend, richer than thee.
Fond Man! what good or beauty can be found
In heaps of treafure bury'd under ground?
Which rather than diminifh'd e'er to fee,   55
Thou wouldft thyfelf, too, bury'd with them be.
And what's the diff'rence? Is it not quite as bad
Never to ufe, as never to have had?
In thy vaft barns millions of quarters ftore,
Thy belly, for all that, will hold no more   60

Than mine does. Ev'ry baker makes much bread;
What then? he's with no more than others fed.
Do you within the bounds of nature live,
And to augment your own you need not ftrive.
One hundred acres will no lefs for you   65
Your life's whole bus'nefs than ten thoufand do.
But pleafant 'tis to take from a great ftore.
What, Man! tho' you 're refolv'd to take no more
Than I do from a fmall one? If your will
Be but a pitcher or a pot to fill,   70
To fome great river for it muft you go,
When a clear fpring juft at your feet does flow?
Give me the fpring which does to human ufe
Safe, eafy, and untroubled ftores produce:
He who fcorns thefe, and needs will drink at Nile, 75
Muft run the danger of the crocodile,
And of the rapid ftream itfelf, which may
At unawares bear him, perhaps, away.
In a full flood Tantalus ftands, his fkin
Wafh'd o'er in vain, for ever dry within;   80
He catches at the ftream with greedy lips,
From his touch'd mouth the wanton torment flips.
You laugh, now, and expand your careful brow;
'Tis finely faid, but what's all this to you?
Change but the name, this fable is thy ftory;   85
Thou in a flood of ufelefs wealth doft glory,
Which thou canft only touch, but never tafte;
Th' abundance ftill, and ftill the want, does laft.

The treasures of the gods thou wouldst not spare,
But when they 're made thine own they sacred are,
And must be kept with rev'rence, as if thou   91
No other use of precious gold didst know,
But that of curious pictures, to delight,
With the fair stamp, thy virtuoso sight.
The only true and genuine use is this,   95
To buy the things which Nature cannot miss
Without discomfort: oil, and vital bread,
And wine, by which the life of Life is fed,
And all those few things else by which we live;
All that remains is giv'n for thee to give.   100
If cares and troubles, envy, grief, and fear,
The bitter fruits be which fair Riches bear,
If a new poverty grow out of store,
The old plain way, ye Gods! let me be poor.   104

VIII. *The dangers of an honest man in much company.*

HONEST and poor, faithful in word and thought,
What has thee, Fabian! to the City brought?
Thou neither the buffoon nor bawd canst play,
Nor with false whispers th' innocent betray;
Nor corrupt wives, nor from rich beldams get   5
A living by thy industry and sweat;
Nor with vain promises nor projects cheat,
Nor bribe or flatter any of the great.

But you 're a man of learning, prudent, juft;
A man of courage firm, and fit for truft.   10
Why, you may ftay, and live unenvy'd here;
But, faith, go back, and keep you where you were.

IX. *The fhortnefs of life, and uncertainty of riches.*

INSERE nunc Melibæe pyros, pone ordine vites.

Go, Melibæus! now,
Go graff thy orchards and thy vineyards plant;
Behold the fruit!   3

I.

WHY doft thou heap up wealth, which thou muft quit,
Or, what is worfe, be left by it?
Why doft thou load thyfelf when thou 'rt to fly,
Oh, Man! ordain'd to die?

II.

Why doft thou build up ftately rooms on high, 5
Thou who art under ground to lie?
Thou fow'ft and planteft, but no fruit muft fee,
For Death, alas! is fowing thee.

III.

Suppofe thou Fortune couldft to tamenefs bring,
And clip or pinion her wing;   10
Suppofe thou couldft on Fate fo far prevail,
As not to cut off thy entail;

IV.

Yet Death at all that fubtilty will laugh ;
Death will that foolifh gard'ner mock,
Who does a flight and annual plant ingraff   15
Upon a lafting ftock.

V.

Thou doft thyfelf wife and induftrious deem;
A mighty hufband thou wouldft feem :
Fond Man ! like a bought flave thou all the while
Doft but for others fweat and toil.   20

VI.

Officious Fool! that needs muft meddling be
In bus'nefs that concerns not thee;
For when to future years thou' extend'ft thy cares,
Thou deal'ft in other men's affairs.

VII.

Ev'n aged men, as if they truly were   25
Children again, for age prepare;
Provifions for long travel they defign,
In the laft point of their fhort line.

VIII.

Wifely the ant againft poor Winter hoards
The ftock which Summer's wealth affords;   30
In grafhoppers, that muft at autumn die,
How vain were fuch an induftry ?

IX.

Of pow'r and honour the deceitful light
Might half excufe our cheated fight,

If it of life the whole fmall time would ftay,   35
And be our funfhine all the day.

X.

Like lightning that, begot but in a cloud,
(Tho' fhining bright and fpeaking loud)
Whilft it begins, concludes its violent race,
And where it gilds it wounds the place.   40

XI.

Oh, fcene of Fortune! which doft fair appear
Only to men that ftand not near.:
Proud Poverty that tinfel brav'ry wears,
And, like a rainbow, painted tears!

XII.

Be prudent, and the fhore in profpect keep;   45
In a weak boat truft not the deep :
Plac'd beneath envy, above envying rife ;
Pity great men, great things defpife.

XIII.

The wife example of the heav'nly lark,
Thy fellow-poet, Cowley! mark;   50
Above the clouds let thy proud mufic found,
Thy humble neft build on the ground.   52

X. *The danger of procraftination.*

———Sapere aude,
Incipe, vivendi qui recte prorogat horam,
Rufticus expectat dum defluat amnis, at ille
Labitur, et labetur in omne volubilis ævum.   4

BEGIN, be bold, and venture to be wife;
He who defers this work from day to day,   5
Does on a river's bank expecting ftay,
Till the whole ftream, which ftopp'd him, fhould be
That runs, and as it runs, for ever will run on. [gone,

JAM cras hefternum confumpfimus, ecce aliud cras
Egerit hos annos.

OUR yefterday's to-morrow now is gone,
And ftill a new to-morrow does come on.
We by to-morrows draw up all our ftore,
Till the exhaufted well can yield no more.   4

XI. *Of Myfelf.*

——Nec vos dulciffima mundi
Nomina, vos Mufæ, libertas, otia, libri,
Hortique fylvæque anima remanente relinquam.

NOR by me e'er fhall you,
You of all names the fweeteft and the beft,
You Mufes, books, and liberty, and reft;
You gardens, fields, and woods, forfaken be,
As long as life itfelf forfakes not me.   5

EPITAPHIUM.

VIVI AUTORIS.

Hic, ô Viator ! sub lare parvulo
Coùleius hîc est conditus, Hîc jacet
Defunctus humani laboris
Sorte, supervacuâque vitâ.

Non indecorâ pauperie nitens,   5
Et non inerti.nobilis otio,
Vanóq; dilectis popello
Divitiis animosus hostis :

Possis ut illum dicere mortuum,
En terra jam nunc qùantula sufficit !   10
Exempta fit curus, Viator,
Terra sit illa bevis, precare.

Hîc sparge flores, sparge breves roses,
Nam vita gaudet mortua floribus,
Herbisque odoratis corona
Vàtis adhuc cinerem calentem.   16

THE AUTHOR'S EPITAPH

Upon himſelf yet alive, but withdrawn from the buſy world to a country life; to be ſuppoſed written on his houſe.

Here, Paſſenger! beneath this ſhed
Lies Cowley, tho' entomb'd not dead,
Yet freed from human toil and ſtrife,
And all the impertinence of life:

Who in his poverty is neat,   5
And even in retirement great.
With gold, the people's idol, he
Holds endleſs war and enmity.

Can you not ſay he has reſign'd
His breath, to this ſmall cell confin'd?   10
With this ſmall manſion let him have
The reſt and ſilence of the grave.

Strew roſes here as on his herſe,
And reckon this his funeral verſe:
With wreaths of fragrant herbs adorn
The yet ſurviving Poet's urn.   16

Latin Epitaph on the Author's tomb in Westminster-Abbey.

ABRAHAMUS COULEIUS,
Anglorum, Pindarus, Flaccus, Maro,
Deliciæ, Decus, Defiderium Ævi fui,
Hic juxtà fitus eft.

Aurea dum volitant latè tua fcripta per orbem,
Et Famá æternùm vivis, Divine Poeta,
Hic placidâ jaceas requie, Cuftodiat urnam
Cana Fides, vigilentq; perenni lampade Mufæ,
Sit facer ifte locus, Nec quis temerarius aufit
Sacrilega turbare manu Venerabile Buftum.
Intacti maneant, maneant per fecula dulcis
Couleij *cineres ferventq; immobile faxum.*
Sic Vovet
Votumq; fuum apud Pofteros facratum effe voluit.
Qui Viro Incomparabili pofuit fepulchrale marmor.
GEORGIUS DUX BUCKINGHAMIÆ.

Exceffit è vita Anno Ætis 49, *et honorifica pompa elatus ex*
Ædibus Buckingamianis, viris illuftribus omnium ordinum
exfequias celebrantibus. Sepultus eft Die 3º *M. Augufti*
A. D. 1667.

THE EPITAPH

Transcribed from the Author's tomb in Westminster-Abbey, attempted in English.

Here under lies

ABRAHAM COWLEY,

THE PINDAR, HORACE, AND VIRGIL,

Of the English nation.

Wᴴɪʟᴇ thro' the world thy labours shine
Bright as thyself, thou Bard divine;
Thou in thy fame wilt live, and be
A partner with eternity.

Here in soft peace for ever rest,   5
(Soft as the love that fill'd thy breast:)
Let hoary Faith around thy urn,
And all the watchful Muses, mourn.

For ever sacred be this room,
May no rude hand disturb thy tomb;   10
Or sacrilegious rage and lust
Affront thy venerable dust.

Sweet Cowley's dust let none profane;
Here may it undisturb'd remain:
Eternity not take, but give,
And make this stone for ever live.   16

CONTENTS.

From the APOLLO PRESS,
by the MARTINS,
Nov. 29. 1777.

THE END.